THE
GARRISON
CASE

THE
GARRISON
CASE

A Study
in the
Abuse of Power

by

MILTON E. BRENER

 *Clarkson N. Potter, Inc./Publisher* NEW YORK

DISTRIBUTED BY CROWN PUBLISHERS, INC.

AUTHOR'S NOTES

MATERIAL FROM WHICH THIS MAN-
uscript was prepared consists largely of affidavits and memoranda of interviews with approximately fifty individuals, reports of investigations,
and almost two hundred other documents accumulated in the course of
my representation of clients involved in the Garrison probe. Much of
the material is contained in files of news clippings totaling about 1,000
pages, including virtually all articles from the local (New Orleans) press
pertaining to the investigation, as well as many news items from periodi-
cals from other communities.

In addition, I have utilized the official records of proceedings in the
Criminal District Court for the Parish of Orleans, and in the United
States District Court for the Eastern District of Louisiana, as well as
transcripts of some of the court proceedings.

Some of the specific sources of various portions of this book are as
follows:

Chapter 1. Information concerning Garrison's early years is contained in *Plot or Politics* by Rosemary James and Jack Wardlow, published by Pelican Publishing House, New Orleans, Louisiana.

Chapter 3. The chronology of the indictments against former District Attorney Richard Dowling and his assistant, and the disposition of the charges, is based upon my own recollection of the events as confirmed by the records of the Criminal District Court. Garrison's attack against the eight judges of the Criminal District Court are from news accounts published in the *States-Item*, October 31st, 1962. Garrison's charges of racketeering influences on the judges are from news articles of November 2nd, as well as from the Bill of Information filed against Garrison by the Attorney General. The account of the indictments against Judge Bernard Cocke is based largely on my own recollection as confirmed by the records from the Criminal District Court.

Chapter 4. Quotations from the bitter battle between Garrison and Superintendent of the New Orleans Police Department, Joseph I. Giarrusso, are from the *States-Item* of March 8th, 1963. Garrison's statement concerning police brutality is from the *States-Item* of May 15th, 1963. The last excerpt quoted from that battle is found in *Plot or Politics*, page 25. Garrison's attack on Governor Davis was quoted in the *States-Item* of October 22nd, 1963. The quotations of Sam "Monk" Zelden were reported in the *States-Item* of April 3rd, 1964. The quotation by Judge John Fournet of the Louisiana Supreme Court is from the case of *State v. Open Hearing Investigation*, 162 So. 2d 565 at p. 569. Garrison's remarks concerning the "hydra of public officials" were quoted in the *States-Item* of June 3rd, 1964. All quotations concerning his accusation of bribery in the legislature are from news reports of July 6th through July 9th.

Chapter 5. Garrison's condemnation of the police investigation of graft in his Office is from the *States-Item* of June 15th, 1965. Examples of his "twenty-one questions" are from the *States-Item* of June 24th, 1965. Garrison's remarks about Aaron Kohn are from the *Times-Picayune* of September 27th, 1966; his attack of the Metropolitan Crime Commission and its special investigator is a press release by his office to all media on October 19th, 1966.

Chapter 6. The opening quotation is from page 74 of the October, 1967, issue of *Playboy* magazine. Jack Martin's self-description is quoted by Merriman Smith in the Dallas *Times Herald* of March 5th, 1967. Quotations by David Ferrie are from his statement to the District Attorney given December 15th, 1966. Materials for this chapter also include extracts from information received from the reports of the Secret Service and the Federal Bureau of Investigation on the interview of

Ferrie and the corroboration of his statements; the reports by the New Orleans Police Department on the arrest of Ferrie (nos. K-13880–63 and K-14238–63), dated May 22nd, 1964; report on the investigation of the complaint by Jack Martin concerning the November 22nd pistol whipping by Bannister (no. K-1263–63), dated November 25th, 1963; as well as personal interviews with Alvin Beauboeuf, Carlos Quiroga, Carlos Bringuier, Rancier Ehlinger, and one of the arresting officers involved in the raid on Ferrie's apartment November 24th. Garrison's reference to the skating rink as the "communications" center and to the entire trip as the "thread that unraveled the plot" are from an article in the *Saturday Evening Post*, April 24th, 1967, entitled "Rush to Judgment in New Orleans," by James Phelan. Both references are on page 24 of that issue. Stories concerning the condition of Ferrie's airplane were recorded in the *Times-Picayune*, February 23rd, 1967.

Chapter 7. The account of the conversation among Garrison, Senator Russell Long, and Joseph Rault is reported in *New Orleans* magazine for April, 1967, page 8; and Rault's conclusion is found on page 60 of this article. In addition, a reference by Garrison to this conversation is found on page 74 of the October, 1967, issue of *Playboy*. Reference to the chess game is from page 23 of the *Saturday Evening Post* article by Phelan. Additional material comes from personal interviews with Beauboeuf and Martens and from copies of statements of these witnesses taken by the District Attorney's Office, as well as from a transcript of the interview with Melvin Coffee. The material concerning Andrews is based upon personal conversations, including, primarily, an interview in December, 1967; Andrews's testimony before the Warren Commission as reported in Volume XI of the Evidence; and the courtroom testimony of Regis Kennedy of the F.B.I. during the Clay Shaw trial, as reported by the *Times-Picayune*, February 18th, 1969. Andrews's admission that Clay Bertrand did not exist is from Volume XI of the Evidence of the Warren Commission, page 334. Andrews's statement concerning the discrepancy in testimony to Bertrand's height is from the Commission Report, page 331. Andrews's television remarks are from the NBC documentary of June 19th, 1967. The charge against Manuel Garcia Gonzales is designated no. 198–483 in the records of the Clerk of the Criminal District Court. The background material concerning Clay Shaw was reported in the local press during the first ten days of March, 1967, and in *Plot or Politics*. William E. Wulf's statement concerning Oswald's Communist convictions in high school are from page 165 of the Warren Report. The information concerning the training camp in St. Tammany Parish is from reports of interviews with Rudolph

Richard Davis, one of the promoters, and Angel Vega, one of the trainees, as well as from personal interviews with Carlos Bringuier and Carlos Quiroga. Garrison's reference to "overt" and "covert" camps is reported, among other places, in the *States-Item* of May 5th, 1967.

Chapter 8. This material is based largely on personal interviews with Quiroga and Bringuier, on copies of memorandums from Garrison to his staff and from various staff members to Garrison, a transcript of an interview with Gordon Novel by news reporters (not published), and press reports of February 22nd and February 23rd, 1967. Lardner's remarks concerning Ferrie are quoted in the *States-Item* of February 22nd. Garrison's reference to Ferrie's death as suicide is from numerous news reports, including the *Times-Picayune* of February 26th. The offer of David Lewis to the U.P.I. is reported in the article by Merriman Smith in the Dallas *Times Herald* of March 5th. Description of the events leading up to the arrest of Shaw is, in part, from the testimony of Salvadore Panzeca, attorney at the trial of Clay Shaw, as reported in the local press.

Chapter 9. Material for this chapter consists of: investigative reports concerning Perry Russo, including statements and sworn affidavits of almost two dozen witnesses; a letter by James Phelan dated June 22nd, 1967, to Garrison containing an exhibit listing nineteen instances of contradictions and errors in Russo's testimony; the Sciambra memorandum of February 25th; the transcript of the preliminary hearing of March 14th through March 17th, 1967; the second Sciambra memorandum, dated February 27th; the transcript of the hypnotic sessions of Perry Russo; and personal interviews with Alvin Beauboeuf and Layton Martens. The information concerning Oswald's departure from New Orleans is from the Warren Report, pages 320 and 321. The facts concerning Brecht Wall are from the James Phelan letter of June 22nd.

Chapter 10. The material in this chapter comes from the official record of the Clerk of the Criminal District Court, which includes the search warrant and the return, and the transcript of proceedings of the preliminary hearing conducted March 14th through 17th, 1967.

Chapter 11. Material for this chapter is taken largely from the Phelan letter of June 22nd; a column by George Lardner, Jr. in the Washington *Post*, June 22nd, 1967; a personal interview with Edward O'Donnell— most of the contents of which have since been made public in courtroom testimony; courtroom testimony of Russo in the trial of Clay Shaw in February, 1969, as reflected by the transcript of his testimony.

Chapter 12. Most materials from this chapter are from press reports of the Andrews's proceedings and personal interviews with Andrews and various reporters. The second questioning of Andrews before the Grand Jury concerning the physical description of Clay Bertrand is from the second Andrews's indictment, no. 198–483 in the records of the Clerk of the Criminal District Court. All Grand Jury testimony is from the indictments. Also utilized was the transcript of the motion by Andrews to recuse.

Chapter 13. This chapter is based largely on my own recollections as reinforced by the official record of the charges against Martens and the transcript of his questioning by the District Attorney's Office.

Chapter 14. Material utilized in this chapter includes a police report of June 12th, 1967, by the Deputy Superintendent of Police concerning allegations of Alvin Ronald Beauboeuf; the statement of Alvin Beauboeuf to the police, dated June 2nd, 1967; the statement of Mrs. Beauboeuf, dated May 17th, 1967; the statement of Alvin Beauboeuf, dated May 17th, 1967; an affidavit of Alvin Beauboeuf, April 12th, 1967, attached to a letter of April 28th, 1967, from Jim Garrison to the Committee of Ethics and Grievances, Louisiana State Bar Association; the transcript of a magnetic tape of the conversation between Hugh Exnicious, Lynn Loisel, and Alvin Beauboeuf certified correct by Exnicious on May 27th, 1967, before David J. Kelly, Notary Public; a letter of Garrison to Louisiana State Bar Association Committee on Ethics and Grievances, dated May 12th, 1967, concerning Burton Klein.

Chapter 15. Primary sources for material concerning the various witnesses are as follows: Gordon Novel—news accounts; Sergio Arcacha Smith—written statements in investigative files; Sandra Moffett—written statements in investigative files and news reports; Carlos Quiroga—personal interview; John Cancler—personal recollections and news articles, particularly States-Item of June 12th, 1967; Miguel Torres—news items of June 20th, 1967, and the NBC documentary of June 19th, 1967; Fred Lemans—news items of June 20th, 1967, and the NBC documentary of June 19th, 1967; Clyde Johnson—written statement in investigative file and press reports; Donald P. Norton—reported in the Albertan (Calgary), August 7th, 1967; Raymond Cummings—local press reports; Clyde Limbaugh—local press reports; Howard Rice Knight—statements in investigative files; Arthur Stout—local press reports.

Chapter 16. Judge Haggerty's warning against pretrial publicity is quoted in the States-Item of March 27th, 1967; Garrison's charge that Oswald was involved with the C.I.A. is from the States-Item of May 8th, 1969. Garrison's statement concerning his desire to talk to Lee Odom is quoted in local press items of May 13th through May 18th.

Lee Odom's statement in response is quoted in the Dallas *Morning News* of May 19th, 1967. Garrison's theory about the assassination is given in an Associated Press report, by Laura Forman, which appeared in the *States-Item* of May 23rd, 1967. The comment concerning frangible bullets is from the *States-Item* of May 26th. Garrison's remarks concerning Gurvich are from press reports of June 26th, 1967. His statements concerning the fourteen-man guerrilla team are from the Nashville *Tennesseean* of June 22nd, 1967. His remarks concerning the Chief Justice are from the *Times-Picayune* of September 5th, 1967. The quotations from interviews in New York concerning the Warren Commission's single assassination theory are from verbatim transcripts. The attack on President Johnson is quoted in the Los Angeles *Free Press* of November 17th. Reports concerning the .45-caliber bullet and the escape through the manhole are from the *Times-Picayune* of December 19th, 1967. Garrison's conclusions as to the "geographical corridor" are from the *States-Item* of February 16th, 1967. The attack on Ramsey Clark is from a District Attorney press release, dated February 19th, 1968, to all media. The interview with the Dutch newsman is reported in the *States-Item* of February 22nd, 1968.

Chapter 17. This material is from official court records and news articles and, in part, from personal recollections.

Chapter 18. All material is from local news reports of the trial and from personal interviews with witnesses to the proceedings. The information concerning the jail sentence of Vernon Bundy is from the *Times-Picayune* of March 20th, 1969.

1

THE STRANGE SPECTACLE KNOWN
as the Kennedy assassination probe of Jim Garrison cannot be fully
understood without some understanding of the man himself and his
tempestuous political career.

He is physically impressive—six feet, six inches tall, handsome, and
well built. His dress is immaculate; his voice is deep and beautifully
modulated. Few experience trouble recalling his name. No one mistakes
him for anyone else.

The favorable first impression deepens upon closer contact, for Garrison is blessed with an easy mastery of the language. Humor is his key
weapon and he has a deft ability to parry the most telling criticism with
pointedly clever rejoinders. They generally obscure to all but the most
humorless their often totally irrelevant nature.

He is possessed of an irresistible confidence in himself and the correctness of his opinion on any matter he deems significant. Contemptu-
ous of details, he is subject to capricious change of opinion on matters
not fundamental to his basic convictions. But the fundamentals of these

convictions are his most cherished possessions. They yield to no evidence.

He sometimes appears to stand in awe of his ideas in the manner of a sculptor or painter regarding his work. His manner in meeting attacks upon them is not defensive; it is one of restrained outrage.

The correctness of his conclusions is thus a matter of high principle; he does not compromise nor admit to the possibility of error. A favorite author is Ayn Rand; a favorite book, *The Fountainhead*, the story of the uncompromising architect. As though anxious to dispel an impression of intractability, he often seems prone to compensate by a ready disposition to yield to all suggestions in matters of less significance.

There is, finally, a quality about Garrison incapable of definition that renders an abiding dislike of the man virtually impossible upon personal contact. The word "charm" is close, but inadequate. I once heard him say of a mutual acquaintance that he possessed a "delicious" sense of humor. The word aptly describes his own. It permeates his private informal conversation no less than his most studied public appearance. His manner is casual and unhurried.

These were traits that were quickly apparent when I first met Garrison in the fall of 1956 upon joining the staff of District Attorney Leon Hubert, who was later to serve as Assistant Counsel to the Warren Commission. Garrison was Hubert's Executive Assistant. First Assistant was Malcolm O'Hara, who was later to serve as a judge of the Orleans Parish Criminal District Court. There was nothing in Garrison's performance to presage what was to come. I knew nothing of his past, which was, in fact, unspectacular. He was born Earling Carothers Garrison in 1921 in Denison, Iowa, and moved to Chicago with his mother at an early age. He served with distinction in the United States Army in Europe during World War II as a pilot of an unarmed observation plane. His legal education was at Tulane Law School in New Orleans, from which he graduated in 1949. After graduation he took a year of postgraduate work, then found employment with a large New Orleans law firm.

Garrison was appointed Assistant District Attorney for Orleans Parish in 1953. Without question, he was the most impressive of the twenty or so lawyers on the District Attorney's staff. He was reputed to be lazy. I, for one, never agreed with that estimate, however, and felt it was born largely of his propensity for writing satirical compositions, often in verse, which he circulated among the staff, and an undoubted knack for delegating both authority and labor.

Like the rest of us, of course, he was not without fault. He did, it seemed, have a tendency to make snap judgments on insufficient facts. He was prone to oversimplify. His abundant ego could, on occasion, be a cause of annoyance. And it is neither exaggeration nor hindsight to recall that in his humor there could at times be detected traces of cruelty.

But these faults, if such they were, seemed relatively insignificant. More prominent were his obvious ability, an easy manner, and a sharp and spontaneous humor. His mind was quick. He seemed incapable, and intolerant, of dullness or ineptitude.

Garrison's earliest political adventures gave little hint of the tempest to follow. In the fall of 1957, with the backing of the then Mayor, de Lesseps S. Morrison, Garrison ran as a sacrificial candidate for the office of Assessor in a district traditionally, and invincibly, in the grip of a political opponent of the Mayor. Morrison himself was running for reelection as Mayor. Malcolm O'Hara was the administration candidate for District Attorney. I agreed to help Garrison with the ritual of posting signs on election day at polling places throughout the district. I was, and remain, ignorant in the ways of politics, but knew it to be minimum accepted procedure that posters be in place before the polls opened at 6:00 A.M. Garrison suggested 9:30 A.M. It was at least 10:30 A.M. by the time we actually started. It amounted to a leisurely cruise through the area punctuated by infrequent stops to post a sign wherever a vacant spot could be found amid the sea of his opponent's posters. His reaction to a 3–1 defeat was mock solemn assurance to me that, had he listened to my suggestion to post additional signs, he would have won.

Morrison was an easy winner. In the race for District Attorney Malcolm O'Hara went into a second Democratic primary, held in January, 1958, against Richard Dowling, an experienced and well-known criminal lawyer. On the night of the second primary election, O'Hara was the apparent winner by five votes out of approximately eighty thousand cast. Even before the final returns were in, most of the assistant district attorneys geared for the court fight that was inevitably to follow such a close election. Ultimately, the result was reversed by the State Supreme Court, which threw out thirteen votes in one precinct as having been fraudulently cast by the polling commissioners. As the commissioners all wore O'Hara badges, the votes were subtracted by Supreme Court edict from the O'Hara column, rendering Dowling the winner. Garrison's acid comments were welcome relief to the general gloom of the assistant D.A.'s. No one saw fit to mention that he had not been seen during the course of the preparation for the election suit, the trial, or the appeal. He had, in fact, not been seen at all following the official counting of the ballots, at which time he had pronounced the controversy to be "all over," the reversal of the vote in the courts to be an "impossibility," and the claim of fraud made by the Dowling forces to be "incredible."

Service in the District Attorney's Office in Orleans Parish is under the spoils system, not civil service. The entire force of assistant district attorneys on Leon Hubert's staff suddenly faced the prospect of immediate relocation, and Garrison entered the private practice of law.

The next four years were tough ones. His sense of humor never dulled, though its target was often his own financial difficulties and his struggle to survive in the practice of law. But he was the embodiment of the adage that one can best hide his poverty by living like a rich man. His dress continued impeccable, his cigars expensive. He would spend several hours at the more plush New Orleans restaurants consuming pre- and post-lunch martinis and liqueurs and entertaining his companions with splendid specimens of wit.

In 1959 Mayor Morrison ran for Governor against Jimmie Davis and lost. For his support in the campaign, Garrison was appointed Assistant City Attorney, a part-time job paying a nominal salary.

In 1960 Garrison ran with the support of Mayor Morrison against a sitting Criminal Court Judge. Sitting Judges have traditionally been considered unbeatable, a myth that was to remain until destroyed by Garrison himself sometime after his election as District Attorney. However, even as early as 1960, it was apparent that Garrison had little faith in this dogma. He ignored the platitudes of his co-candidates for other judgeships and launched an aggressive attack on the poor work record of the incumbent. Garrison lost by a mere few thousand votes. It is interesting to speculate on the nature of his judicial career had he won.

Sometime shortly thereafter Garrison formally changed his name to "Jim Garrison," the name by which he had always been known.

In 1961 he qualified to run for District Attorney against the incumbent, Richard Dowling, with a well-written blast at Dowling's laxity in pursuing prosecutions and, generally, in attending to the duties of his office. It was a charge often made by others throughout Dowling's four-year term, but Dowling, a tough warrior by any standards, appeared unbeatable. Garrison sought the support of Mayor Victor H. Schiro, who had been chosen by the City Council to succeed Morrison upon the latter's appointment as Ambassador to the Organization of American States. Despite Schiro's reluctance to be burdened with Dowling's spotty record on law enforcement, he refused to buck a District Attorney considered to be a likely winner. Dowling's major opposition appeared to be defense attorney Irvin Dymond, later to appear as chief counsel for Clay Shaw, the man accused by Garrison of conspiracy in the assassination of President Kennedy. Dymond had the backing of a major mayoralty candidate. Another candidate in the District Attorney race was Frank Klein, likewise backed by a mayoralty candidate. Garrison had no backing at all. He was without support or money of his own. On one occasion I spoke to him in the Civil Court Building and inquired if he were still in the race. He lamented that the deadline for withdrawals had passed and complained that he could not get the support of Mayor Schiro as he, Garrison, had been "finessed," referring to a purported agreement whereby Schiro and Dowling would not oppose each other.

About a month before the first Democratic primary, there occurred one of the few truly decisive events in New Orleans politics. All of the District Attorney candidates were invited to appear on an open-end panel discussion to be broadcast live on all four television stations operating in the New Orleans area. Dowling, acting on the advice of his supporters that he had nothing to gain by offering himself as a live target for the various challengers, bowed out with a prior out-of-town engagement. His absence did little, however, to abate the vigor of his opponents' attacks. Garrison said virtually nothing until well into the program when, with the calm of a man with little to lose, he began an authoritative discourse about the current narcotics problem, its roots, its scope, and the "incredible" failure of the incumbent to attack it. This was the first exposure of consequence of the people of New Orleans to the beautifully modulated self-assured voice and the superbly effective forensics of Jim Garrison. Garrison looked and spoke like a District Attorney. And he had a captive audience. There was nothing else to watch on television in New Orleans that night.

Presently, the moderator turned to the question of the "fulltime District Attorney" prompted by the repeated criticism of the incumbent for having allegedly neglected his office in order to pursue his private civil-law practice. All but Dymond quickly promised to divest themselves of all outside interests. For the $17,000 yearly salary, they would devote all of their time and energy to the public. Few of the viewers realized that none except Dymond had any practice of consequence to surrender. The question gave Dymond more trouble. After preliminary skirmishing, Dymond in a moment of brutal candor said:

> Let me say this. I make more than $17,000 per year and I intend to go on making more than $17,000 per year. And if the people of New Orleans want a $17,000 per year man as their District Attorney, I'm not their boy.

His candor may well have earned him the votes of a number of people earning more than $17,000 per year. Undoubtedly, however, he lost a considerable number of votes from those who manage to get along on less. It was an uneven swap. The remark deserves to live in history with "Rum, Romanism and Rebellion." The program not only finished Dowling, it all but eliminated Dymond as a major candidate. But Garrison had projected beautifully, and the response was tremendous. Support developed; contributions trickled in and TV appearances were possible. In each of them, more and more voters became fascinated by the image of this giant of a man and his flawless delivery.

"Let me show you the record of my opponent on some of the more important narcotic offenders," he proclaimed. His melodious voice boomed with promise of fascinating and shocking things to come. He turned to a blackboard containing the names of the offenders: "If I told you, you wouldn't believe it." He termed Dowling "The Great Emancipator." Said Garrison, "He let everyone go free."

"Get a new District Attorney," said Garrison. He named several of his opponents, including Klein, as all being good men. "If I'm not your cup of tea, vote for one of them, but get a new District Attorney." By friends he was soon dubbed "The Jolly Green Giant." The name stuck.

In the first primary Dowling fell far short of the needed majority. Garrison was a close second; Dymond a very poor third. Klein was fourth. With the votes of Garrison, Dymond, and Klein clearly constituting anti-Dowling votes, Garrison's second primary victory seemed almost assured.

There was a second open-end panel. Now, however, there were only two opponents: Dowling and Garrison. This time Dowling appeared, and the result was quite different. Garrison was not in his element. The free flow of uninterrupted discourse was not possible as Garrison was placed permanently on the defensive by the tough and experienced courtroom lawyer. Nor did he do a creditable job of defending. Hard facts have never been Garrison's forte. One disappointed Garrison supporter opined the following day that at the conclusion of the program Garrison looked as though he had been hit with a wet mop.

It made no difference. Unfortunately for Dowling, it was too late. Garrison won the second primary by about 6,000 votes out of approximately 130,000 cast. Schiro was reelected Mayor by a comfortable margin.

Garrison picked Frank Klein as his First Assistant; his top investigator was Pershing Gervais, a controversial figure, previously dismissed from the Police Department for misconduct, and a former witness against fellow policemen during a graft-system scandal of major proportions. The appointment was to cause Garrison embarrassment and complications throughout most of his first four years. But the two men were fast friends and Garrison has always repaid loyalty with intense loyalty of his own.

Instead of the three or four civilian investigators usually employed by the District Attorney's Office, Garrison asked for and received about a dozen top policemen as his investigative force.

I spoke to Garrison about serving in a part-time position on his staff, one that could be pursued without interference with private civil practice. He responded by appointing me to supervise prosecution of all narcotic cases. In the course of my seventeen months in his office, I was assigned considerably more varied duties, but neither I nor most who have served on his staff could find reason to complain about Garrison as a man to work for. He was appreciative and respectful of each man's efforts.

In May, 1962, Garrison and his staff were sworn into office. The major apprehension being voiced by his political opponents and detractors was the tired complaint that Garrison was lazy. It was going to be nigh impossible to get this slow-moving gangling giant to act. This was going to be a do-nothing administration.

Or so they said.

2

THE CRIMINAL COURT BUILDING IN
New Orleans is a huge four-story stone building occupying an entire
square at the intersection of two large avenues, Tulane and Broad. In
1962 it was fairly bursting at the seams, the demands upon it having
long outgrown those of 1930, the year of its dedication. It housed the
offices of Police Headquarters, including its vast record room, identification bureau, detectives' office, narcotics office, and homicide office,
among many others, as well as the offices of the District Attorney, the
Clerk of the Criminal District Court, the Coroner, the Criminal Sheriff,
and Criminal Division of the Legal Aid Bureau—all in addition to the
eight courtrooms and chambers comprising the Criminal District Court.
Not until mid-1968 was the strain relieved somewhat by the construction
of a new Police Headquarters Building.

Most of the principals who labor at the building are on a first name
basis with each other, as they are with many other public officials and
the few dozen or so lawyers who regularly appear in the criminal courtrooms. Of these, less than a dozen are devoted almost exclusively to the

practice of criminal law. New Orleans is one of the few cities in the land maintaining separate civil and criminal judicial systems. As a result, the criminal judges, lawyers, clerks, sheriffs, and court attachés live in a world apart from their civil counterparts, who dwell about two miles away in the New Orleans Civic Center. They often feel, sometimes with justification, like stepchildren of the city administration. Their pleas for physical improvements and less-cramped quarters went long unheeded.

The judges, chosen by popular election for twelve-year terms, necessarily come almost exclusively from that small band of criminal practitioners and assistant district attorneys, who number about twenty at any given time and serve at the pleasure of the District Attorney. Of the eight judges on the criminal bench during 1967, all but one had served for varying terms as assistant district attorneys. Most had also served with varying degrees of experience as defense attorneys.

By and large, the judges are neither better nor worse than other mortals. They possess all the weaknesses and strengths of ordinary men. If they are not as wise or knowledgeable or coldly objective as believed by many, neither are they corrupt nor totally unprincipled, as suspected by others.

The building is often referred to by the criminal practice fraternity as "Tulane and Broad." The pious pronouncement across its imposing facade on Tulane Avenue—"The Impartial Administration of Justice is the Foundation of Liberty"—has been the butt of countless jokes, sometimes crude, sometimes clever, by those familiar with the hit-and-miss nature of the administration of criminal justice within. The building houses many public officeholders and others who aspire to unseat them. Political rivalries and ambitions permeate the vast hallways and cavernous corridors and offices. It is also frequented on a more or less regular basis by many of that unfortunate species to whom trouble is a way of life, and many whose legitimate businesses are operated on the outer periphery of the law. Small-time politicians seeking favors from judges or assistant D.A.'s for constituents can be found on almost any morning, mingling with bondsmen, jurors, and attorneys in the hour or so before courts convene at 10:00 A.M. Over the years Tulane and Broad has assumed a character of its own. Those knowledgeable in the petty intrigues and jealousies among its occupants, and with the pressures of public interest in controversial cases, can often sense the rise and fall of tension by merely strolling the crowded hallway. It has also been the scene of many celebrated New Orleans trials, in several of which participants in Garrison's "assassination probe" have taken part.

When Garrison took office as District Attorney in May, 1962, it was with the active support of many in the building and with the goodwill of practically all. The officeholders and their deputies, political animals all, had long learned the value of friendship with winners. Beyond the observance of basic amenities, as exist in all business affairs, political officeholders value cooperation among each other as a vital contribution to their mutual interests, namely, self-perpetuation in office. It is part of the system.

But Garrison despised the system and often appeared to look contemptuously on its members as petty, unprincipled men, unworthy of being treated on an equal basis. His disdain for the other occupants of Tulane and Broad made itself felt in a number of minor but irritating ways. Though he was tactless and a trifle arrogant, I felt, as did most who knew Garrison, that his innate honesty was genuine and beyond question. The seeds for his abuse of office, it would develop, lay elsewhere.

By virtue of his office, the District Attorney is potentially the most powerful of the public officials domiciled at Tulane and Broad. That he is potentially the most powerful in the city can be respectably argued. However, until 1962 the full extent of his strength had been convincingly impressed neither upon the community in general nor upon the politicians themselves. It lay largely unused in the statute books. Not until the advent of Jim Garrison was the realization driven home of the large extent to which the D.A.'s power had remained untapped—whether through responsible restraint on the part of former district attorneys, timidity, a lack of political ambition, or a combination of all three.

The District Attorney in Louisiana can charge any individual with any crime other than a capital offense by the mere signing of his name to a bill of information. By a stroke of the District Attorney's pen, headlines are made. Individuals are publicly embarrassed and compelled to undergo the financial expense of bail and legal representation and the emotional drain of public trial. This last cannot be fully comprehended, save by those who have experienced it. Likewise, by the signing of his name, the District Attorney can dismiss any charge, including capital charges; he need not seek the permission of the court.

Then there is the Grand Jury, which is, in truth, the District Attorney's toy. It is, in modern America, an anachronism, a relic from the legal Stone Age. It once served a legitimate function; however, like the human appendix or the little toe, it has outlived its usefulness and remains only an irritant to the modern administration of criminal law.

Grand Juries in Orleans Parish are selected for six-month terms by one of the eight judges in the Criminal Court, who then makes any necessary judicial determination in the course of that Jury's term. The duty of Grand Jury selection and judicial supervision is rotated among the judges. Selection of the twelve men who make up the jury is made by the judge from a panel of sixty or so citizens chosen at random from the Jury lists. They hear all capital cases, as such charges can only be tried upon a Grand Jury indictment. In addition, they may hear any other cases and likewise return an indictment if they feel the evidence so warrants. Proceedings are secret. Only the jurors and the District Attorney or his assistants, without limit as to number, are present to hear the witness. The judge is not. Some district attorneys, and many of their assistants, believe the requirement of secrecy of the Grand Jury proceedings to have been handed down with the Commandments at Mount Sinai.

It is understandable that secrecy of the proceedings is so zealously guarded for, often, they are a travesty. Among the members of a typical Grand Jury none will have any special training or experience and most will have no special ability to qualify for the exercise of investigative authority. Yet within the confines of the Grand Jury room, they reign supreme.

The sudden acquisition of authority and power over men apparently has an exhilarating effect. They need not be awed or bewildered by the new responsibility, however. Their legal adviser is the District Attorney. A strong camaraderie quickly develops. And it is not all work. Dinners and drinks are at State expense, and the expense itself has been the subject of news articles by more than one inquiring reporter.

Except in rare instances, the Jury will hear only those witnesses the District Attorney wishes them to hear. They are preconditioned by what the District Attorney has told them of the matter under investigation. There is no judge to strike any of his remarks as prejudicial. No representative of the defendant or prospective defendant is present; none of his witnesses will be heard, except as the Jury might wish to hear them. In this, as in all other matters, most Grand Jurors will be guided by the advice of the District Attorney.

Hearsay and opinion evidence are the rule, not the exception. There is no one to object. Witnesses deemed hostile or untruthful by the District Attorney, arbitrarily or otherwise, may be pointed out in advance. Most judges will permit only one counsel for a side to cross-examine a witness in the course of a trial. In the Grand Jury room, a witness may be badgered by all twelve jurors, plus the District Attorney and as many of his assistants as happen to be present. The questions will be in no particular order. Everyone will speak at once. There will be argumentative questions, abusive questions, questions such as would never be permitted in open court. The jurors are not deliberately chosen for their incivility; they are generally respectable citizens. But the metamorphosis that transpires when twelve such persons are given unbridled authority in secret proceedings merits scrutiny by serious students of human nature.

The prospective defendant himself is normally not heard unless he requests it. Most lawyers would stand aghast at any suggestion that a client suspected of crime should voluntarily appear before the Grand Jury. Testimony of a prospective defendant who has not been warned of his right to refuse to answer incriminating questions and to sign a waiver of his rights may result in a dismissal of an indictment brought against him.

Prior to 1962, most District Attorneys used the Grand Jury primarily as a buffer between themselves and adverse criticism in unpopular matters. Charges against an important public official or citizen, or on a controversial matter that the District Attorney wanted tried, were usually submitted to the Grand Jury. If indictment followed, no one could criticize the District Attorney. If the public clamored for the filing of criminal charges that the District Attorney felt were not warranted, or were politically unpalatable, the case was submitted to the Grand Jury. If a no true bill was returned, the District Attorney's skirts were clean. Few realized and none dared say publicly that the Grand Jury was, in practice, the puppet of the District Attorney. There were such phenomena as "runaway" Grand Juries, but these were rare and generally more disruptive to the legitimate administration of criminal law than the obedient ones.

Hence, if the Grand Jury was of benefit to the District Attorney, it was in a negative sense. The District Attorney is on the firing line; and most wage a constant battle against adverse publicity. Most D.A. elections are more savagely fought than those for any other Parish office, including that of the Mayor's, as, among other reasons, the ammunition is more plentiful. Thousands of cases are processed each year and honest errors and mistakes of judgment are inevitable. They make excellent fodder for the news-hungry press, as well as for political opponents. The smart District Attorneys have learned to live with the press as they would with an untamed carnivorous animal. It was constantly to be sated and pacified with newsworthy items of a harmless or innocuous nature, and as long as the animal lay sleeping, so much the better. They would not arouse it.

But Jim Garrison did not think defensively. No one had previously sought to use either the news media or the Grand Jury as offensive weapons. But all of that was to change.

3

GARRISON'S CRITICS TO THE CON-
trary, certain positive accomplishments must be credited to him with
respect to the internal operation of his office. His staff has built an impressive record of prosecutions. Beginning in October, 1963, he went
beyond his campaign promise of a full-time devotion to office and required all assistants to virtually divorce themselves from the private
practice of law. He aggressively pursued forfeiture of bonds of absent
defendants and used the proceeds to purchase much-needed modern
equipment and to renovate completely his own office, as well as those of
all assistants and ultimately the eight judges of the court. Whether his
office is the "best in the country," as he has often claimed, may be
another matter. However, the office does compare favorably with the
best of prior administrations in New Orleans and none but his most
bitter detractors could deny that his qualities of imagination and aggres-
siveness have, in many respects, been good for law enforcement.

Garrison's major preoccupation has not been with internal operations,
however. Responsibility for the routine administration of the office,

which is the prosecution of the thousands of cases, including murder, rape, and robbery, as well as gambling and prostitution, was quickly delegated to others almost in its entirety. For almost immediately upon his entry into office, Garrison demonstrated a preoccupation with matters whose genuine connection with the legitimate function of his office has been hard to discern.

Shortly prior to Garrison's assumption of office, an assistant district attorney of Richard Dowling, the outgoing D.A., dismissed charges in two pending cases without serious explanation. The dismissals were the subject of considerable publicity and the inference by the public of corruption was undeniably strong. However, those who knew him had little reason to question the assistant's honesty. He was over fifty years of age and such faults as he had ever exhibited, in or out of office, were ascribed by practically all of the Tulane and Broad establishment to be those of poor judgment, not of corruption. More to the point, however, there was no evidence of corruption, nor was any developed in the course of the Grand Jury investigation relentlessly pursued by Garrison upon his assumption of office. Among those subpoenaed before the Jury was the former assistant D.A. himself. Notwithstanding a total failure to develop evidence of bribery, Garrison sought and obtained Grand Jury indictments for "malfeasance in office"—a loosely defined statute well-suited for use, and frequently used, by Garrison during his first years in office, against those he deemed political enemies.

The indictments garnered large headlines. The cases were dismissed by the Court in July, 1962, on the ground that the Grand Jury indictments were tainted with the compulsory appearance before that body of the suspected offender in violation of his constitutional rights. Despite his publicly stated intention to do so, no appeal was taken by Garrison.

In early August, however, there followed nine additional charges of malfeasance against the same former assistant. The purported "malfeasance" consisted of routine dismissals of other prosecutions in none of which had there even been a suspicion of corruption. The new cases likewise were front-page news. Nothing further was heard of these, however, and some were quietly dismissed in the latter part of 1966. Others still remain open on the docket books. None were ever prosecuted further. Nor should they have been. Nor does there appear to be any valid reason for their having been filed.

A few days following the multiple indictments of the assistant, Garrison turned his fire on Dowling himself. Dowling was the subject of four Grand Jury indictments based upon routine dismissals of cases by Dowling during his administration as District Attorney, all for reasons apparently deemed insufficient by his successor.

These baseless indictments caused some anguish even to many of Garrison's supporters. His record as D.A. had been far from perfect, but Dowling, over seventy years of age, had given none the occasion to question his honesty. In Dowling's presence, in the second television open-end discussion, Garrison had disclaimed any reservations as to his opponent's integrity. In his public response to the indictments, Dowling suggested that Garrison was seeking publicity.

Many agreed. For several months Garrison's investigators, accompanied by some of his assistants, were staging nightly raiding parties on Bourbon Street, New Orleans's famous nightclub strip, while Garrison loudly proclaimed war on vice and vowed to clean up the street. There were many who, almost as loudly, insisted that Garrison was motivated more by a passion for publicity than by revulsion at the rampant B-drinking that flourished along the street. I personally feared that such transparently vindictive action as the malfeasance indictment of his former opponents would lend credence to the claims of Garrison's enemies as to his mania for publicity and would demolish public support. I had much to learn.

The Dowling indictments were promptly thrown out as stating no criminal offense recognizable in law. Despite Garrison's announced intention to appeal, no appeals were taken. The public promptly forgot the entire matter.

Meantime, Garrison's crusade against sin continued with increasing intensity. Nightly raids against honky-tonks and clip joints along a certain segment of Canal Street, the city's main stem, paid off relatively quickly when the clubs folded in the face of repeated arrests of employees and the consequent expense and interruption of business. Garrison was angered by the claims of his critics that no trials or convictions resulted from these nightly arrests and replied indignantly that he had closed the clubs and that trials or convictions were immaterial.

The Bourbon Street clubs were more formidable, however, and the attacks were costly. Under the law, one judge had to approve any expenditure by Garrison from the "fines and fees" fund which was used to finance this crusade, and Garrison was quite reticent about revealing details of the expenditures. Further, the judges had reservations about his use of a dozen or so investigators as a "second police force," as they termed it. It had never before been done and that was sufficient prohibition for them. Few of the judges were burdened with excessive imagination. Neither were they quite prepared to authorize the lavish redecorating of the District Attorney's office being undertaken by Garrison. The judges suspended all authorizations of funds until the entire Court returned from vacation in October. Garrison made a personal $5,000 loan from a local bank to continue the crusade until then.

In October, however, more complications developed. The judges agreed at a joint meeting that no expenditures would be approved except by a majority vote of all judges.

The first inkling I had of the considerable friction that was developing was Garrison's announcement at a staff meeting that he had finally located the trouble at Tulane and Broad. "There is," he said, "a conspiracy among the judges to wreck my administration."

On October 31st Garrison retaliated with a hammer blow. At noon he gave an after-dinner speech to a Jewish Temple Brotherhood. He had had the foresight to invite representatives of the local television stations to be present. That evening, large headlines informed the city of Garrison's after-dinner remarks to the effect that the Parish Prison was becoming dangerously overcrowded with prisoners awaiting trial—the reason being that the eight judges of the Criminal District Court were running a "vacation racket." They were, he said, enjoying 206 holidays a year, not counting legal holidays like "All Saints' Day, Huey Long's Birthday, Memorial Day, and St. Winterbottom's Day," while prisoners languished in jail. The only possible way to put an end to this holiday system was to publicize the "racket." "No point in trying to talk to them," said Garrison. "They (the judges) are comparable to the sacred cows of India." That night the viewing public was treated to an entertaining TV film of Garrison's blistering attack and undoubtedly many joined in the obvious delight of Garrison's Temple Brotherhood audience.

Singled out for special attack was Judge J. Bernard Cocke with whom a bitter feud was developing. Garrison caustically pointed out that Judge Cocke treated himself to a three-day weekend each week and did not hold court on Fridays. "However," said Garrison, to the laughter of his audience, "he takes only one Friday off each week."

The issue of Judge Cocke's Friday "vacation" was to outlive Garrison's feud with the judges and was to play a part in Cocke's defeat some eighteen months later. Judge Cocke had an unfortunate disposition and had alienated innumerable lawyers, as well as jurors and witnesses, during his twenty years or so on the bench. In a world where all judges are brilliant, energetic, and courageous, this would, of course, be a major fault. However, the judges bring with them to the bench all forms of human frailties, many of which are more serious than discourtesy. Judge Cocke was generally recognized by the Bar as a conscientious, industrious, and fearless jurist. He could be found any Friday doing research in the Supreme Court Library. The Criminal Court was without research assistants or adequate research facilities.

Although most among the Bar and among the politicians and habitués of the building considered the attack to be unjustified, such individuals are relatively few in number and together with relatives and close friends do not constitute a potent factor in any election. The officeholders, politicians, lawyers, and professional men of New Orleans, as of any other city, are but a negligible part of the electorate. The bulk of the 200,000 registered voters of New Orleans, as elsewhere, consists largely of men and women too preoccupied with the daily necessity of earning a living to read beyond headlines. The workings of government and of courts remain a mystery. They are often deeply suspicious of all who constitute a part of this incomprehensible apparatus. The motives and honesty of men in public life are forever suspect to countless citizens who deem them unreal people living in an unreal world known only through newspapers and television.

What was becoming increasingly clear to many was Garrison's remarkable ability to respond to the prejudices and misconceptions of the great mass of voters beyond the circle in which he worked and lived. Garrison did not at all jibe with the generally accepted image of a politician. The thought of Garrison conducting a door-to-door campaign or shaking hands at random with members of a crowd is ludicrous to those who know him. His acquaintances are by and large a select group of lawyers and politicians, as well as a few other close personal friends. The group was far smaller in 1962 than in later years. How this aloof individual has consistently sensed the mood of the invisible crowd beyond his acquaintances and established a rapport with them with unerring instinct remains the greatest enigma to friends and enemies alike.

There was no mistaking the gathering shape of public opinion. Garrison had hit where the judges were vulnerable, and the fact that his charges were grossly exaggerated or unwarranted or intemperate made an adequate reply no less difficult. The judges, indeed, were in a difficult position. Beyond pointing out that the attack was motivated by their refusal to permit Garrison to "throw money away with both hands" and that he had never complained to the judges personally of the overcrowded conditions in the Parish Prison or of excessive vacations, the response was most moderate under the circumstances, gently taking Garrison to task for intemperate statements. They called for an investigation by the Bar Association into the ethics of Garrison's blast.

Judge William O'Hara, who had recently retired from the bench after nearly thirty years of service (and whose vacancy had been filled by his son, Malcolm), issued his own public statement to the effect that any blame for the crowded conditions of the Orleans Parish Prison must rest with the District Attorney. The statement was factual in tone and attempted to explain the operational deficiencies in Garrison's office that were responsible for the increasing backlog of cases. Judge O'Hara pointed out that Leon Hubert, under whom Garrison had served, had sharply reduced the population of the Parish Prison and the backlog of cases awaiting trial. He suggested that by use of similar methods Garrison could do the same. Garrison responded publicly with a lengthy press release in which, after a properly outraged defense of the conduct of his own office, he turned his fire on the judges whom he accused of showing a "remarkable lack of sympathy" with his drive on vice. After some amplification of this he homed in:

> The judges have now made it eloquently clear where their sympathies lie in regard to aggressive vice investigations by refusing to authorize use of the D.A.'s funds to pay for the cost of closing down the Canal Street clip joints. We have closed them, despite their obvious attempts to block me, and they now seek to slap the D.A. on the wrist by making him pay for this successful operation out of his pocket. . . . Again, the message is clear: "Don't rock the boat, son. You are not supposed to investigate anything." This raises interesting questions about the racketeer influences on our eight vacation-minded judges. This is a matter regarding which I will have much to say a little later.

The rest was colorful if anticlimatic. In view of events to follow in four years, however, it bears repeating:

> The first discernible interest on their part with regard to the District Attorney's handling of vice cases arrived the past summer when it became apparent that this office was achieving success in its effort to eliminate the B-drinking racket in New Orleans. . . . The efficiency and dispatch with which the judges of the present court stopped my undercover investigation of B-drinking and the resolve which they demonstrated in their uniform opposition to any continued vice investigation by this office would gladden the heart of any efficiency expert.

The judges were infuriated. A charge of racketeering influences was not one to be ignored. Petty differences and some not so petty between the judges were forgotten as they sought public vindication of their

good names. All eight signed a charge of criminal defamation, a mis-
demeanor triable under Louisiana law by a judge alone. The judges thus
met Garrison's challenge squarely. It was the last time they were to do
so. The circumstances of the battle that followed justify scrutiny as they
are not without bearing on the events of 1967.

The charge filed by the judges was promptly dismissed by Garrison's
First Assistant, Frank Klein, Garrison having determined that it was
baseless. The judges called in Louisiana's Attorney General, Jack Gremillion, to supersede Garrison and to file and prosecute the charges of
defamation. Gremillion accepted the request, claiming that the "integrity of the judiciary is at stake." Judge William Ponder of Many,
Louisiana, was assigned to hear the case.

Bar Associations and civic groups sought to heal the wounds and to
avoid the unseemly spectacle that was brewing.

Garrison's foes publicly demanded full apologies. Privately it was
hinted by the judges that a watered-down statement would suffice.
Garrison's friends counseled that some explanation or apology could be
made without loss of face. Garrison was intractable. He was the one due
an apology.

Many felt that the feud would die a natural death without a trial. But
seldom more than a few days could pass without some rhetoric or
humorous observation by Garrison adorning the front page of the daily
papers. Reporters beseiged him for interviews and he was a willing
subject. Several assistants, myself included, suggested to Garrison that
silence on his part would probably result in a loss of public interest in
the feud and a gradual détente with the judges. Garrison generally
agreed and was undoubtedly sincere in his agreement. But his resolve
generally lasted only until the approach of the next reporter. The press
seldom went away from the building empty-handed and Garrison continued to supply the fuel that kept the feud alive.

In January, 1963, the trial was held. One by one the judges paraded to
the stand to assure the Court and the public that they were not shirking
their duties and that they were not at all influenced by racketeers. The
cross-examination, ably handled by Garrison's friend and attorney,
Donald Organ, was often embarrassing. One judge admittedly did
consort with known gamblers. One judge's deceased mother had at one
time been part owner of a lottery company. One judge had been accused
twenty years ago by a political opponent of being in cahoots with
racketeers while serving as District Attorney. These revelations were the
subject of large headlines for three days and were devoured by thousands. That it amounted to something less than proof of racketeering
influences, or that there was not a whisper concerning such influences

on fully half of the judges, was of no moment to most of the public. The judges took their lumps willingly in anticipation of Garrison's own appearance on the witness stand. Indeed, he had much to answer for. Why had he not spoken to any of the judges about his concern over the increasingly crowded conditions in the Parish Prison? Why had he not spoken to them about his belief that they were taking an excessive number of holidays? Had any of his trial assistants ever complained to him of any racketeering influence on any of the judges? Tough questions indeed!

On the day the prosecution was to close its case, Garrison's numerous critics crowded the courtroom. They were undoubtedly looking for a repetition of the Garrison-Dowling debate. They were to be surprised and disappointed. Following the Attorney General's announcement that the prosecution rested, Organ was on his feet:

"Your Honor, the defense also rests."

Probably most of the public felt as did one who expressed to me his keen disappointment. He had, he said, read all about the trial of the judges and felt that they should have been convicted. Now, however, how could he determine if Garrison had done anything wrong or not?

The decision to rest without evidence was Garrison's alone. The night before the prosecution was to close, I heard firsthand his vivid description of his enemies sitting patiently for three days, salivating, as he described it, over the prospect of his denouement on the stand, and his argument that he had nothing to gain and everything to lose in the eyes of the public—the only court that concerned Jim Garrison.

Garrison was duly convicted. He was sentenced to pay a fine of $1,000. But long before his conviction was reversed by the United States Supreme Court in early 1965, it was clear to all, the eight judges included, that he had won and the judges had lost. The Supreme Court reversal followed an affirmance of the conviction by the Louisiana State Supreme Court and was based on the unconstitutionality of the defamation statute insofar as it applied to defamation of public officials, such as the judges. In such cases, said the United States high court, there must be proof of actual malice. Such proof, according to the Court, was lacking. Garrison celebrated the occasion to remark that the unconstitutionality of the statute was apparent to everyone except the State Supreme Court. The absence of proof of racketeering influences was again lost from view.

Meantime, during the pendency of his defamation trial Garrison had turned to two trusty weapons, the Grand Jury and the malfeasance statute, to gain some measure of vengeance against his major antagonist, Judge Bernard Cocke. Cocke had asked a witness in the course of a

preliminary hearing in open court if his, the witness's, testimony had
been the same before the Grand Jury. For this the Judge was cited for
contempt of the Grand Jury, for alleged violation of Grand Jury secrecy.
Then, shortly following his conviction for defamation, Garrison sent an
assistant district attorney with a voucher for undercover work in connection with Garrison's Bourbon Street campaign to Judge Cocke to seek
Cocke's signature. The Judge, along with all of his colleagues, had long
since made known his position that such expenditures by the District
Attorney were not authorized. A second assistant was sent as a witness.
Cocke refused and an indictment of malfeasance followed.

On both occasions Judge Cocke vehemently denied any wrongdoing.
But so do all defendants. A judge from another parish was appointed to
hear the trials, which were held less than two weeks after the second
charge, and Judge Cocke was promptly acquitted. Garrison was forced
to try the case himself when his assistants refused. He had also invited
Attorney General Gremillion to prosecute, noting that "the integrity of
the judiciary may be at stake," but Gremillion declined the offer. It was
Garrison's second court appearance since assuming office. His own
defamation trial was the first. The acquittals were expected even by
Garrison, but the humiliation to his antagonist of being forced to sit at
the bar as a common criminal was apparently sufficient.

I had felt that such almost childishly punitive measures and blatant
abuse of the Grand Jury would cause wide public condemnation. Again
I had overestimated the public and underestimated Garrison. Even the
irascible Cocke realized that in the eyes of the public Garrrison had
undoubtedly won again. For after all, what could be expected of any
Judge but to acquit his colleague?

By early 1963, in civil proceedings before civil judges, Garrison had
successfully "padlocked" as public nuisances about a half dozen Bourbon Street night clubs. I had assisted in the trial of these cases and later
in May, 1963, successfully tried similar cases against an additional six
clubs. I knew that the effectiveness of the padlocking was somewhat less
than the word implies. They were permitted to continue operation upon
posting of bond to guarantee against any further B-drinking or related
vices. The penalty for any violation was $100. Whether any significant
change in the Bourbon Street routine was effected has been a matter of
dispute. The psychological effect of his victories was not disputed at all,
however. By early 1963 Garrison had confounded friends and enemies
alike with his increasingly favorable image with the public. There was
no question about who was in command at Tulane and Broad. He was
ready to go on to other battles.

4

THE SUPERINTENDENT OF THE NEW
Orleans Police Department is Joseph I. Giarrusso, a dedicated, highly
competent policeman who reached his position from the ranks. He was
selected by Mayor Morrison for the top position with the Department
in 1959, after having served a number of years as head of the Department's Narcotic Squad, which he had developed to a high degree of
excellence. His honesty is beyond question.

The opening salvo in a long and bitter battle between Garrison and
Giarrusso was fired at the height of Garrison's Bourbon Street campaign
when he accused the Department of displaying "monumental disinterest" in his drive against vice. Giarrusso was thus allied with the judges on
the side of the racketeering element. The "monumental disinterest"
phrase was catching enough to warrant constant repetition by the press
in the manner of a child entranced by his first syllable. Stunned by the implications of this criticism, as well as by Grand Jury chastisement for having failed to gather evidence to padlock the Bourbon Street clubs as Garrison had done, Giarrusso responded. In March of 1963 he staged raids on a

number of the strip joints and booked owners and employees on charges of obscenity growing out of the striptease performances. Giarrusso referred the evidence to Garrison's office for padlocking action. If he expected approbation from Garrison, he, too, had much to learn. Garrison responded by terming the cases "the purest garbage." Said he:

> The cases of which he speaks are not what he represents them to be, not what they should be, and would not provide a solid basis for padlocking a bird cage.
> I am not sure Chief Giarrusso knows this, for he has been around some time now and during this time not a single racket has left the city.

In words that allowed little room for doubt, Garrison accused Giarrusso of siding with the underworld against his office. The raids, he said, were made purely for the purpose of providing statistics.

> This is your police department. These are a few examples of how it functions behind the facade of statistics. The fact that there are many good men in it makes it all the more of a pity.

Giarrusso's response, like that of the judges, was mild:

> The District Attorney is a responsible public official. I call on him to cut out all of this bickering and join me in getting down to work . . . and vigorously prosecute the criminal element of this community.

A lull in the feud lasted until mid-May, at which time Garrison again made headlines by a dinner speech to the Young Men's Business Club in New Orleans during which he announced a crusade against police brutality. Sensational charges of several specific instances of severe beatings, complete with exhibits consisting of blown-up photographs, were displayed. As with the judges, Garrison again sensed a conspiracy:

> There exists a pattern of systematic brutality which is not sanctioned by those in official capacities within the New Orleans Police Department. At the same time, there is no apparent organized effort being made to stop this brutality, but rather an organized system of covering up these instances.

Garrison referred to the brutality as "an old New Orleans custom" that he was going to end.

The following day nine policemen were charged in connection with the supposed beating of prisoners; the public reaction, however, was not at all what Garrison had expected. Giarrusso stuck by his men, refusing to dismiss them as is customary in such instances, and accused Garrison of double-talk. Many publicly-voiced reactions, including editorials in the local press, queried the extent to which Garrison's craving for publicity was the motivating factor. But Garrison demonstrated hitherto unknown qualities of reverse-field ability, if not overwhelming confidence in the charges he had filed. He announced his dismissal of the charges and referral of the matter to the Grand Jury. The chastened Garrison explained that he was doing this for the purpose of demonstrating the impartiality of his office. He decided, he said, that the most effective way to eliminate police brutality was to cooperate with the department. Nothing more was ever heard of the charges. The Grand Jury made no return, neither true Bills nor no true bills. The matter was forgotten, as were scores of charges resulting from the raids on Bourbon Street.

It was not at all the end of the dispute, however. Some of the most poetic passages to be penned by Garrison were products of his continual publicity barrage against Giarrusso, as witness the following:

> The police here are like an army that has a mission to capture an enemy hill. Years ago they went out, surrounded it, and then dug in. They've been dug in for so long that they've forgotten what they are supposed to do. They have made friends with the enemy, and even exchanged birthday and Christmas presents. So why capture the hill and end all the fun?

*　　*　　*

In August, 1963, Executive Assistant Frank Shea was one of the eleven candidates that qualified for a Criminal Court judgeship vacated by the death of Judge Shirley Wimberly. Many of the other candidates had political support in varying strength. Shea had no support, save that of his boss, Jim Garrison. He led the field in the first primary and entered a second primary with the runner-up, Guy Johnson. In the second primary, almost to a man, the defeated candidates threw their support to Johnson, who also garnered practically all organized political support, as well as the endorsement of the city's newspapers. Unabashed, Garrison scheduled a victory party for election night at one of the city's major hotels. The gathering was not to be disappointed. Shea's margin of victory was just enough to discourage a contest of the results. Garrison now had a friend on the bench.

This was the first public test of Garrison's popularity. The significance was not lost on the judges, as was soon to be demonstrated.

*   *   *

In early September, 1963, trial was scheduled for a New Orleans abortionist, one Juliette Pailet, on charges developed by painstaking police work. I was assigned the case for trial. Garrison savored the prospect of conviction as another first for his office as there had been no trials for abortion in New Orleans in many years.

Two days before the scheduled date of trial, Mrs. Pailet's defense attorney, Irvin Dymond, informed me that his client had suffered what he described as a nervous breakdown and would not be able to stand trial as scheduled. The information was verified in essence by her psychiatrist.

Garrison, moving quickly to thwart what he immediately perceived to be an attempt to delay the case by feigning illness, had her examined by another psychiatrist and by the Orleans Parish Coroner, Dr. Nicholas Chetta. The two State experts disagreed with the defendant's doctor as to her ability to stand trial at that time and the question of the delay was argued before Judge Oliver Schulingkamp.

The Judge that afternoon announced that he was granting a delay until early November, there being no jury panel scheduled for the month of October. Garrison's appeal from the decision was to the public through the press. It appeared in the *Times-Picayune* the following morning.

He was "shocked" at the decision, said Garrison, for there was "absolutely no basis" for it. The Judge's reasons for postponing the case were termed "incredible" in view of the "uncontradicted testimony by experts" that she was able to stand trial.

I had been present at the hearing; Garrison had not. I had disagreed with the Judge's decision, but I could hardly have called it incredible, nor could I have called the testimony of the State's doctor uncontradicted. The implications of the statement were such that I felt a charge of contempt to be inevitable. However, Judge Schulingkamp had stood in opposition to Garrison in company with his seven colleagues on the bench in a battle for public opinion and lost. Now, he was alone, and he had little stomach for a battle with the garrulous D.A.

A motion for reconsideration of the continuance was filed and heard the following day. The decision was reversed. The case went to trial in late September, and Mrs. Pailet was convicted.

The trial was my last assignment for Garrison. I and three other assistant D.A.'s left the Office the end of September as a result of his new policy prohibiting substantial civil practice by his staff. But it was not the last the public was to hear of the Pailet case.

Less than three weeks following the trial and Mrs. Pailet's sentence to a term of seven years in the penitentiary, she was released from the Orleans Parish Prison pending her appeal as a result of a reprieve by Governor Jimmie Davis. Convicted defendants sentenced to more than five years in the penitentiary cannot be admitted to bail under Louisiana State law during the pendency of an appeal. The Governor ascribed his action to Mrs. Pailet's ill health and the statement of her doctor that she was in need of medical attention. The reprieve was temporary in nature and did not serve to mitigate the sentence which would begin when and if the conviction were affirmed upon appeal to the State Supreme Court.

Garrison's reaction was swift and lacked none of his customary vigor or color. Referring to the Governor's own description of his reprieve as "an act of human kindness," Garrison retorted:

> The fine words with which Governor Davis described his act should not conceal from anyone that he has interfered with the judicial process of the Parish of Orleans.
>
> And the surrounding circumstances of his actions raises questions about his motives and propriety in reprieving Mrs. Pailet.

Garrison obviously was not to be awed by high office. He continued:

> I think the Governor's action should be investigated and all of the circumstances of the so-called "act of kindness" should be put under the light of public scrutiny in order to determine what laws Governor Davis may have violated.

And lest there still remain any doubt:

> I will study how an investigation of Governor Davis's bizarre act can be begun.
>
> Governor Davis may call it "an act of human kindness" if he wishes, but it looks like an old-fashioned fix to me.

Nor could he resist a side thrust at the man who had prosecuted him for public defamation:

> Normally such an investigation of such questionable action
> by a Governor would be conducted by the Attorney General.
> But Louisiana has no Attorney General.

Mrs. Pailet remained free until her conviction was affirmed on appeal a few months later, whereupon she commenced serving her term in prison.

If anything ever came of the investigation of Governor Davis, or if any evidence was developed of any "fix," it was never made public.

Quite likely the suspicions voiced by Garrison ran through the minds of others or were voiced frequently in private conversations. The public normally does not ascribe such flimsy underpinnings, however, to public pronouncements by officials. Most will assume that substantial evidence must necessarily underlie any such accusation by a D.A. This distinction is one that Garrison has had considerable difficulty in grasping.

*   *   *

Davis's term as Governor was due to expire in May, 1964, and under the law, he could not succeed himself. In January of 1964 John J. McKeithen was elected to the Governorship. Garrison had supported McKeithen and the latter publicly acknowledged his indebtedness. McKeithen's gratitude was such that there was, he said, nothing that Garrison wanted that he would not feel obliged to help him to obtain.

Shortly thereafter, the D.A. was back in action. In early 1964, three men, Sidney Hebert, James Martin, and John Scardino, were sentenced by Judge Malcolm O'Hara to serve three and one-half year terms in the State Penitentiary for the crime of simple kidnapping. Twenty-eight days later, after having served but thirteen days of their sentences, Hebert and Martin were paroled by the State Parole Board. Scardino was also serving time as a narcotics violator and was ineligible for parole. The Parole Board consists of five men, all appointees of the Governor, and sits in Baton Rouge, Louisiana, about ninety miles north of New Orleans, well outside of Garrison's jurisdiction. However, the D.A. was not to be deterred. The action of the Board was the subject of public indignation and the D.A. was never one to become enmeshed in fine legal technicalities when he smelled blood.

Dusting off a seldom-used statute authorizing the District Attorney to conduct an "open hearing" whenever he "shall have been informed that a crime or crimes has been committed," Garrison petitioned for such a hearing, alleging that he had been informed that money changed hands in a conspiracy to arrange two quick paroles. He had learned, he said, that money was given to an intermediary, who was to turn it over to "certain public officials" in return for their using their influence to effect the paroles. All five members of the Parole Board, together with a mass of documents and records, were subpoenaed. The hearing, commencing April 1st, was marked by the third courtroom appearance of Jim Garrison since assuming office. Judge Edward A. Haggerty, later to preside at the trial of Clay Shaw, quickly made known the nature of the hearing that was to come. Objections by attorney Sam "Monk" Zelden, representing the Board members, that the hearing was a "vicious proceeding whereby the District Attorney can go on a fishing expedition" were met by the Judge with the retort that Zelden had no standing to object or to be heard. The Parole Board members were witnesses only, said the Judge, and he, Zelden, had no right even to address the Court. No one would have a right to cross-examine any witness produced by the State, nor to object to any evidence to be admitted, for there were no defendants, only witnesses in this hearing. The State Supreme Court refused to interfere, and the hearing commenced.

Garrison called his surprise witness, John Scardino. The twenty-eight-year-old convict from the State Penitentiary testified that he had been told by Martin and Hebert that they were "buying their freedom for $3,500 through a certain New Orleans lawyer who was named both in the testimony and in the public news reports of the hearing. Scardino was also to testify that he "learned" at Angola, the Louisiana State Penitentiary, that convicts were acting as agents for the Parole Board in effecting paroles and that "everyone on the Parole Board took money."

All of the members of the Board, as well as the attorney named by Scardino, vehemently denied wrongdoing in public statements to the press. More prominently featured, however, was their in-court testimony, consisting largely of denials of questions pertaining to their purported dishonesty. Somehow, the implication of such questions is never completely removed by disavowal of the witness.

Credible proof of acts of public bribery might not have been too surprising to all segments of the public. Nor would it have been surprising to other segments, however, to learn that guardhouse talk among convicts is not always accurate, or that there exists a tendency among members of the convict element to boast of their prowess in raising large sums to buy favor in high places.

The untested charges of Scardino were sensationalized in the press. Encouraged, Garrison announced plans to subpoena the Governor, clearly impossible under State law due to executive immunity. Attorneys

for the hapless Board members and the alleged lawyer intermediary
returned to the Supreme Court the following day again seeking a form
of help known by lawyers as "extraordinary writs."

The flagrant nature of the testimony prompted a more serious ap-
praisal of the implications by the Supreme Court. A divided Court
finally agreed to allow the hearing to continue. A minority of two,
including the Chief Justice, John Fournet, were in favor of stopping the
proceedings in their entirety. Said the Chief Justice in his dissenting
opinion:

> It may be well to note that:
>
> 1. Not one scintilla of credible evidence has been pro-
> duced to show that any of the alleged crimes have been
> committed in Orleans Parish, or anywhere else for that
> matter.
>
> 2. The only evidence adduced is the testimony of a con-
> vict brought here from the state penitentiary to give hear-say
> evidence to the effect that rumors exist among the inmates of
> the penitentiary indicating a parole may be bought for a
> certain price when certain attorneys and members of the
> legislature—whose names are boldly proclaimed and pub-
> lished throughout all news media—are employed by a con-
> vict to secure it.
>
> 3. The members of the parole board have been subjected
> to harassment by questions that are suggestive, insinuating,
> and full of innuendoes intended to leave the impression they
> are actually guilty of some kind of crime or crimes. Such
> evidence could not be admitted in the trial of any case in any
> court of justice in the land, either civil or criminal.
>
> 4. To add to this disgraceful spectacle, I note by the news
> media the Governor of Louisiana has been subpoenaed as a
> witness.
>
> It would seem to me that if the District Attorney actually
> has, or felt he had, any information whatsoever that a crime
> has been committed in Orleans Parish, he should have at
> least SOME CREDIBLE EVIDENCE to support that
> belief, and that he would have first produced it to establish
> Orleans Parish as the legal jurisdiction in which to engage in
> such a "fishing expedition" before allowing the character of
> the individuals involved to be destroyed by such rumors,
> innuendoes, and completely unreliable hear-say evidence.

However, in permitting the hearing to continue, the Court's majority
imposed a series of procedural rules to be followed. They were not at all

earthshaking, but did require that the hearing be conducted under certain rather basic rules: All witnesses were to have the right to counsel; no witness was to give hearsay testimony; every person accused was to have the right to be confronted with the witnesses against him; should there be evidence showing the commission of a crime by a named person being investigated, then such person would have a right to be heard, to appear with counsel, to cross-examine witnesses, and to subpoena his own witnesses.

Hardly anything new or novel.

Garrison's response to the Supreme Court edict was delivered as concluding remarks to Judge Haggerty in open court. He was, he announced, shifting his probe to the secrecy of the Grand Jury. He gave as one of his reasons an alleged attempted suicide by Scardino. There was more testimony to obtain from Scardino, said Garrison, but he was too much in fear of his life to testify publicly.

Further, said Garrison, there was a second reason for concluding the open hearing and removing the matter to the secrecy of the Grand Jury room.

> . . . The Louisiana Supreme Court has added a fantastic new galaxy of ground rules which, in effect, means the end of open hearings in Louisiana. . . . I do not know what their authority is for the arbitrary invention of these so-called ground rules. They are certainly not in the statute which the legislature passed. They have, so far as I can see, been pulled out of thin air. They have the effect of completely destroying the investigative effectiveness of the open hearing. They place burdens upon the court itself which unavoidably would slow any hearing to a snail's pace.
>
> As a result of this invention of so-called ground rules, this is probably the last open hearing that will ever be attempted in Louisiana.
>
> Your Honor, the District Attorney's Office does not intend to be further obstructed after all the other obstacles we have encountered by this legal destruction of the open hearing. In our judgment, the paroles of Martin and Hebert—and their continued freedom—represent an illegal and improper action by the Parole Board. We intend to get to the bottom of it. Accordingly, we now have commenced a Grand Jury investigation into these strange and highly flagrant paroles. . . .
>
> Your Honor, we have completed taking our depositions in this Honorable Court. Our open hearing is concluded.

If any evidence was ever developed as a result of the Grand Jury investigation, it was never made public. There were no convictions, trials, charges, or arrests. Nor did anyone hear any more about it.

*   *   *

In June Garrison was briefly back in the headlines. Following certain general and perfunctory criticism of the State Pardon Board by the local press, he intended, he said, to subpoena the Attorney General and the Lieutenant Governor, both ex-officio members of the Board (a distinct entity from the Parole Board), to explain their actions publicly. Specifically what actions they were to explain was never mentioned. Garrison announced that he was developing an "arsenal of law and precedent" to insure that a public hearing on the Board was not blocked in the criminal District Court or in the Louisiana Supreme Court.

It appeared that, once again, Garrison had sensed a conspiracy:

We see the outline of a hydra which is made up of public officials who have invisible alliances with each other and who maintain in effect an invisible mutual assistance pact.

Before we have successfully called all public officials involved, and we will, we will see part of the hydra flinging violently to block, distort, or end the hearing.

As far as is known, there was never an investigation. If so, it was certainly not public. In any event, there were neither charges nor arrests.

*   *   *

Next came the Legislature. In May, 1964, Governor McKeithen was inaugurated and the Legislature convened immediately thereafter for its regular 1964 Session. There were many new faces in Baton Rouge that year and there was general promise of a substantial improvement in performance over legislatures of prior years. Throughout the normal sixty-day period of the session through May and June, the long-tarnished image of the lawmaking body brightened. Much commendable legislation passed. One of the bills adopted, not necessarily one of those of merit, permitted bail bondsmen six months rather than sixty days in which to return fugitive defendants in lieu of forfeiture of bail. Garrison, whose major source of operating funds had been the "fines and fees fund" comprised to a substantial extent of funds derived from forfeiture of bonds of fugitive defendants, had strongly opposed the bill.

On July 6th, 1964, as the Legislature continued in overtime session, banner headlines around the State announced that Garrison had accused the Louisiana Legislature of public bribery. As in the case of his accusation of racketeering influence on the "judges," no individuals were singled out.

Said Garrison:

> I am convinced that public bribery occurred in passage of House Bill 894 (the Bail Bondsman Bill). Some of the bribery occurred in this Parish.
> I am doing two things: (1) asking the Grand Jury to call in all New Orleans bondsmen and find out how much they contributed, (2) I am asking all District Attorneys in the state to do the same thing in their Parishes.

The other District Attorneys seemed something less than interested. None of them responded. Garrison's source for the supposed bribery was the statement of eight New Orleans bail bondsmen that they were approached by another of their profession for the purpose of contributing $1,000 each to "get this bill passed in the Legislature. It takes money to get a bill passed up in Baton Rouge." There was no indication that any money was actually paid or, if paid, the use to which it had been put by the bondsman in question.

Said Garrison:

> We know that some Legislators were conned. We know that bribery occurred. We want to find out where.

Like most of the targets of Garrison's attacks, the legislators were incensed. There was serious talk of addressing him out of office; however, the Governor's political obligations to Garrison indicated the certainty of a far milder response. Garrison addressed himself to the talk of ejectment, however:

> This seems to be a Legislature in which bail bondsmen out vote District Attorneys by 100 to 1. So it would look like—if such an attempt is made—I won't have an abundance of support.
> Undoubtedly, I would be in a much better position with the Louisiana Legislature if I were a bail bondsman rather than a District Attorney because then I would be able to block any sort of action I chose.

Two days later, the Legislature unanimously censured Garrison for his accusations. Garrison was not abashed. He was, he said, honored by the

Legislature's unanimous censure of him because he "received more votes than the Bail Bondsmen Bill." "The resolution in fine, gentlemen. Now I would like to ask: Where is the money?" Garrison further informed the public that his office had censured the Legislature. He had spoken to each one of his assistants, he said, and they had unanimously concurred in the censure. "The Legislature reminds me of Humpty-Dumpty, who said the most humiliating thing was to be called an egg," said Garrison. "However, if you are an egg, it is not humiliating."

One legislator lamented on the floor of the House of Representatives that in the closing days of the session "A big, dark cloud came out in the headlines . . . the Legislature's guilty of receiving bribes. That's what the headlines said, regardless of what the small print said. The dark cloud which has been created by the political garbage hangs over us. I don't want to make him [Garrison] a martyr, he isn't worth it."

The Governor signed the Bail Bondsmen Bill "to show his confidence in the Legislature." He pointed out that the District Attorneys Association of Louisiana had not put itself on record in opposition to the bill and that in a poll of its members they took no clear-cut position on the matter. Several bondsmen and others were subpoenaed before the Grand Jury. No indictments were returned. Nor was anyone charged or arrested.

*   *   *

Later that summer, Rudolph Becker, a veteran criminal attorney and former Assistant District Attorney, ran for the Judgeship of Division "E" of the Criminal District Court in opposition to Judge Cocke. A number of Becker's newspaper advertisements, as well as his campaign literature, bore the unmistakable imprint of Garrison's clever and fertile creativity. Cocke was an inept campaigner, and his support by several former District Attorneys, State legislators and other city officials, as well as many members of the Bar was scarcely adequate to answer the ridicule heaped upon him. Toward the end of the campaign, Garrison actively and openly supported Becker, who entered a second primary with Cocke. Cocke was ultimately defeated. Becker became the second judge to be elected with Garrison's support.

For a number of months thereafter, it was mercifully quiet. It almost seemed as though there were no more worlds to conquer. The major event was the departure from office of First Assistant Frank Klein, who lost out in a power struggle with Chief Investigator Pershing Gervais. Klein quit in a huff when it became clear that Garrison considered Gervais his chief lieutenant. Gervais' status was never questioned thereafter. Charles Ward became Klein's successor as First Assistant District Attorney.

If Garrison's repeated and dramatic assaults on high office produced little by way of results, he nevertheless captivated the public with his daring. He was now unquestionably one of the most powerful political figures in the State—certainly the most feared by politicians. His position was, indeed, enviable. But Garrison wore his crown precariously. It would be defended violently against even the mildest attacks. There would be a vigorous reaction to the faintest sign of hostility from whatever quarter. And by June of 1965 another city-wide campaign for Mayor, District Attorney, and other city officials was about to swing into high gear.

5

GARRISON'S NAME HAD BEEN widely mentioned as a possible candidate for Mayor and the city was sprinkled with bewildering billboard advertisements reading "Vote for Garrison" without specifying the office.

On June 10th an eruption of volcanic proportions broke an uneasy calm. The targets of Garrison's wrath were Mayor Schiro and Superintendent Giarrusso. The facts that precipitated this conflagration were simple. The ramifications were not.

In November, 1964, a barroom owned by one Clarence Bielosh had been burglarized and a four-hundred pound safe was removed. The safe was recovered. Several months thereafter, Giarrusso's office received a memorandum to the effect that confidential information had been received that Bielosh made a payment of $600 to a member of the District Attorney's staff for withholding or destroying football cards that were contained in the safe. Though the mere possession of football cards is not in itself illegal, the only practical use for such cards is in connection with illegal gambling operations.

Giarrusso, not at all anxious to irritate the volatile District Attorney, furnished a copy of the memorandum to Garrison and requested his consideration as to the best method of proceeding. Said Giarrusso with considerable understatement: "It was realized that this was a sensitive matter and should be treated in that light." Garrison was on duty with the National Guard in Arkansas, but First Assistant Charles Ward made an effort to have Bielosh come to the District Attorney's office for questioning. He later advised Giarrusso that he was unsuccessful and asked police cooperation. In May, Giarrusso was successful in obtaining Bielosh's presence in his office, whereupon the bar owner was questioned by Giarrrusso, Garrison, and Ward. Copies of this statement, as well as all aspects of the investigation thereafter, were furnished Garrison. Neither Giarrusso nor any other member of the Police Department ever publicly named the alleged recipient of graft in the District Attorney's office. However, Garrison in many of his subsequent public releases on the matter made clear that the party in question was Garrison's Achilles heel, Pershing Gervais.

On June 10th the story broke in the local newspapers that the Grand Jury was investigating possible bribery and that District Attorney aides and police were said to be involved. Garrison, from Fort Chaffee, Arkansas, quickly decided that the investigation, which was being conducted by a police major and a member of the Police Bureau of Investigation, must cease. He publicly suggested that Giarrusso should probe his own investigators to determine the extent of "possible outside influence" involved in their probe of Gervais. The next day Garrison again issued a release referring to the "election year political game and a phony fishing expedition." "I know what's going on, but I must find out who's behind the woodwork," he continued. Said the man who had accused the Governor and the entire Legislature and the Parole Board of bribery and the entire Criminal Bench of influence by racketeers:

> I react very strongly to political investigations of my office and I am going to be very aggressive in bringing about the exposure of whoever is responsible for attempting to damage the morale of my office and to discredit the reputation which we have worked so hard to build up.

Garrison next instructed Ward, as Acting D.A. in his absence, to refuse to allow any member of the D.A.'s staff to be drawn into an "outlaw kangaroo political election year inquisition like the one going on now."

As usual, Garrison improved as he warmed to the subject:

Once again I call on Schiro to make available to the people, in its entirety, the whole of this phony investigation on which his Chief of Police has been working so hard for so many weeks. This will show the people that the investigation which Schiro has stealthily launched into my office ended up with absolutely no evidence.

Evidently, my exposure of Schiro's investigation for what it is has touched a highly sensitive nerve. For his statement Tuesday is the first positive statement this man has made since he stumbled into the mayoralty.

When the people of New Orleans learn how this smirking, smiling, glad handing ribbon cutter has attempted to make a weapon out of his Police Department they will dump him in the garbage can.

Responses by Schiro and Giarrusso were muted. Said Schiro:

The investigation will be pursued to its ultimate course no matter how loud anyone screams . . . I request that Mr. Garrison join with me in asking the Criminal Bar Association or any qualified group to determine was it I or was it the District Attorney himself who injected politics into this matter.

It is my fervent hope that this matter can be promptly concluded and that we can get on with the job of fighting the criminal element of this community.

Garrison's retort was a letter to the Mayor demanding that the results of the investigation to date be made public. At a news conference Schiro quoted part of Garrison's letter in which it was claimed that the investigation by the Police Department of "a member of my staff has taken a wrong turn and ended up in your Police Department."

"Isn't that cute?" grinned the Mayor.

To a suggestion that the dispute be submitted to a Citizens Committee, including the deans of the local law schools and other prominent citizens, Garrison said, "It would not matter if he recommended the Queen of England and the President of the United States as members of a committee. By being recommended by Schiro, they are automatically disqualified, as far as any chance of my ever appearing before them."

Among those testifying during Garrison's Grand Jury probe of the matter was Clarence Bielosh. He was promptly charged with perjury—a gambit later developed by Garrison to a high degree of effectiveness. But the matter did not stop there.

By the end of June, Garrison announced a major investigation into what he termed irregularities in the Mayor's office. A letter by Garrison to Schiro read in part: "I am sure you understand that the employment of a Police Department or member thereof to accomplish a political objective is a violation of Revised Statue 14:134 (malfeasance in office)." The D.A.'s old standby!

But he was only beginning. "Naturally, your position as Commander-in-Chief of the forces involved in this curious expedition makes it necessary—if we are to clear the air—that our inquiry begin with you," continued Garrison's letter. Garrison then outlined twenty-one questions pertaining to subjects varying from supposed irregularities in the street-improvement program to private business ventures by members of Schiro's administration. Few of the questions had any semblance of relevancy to the Bielosh case, though most of them were generally conceded to be of far more interest to the public. Some typical questions by Garrison:

> Is it not a fact that you have been informed that a high-ranking member of your staff often accepts cash gratuities? If so, what investigative steps have you initiated?

> Is it not a fact that one of your closest personal friends had the exclusive catering contract at the Municipal Auditorium and that any persons using this public building are forced to use this catering service?

During the next few days District Attorney assistants and investigators were engaged in a feverish examination of records at City Hall. Earlier Giarrusso had publicly said, "Had Mr. Garrison given the Department of Police the opportunity to conclude this investigation, it could very well have been a routine investigation without all the fanfare and sensationalism that has been attached to it." Garrison had other ways of ending the investigation without fanfare. Quietly the investigation of Gervais stopped. Simultaneously and just as quietly, his investigation of City Hall folded. No one heard any more of either probe. Neither was anything heard again of the perjury charge against Clarence Bielosh.

*   *   *

Garrison did not run for Mayor. He ran for reelection as District Attorney. He was opposed only by Judge Malcolm O'Hara, who took a leave of absence from the bench to do so. O'Hara's opposition was a

major surprise. By laymen and attorneys alike the judiciary is considered
more attractive and prestigious than the office of District Attorney.
O'Hara explained that he had hoped to the last that someone would
offer Garrison major opposition; that he had entered the race only at the
last moment when it appeared that the office might go to Garrison by
default.

The campaign was exceptionally bitter. O'Hara quickly made clear
that a major target would be the record and character of Pershing
Gervais. Gervais promptly resigned as Chief Investigator. He has never
returned as a member of the staff, but his influence with Garrison and
upon the office is widely believed to continue without abatement.

O'Hara struck hard but inept blows. Garrison was never called to
account for his numerous freewheeling and unsubstantiated attacks.
O'Hara did, on one occasion, refer to "the ugly force in him which
compelled him [Garrison] to destroy every one who fails to bow to his
will." "It used to be called a Napoleonic complex," said O'Hara. But it
was a mere fleeting thrust at an area that would have been difficult to
defend against a sustained and documented attack. Instead, O'Hara's
blows were wasted on matters much more easily defended. Garrison
won by slightly more than 60 percent of the vote.

In March, 1966, a vacancy was created on the Criminal Court Bench
by the retirement of Senior Judge George Platt. Under State law,
Governor McKeithen could fill the vacancy with his own appointee. At
the urging of the District Attorney, the Governor selected Matthew
Braniff, a close friend of Garrison. He was the third man to ascend to
the bench through Garrison's efforts.

*   *   *

In May, 1966, Garrison began his second term in office. Again, a calm
settled over the office only to be shattered by the D.A.'s explosive reaction to a public statement he deemed a reflection on his administration. Once again, the ramifications of the incident were far more complex than the immediate facts at issue. Garrison's target this time was
the Metropolitan Crime Commission, a nonprofit organization of local
citizens, and most particularly, its Managing Director, Aaron Kohn.

Kohn and Garrison had for years been on friendly terms. Following
Garrison's induction into office in 1962, Kohn had frequently been
laudatory of some of Garrison's major efforts and had, even when
critical, been far less so than in prior administrations.

However, in the summer of 1966 a series of reprieves by Garrison's
friend, Governor John McKeithen, kept a Bourbon Street stripper,

Linda Brigette, from serving any part of a thirty-day jail term imposed by a District Court Judge against the stripper for obscene dancing. In the fall of 1966 she applied to the State Pardon Board for a full pardon. It was vigorously opposed by the Metropolitan Crime Commission. Among the many statements issued on the subject, the Crime Commission declared that Linda Brigette, a featured attraction at one of the more prominent Bourbon Street clubs, was important to certain "organized crime" elements. The term "organized crime" stung Garrison to the quick. There could be no organized crime in New Orleans because Garrison in his four years in office had rid New Orleans of organized crime. Garrison took the remark as a personal affront. He revealed that it was he who had interceded in behalf of the convicted stripper. In seeking a full pardon by the Governor, Garrison claimed that new evidence indicated that testimony given by the State witnesses at her trial was not true. His previous activity in her behalf came as a surprise to all, including the Crime Commission. Garrison's keen interest in the case remains something of a mystery to this day.

Kohn and the President of the Crime Commission were subpoenaed to appear before the Grand Jury. Publicly Garrison said that Kohn would be obliged "to put up or shut up." He freely predicted that Kohn would be unable to substantiate the economic importance of Linda Brigette to organized crime. In advance of Kohn's appearance, Garrison mocked at the coming testimony:

> We will undoubtedly learn that I have been seen on a streetcar at the same time as Bugsy Schwartz, the famous burglar, or that I was in New York City at the same time as Machine Gun Brady. . . .
>
> His standard technique in such encounters is to use guilt by association. This is very much like the squid, which when attacked injects black fluid into the eyes of his opponent.
>
> When I have finished exposing Mr. Kohn's half-truths, however, he will be the one that is backpedalling and not me. . . .
>
> When Mr. Kohn told a series of lies to the people of New Orleans about the office which we have built up, that was the day as far as I am concerned that his career of using half-truths and worse about public officials started coming to an end.

Kohn and the Commission President were subpoenaed for 10:00 A.M. on September 28th. They were allowed to cool their heels in the hallway adjacent to the Grand Jury Room for four hours. They carried with them a large box which they claimed to contain evidence to be shown the Grand Jury for the purpose of supporting their allegations of organized crime and a prepacked lunch of sandwiches.

Garrison, due to the sacredness of the Grand Jury secrecy, claimed that he was prevented from stating publicly what occurred during Kohn's appearance before the Jury. He pointed, however, to the fact that no indictments were returned as proof that Kohn had been proved a liar. He added:

> I now want to invite anyone else who thinks that they see organized crime flourishing in this city to come tell us all about it. Persons without evidence should not apply.
>
> I asked the Director of the Metropolitan Crime Commission to put up or shut up about organized crime flourishing in New Orleans. He appeared before the Grand Jury for four hours. The Grand Jury took no action and made no indictments. . . . The Metropolitan Crime Commission should turn its attention to raising camellias.

In rare criticism of Garrison's conduct, the New Orleans *States-Item* in an editorial on October 1st said:

> It would be more seemly of Mr. Garrison to spend less time ridiculing the efforts of solid, well-intentioned citizens and more time working with those genuinely concerned with prevention, exposure, and punishment of crime.

Garrison's response was to accuse the press of being unfamiliar with the facts and to accuse the Crime Commission of "the big lie." In a speech before the Young Men's Business Club, Garrrison listed six areas of organized crime, all of which he said had been eliminated or placed well under control, largely by the efforts of his office. Before the end of October, a special investigator, hired by the Crime Commission to extract information from the record room of the Clerk of the Criminal District Court was the subject of a lengthy news release by Garrison. Said he:

> The Metropolitan Crime Commission recently has hired a special investigator to help in the obtaining of evidence. . . . It is quite obvious that his assignment is to see, if possible, if he can find something wrong with the handling of these cases by my office. Since we have nothing whatever to fear, either in that area or any other area, he is more than wel-

come to investigate. However, it would save the Crime Commission and its contributors a great deal of money if he would just walk openly into my office and tell us what information he wants.

We will be glad to make one of our investigators available to help him. We will even have a member of our staff assist him in finding his way back to his hotel at the end of the day. . . .

Garrison, proving himself as prolific as ever, continued with page after page of bitter invective against the Crime Commission and its Managing Director, Aaron Kohn. The depth to which Garrison had been stung by the midsummer comment of Kohn concerning the existence of organized crime was revealed when, two months later, he answered a routine inquiry by the President of the Crime Commission with an angry blast which he did not bother to make public:

. . . After a grandiose statement of the positive existence of organized crimes and of their flourishing existence in New Orleans, I have not heard a scintilla of testimony or one iota of proof that would indicate that there was any truth to these statements.

Therefore, said Garrison, he would not engage in any dialogue with the Managing Director or any of the directors of the Crime Commission. Garrison's letter concluded:

Finally, you can save yourself a lot of stationery by not burdening this office with any further correspondence. I have instructed my staff to return to you unopened all further communications from your organization.

The date of the letter was December 21, 1966. For a number of months by this time, Garrison had, in fact, been greatly preoccupied with other matters. But obviously, the scar left by the thrust of Kohn's remarks concerning organized crime had not healed.

*   *   *

So it went. If it were true that the demoniacal ferocity of Garrison's fusillades was still increasing in tempo in his fifth year in office, there was some solace in the fact that they were in essence defensive measures. Not since the election had there, in truth, been a major offensive mounted in the manner of the attack on the judges or the Legislature.

*   *   *

One day in early January, 1967, I was standing in the reception room of the District Attorney's office. I was approached by a former assistant district attorney under Garrison, one whose departure from the office coincided with mine in September, 1963. He obviously had something to say.

"The more things change around here, the more they stay the same." His tone was a mixture of amusement and disbelief. "Do you know what Garrison's investigating now? The assassination of Kennedy!" The incredulity I felt must have shown clearly, for my friend continued, as though trying to convince me. "He has investigators going all over—to Miami, San Francisco, Dallas—he's supposed to be trying to find some kind of conspiracy."

I laughed. Even the Warren Commission had never excluded the possibility that a plot existed, but if such a conspiracy were ever to be uncovered, I would have assumed it would be by someone capable of an infinite capacity for quiet, thorough, and tedious investigation. I had seen something of the D.A.'s probes, and I doubted, if a plot in fact existed, that it was going to be discovered by Garrison.

"Where is the press?" was my first reaction. Of all of the trivia that finds its way into print, I wondered, why hadn't this been exposed? I assumed that one good blast of publicity would suffice to end whatever spectacular was in the making.

The publicity was not long in coming. On February 17th, 1967, the States-Item ran large headlines and a lead story about the investigation. But it was not the end of the matter at all. Once again I had grossly underrated Garrison's instinctive insight into the public temper.

6

IN AN INTERVIEW PUBLISHED IN
Playboy magazine in October, 1967, Garrison explained how his investigation into the assassination of John F. Kennedy began:

> . . . I'll have to tell you something about the operation of
> our office. I believe we have one of the best District Attorney's offices in the country. We have no political appointments and, as a result, there's a tremendous amount of *esprit*
> among our staff and an enthusiasm for looking into unanswered questions. That's why we got together the day after
> the assassination and began examining our files and checking
> out every political extremist, religious fanatic, and kook who
> had ever come to our attention. And one of the names that
> sprang into prominence was that of David Ferrie. When we
> checked him out, as we were doing with innumerable other
> suspicious characters, we discovered that on November 22nd
> he had traveled to Texas to go "duck hunting" and "ice
> skating."

The naked facts are considerably more prosaic. It had started with a telephone call to an assistant district attorney two days after the assassination, Sunday, November 24th, 1963. The party calling was Jack Martin. The message:

> Ferrie had been in Dallas about two weeks previously; Ferrie had been corresponding with Oswald; Ferrie taught Oswald how to shoot.

Who was Jack Martin? He has described himself as an expert on electronic eavesdropping, an author, newspaperman, professional soldier, adventurer, and philosopher. Descriptions by others have been less flattering.

Martin has had firsthand experience with prison cells and mental wards in two states. He was forty-seven at the time of the assassination but appears considerably older than his years. He has a knack for turning up in the middle of controversial matters, though he contributes little. As Ferrie himself was later to tell the District Attorney: "Martin somehow gets to be near the bride at every wedding and the corpse at every funeral."

Martin was employed as an assistant to Guy Bannister, one of two partners of Guy Bannister Associates, Private Investigators. Bannister himself had been a former Assistant Superintendent of Police until he was dismissed from the Department in 1957 for pulling a pistol in a French Quarter bar in the course of a quarrel. He was a tall, white-haired, distinguished-looking fanatical advocate of right-wing causes. Guy Bannister Associates was in the Newman Building at the corner of Lafayette and Camp Streets. It bore two municipal addresses, 544 Camp Street and 531 Lafayette Street. Bannister's company used the Lafayette Street address.

Martin will talk for hours on end upon the slightest provocation. Any information or misinformation he possesses is available for a drink. There will generally be considerably more of the latter than the former and only the least discriminating rely upon "facts" learned from him. They do so at their peril.

Martin subsequently admitted to both the Secret Service and the Federal Bureau of Investigation that the alleged connection of Ferrie with Oswald was a figment of his imagination. He acknowledged that he was drunk, a not infrequent occurrence, and that when drunk he frequently suffers from "telephonitis." To others he has denied the incident occurred at all.

In fact, Ferrie had not been to Dallas, as far as is known, for at least six years. Nor has any correspondence or other connection with Oswald ever been reliably established.

The motive for the call? Many have speculated. Some say merely that Jack Martin needed no motive. Others maintain that he was piqued at having been excluded by Ferrie and Bannister and by a criminal attorney, G. Wray Gill, from any involvement in the investigative phase of the defense of Carlos Marcello, reputed boss of the Louisiana branch of the underworld, on charges of illegal entry into the country. Ferrie was an investigator for Gill who, with New York lawyer Jack Wasserman, represented Marcello. On one occasion in the course of trial preparation, Ferrie ordered Martin out of Bannister's office. The case was concluded and Marcello acquitted in the early afternoon of November 22nd, 1963. News of the assassination had come to the participants of the trial as they waited for the jury's verdict. Another hypothesis is that the call was in retaliation for a pistol-whipping Martin had received from Bannister the night of the assassination. The fracas occurred in a tavern near Bannister's office and arose out of an argument over unauthorized long-distance telephone calls by Martin. Martin was treated for lacerations of his head, but he refused to press charges. Still another view is that Martin resented Ferrie's ill-concealed disdain for him. Ferrie, unlike Martin, was a brilliant man of varied talents. The two apparently had little in common except a conglomeration of weird and often freakish attributes.

According to Martin himself, he hatched the idea upon hearing on TV that Oswald was once in the Civil Air Patrol in 1955 or 1956, an organization in which Ferrie was quite active.

Whether Martin knew that Ferrie had left with two companions that night for a weekend in Texas following the Marcello trial, has never been clear. It is doubtful, for he did not relate this fact to the District Attorney's staff.

And David Ferrie? In 1963 he was forty-six, a former airline pilot by profession, having been fired by Eastern Airlines in 1961 for misconduct. Thereafter, he did free-lance flying and pilot instruction at the New Orleans Lakefront Airport. An exhaustive investigation was compiled by Eastern Airlines to attempt to substantiate dismissal for cause. Sexual deviation was alleged and the dismissal had, in fact, followed an arrest of Ferrie in August, 1961, on charges of crime against nature with a juvenile. More important to the airline, however, was that the other pilots refused to fly with Ferrie. Their complaint: he was physically filthy. Others have described him in the same manner.

There were other aspects of Ferrie's appearance that disturbed the more sensitive. His clothes were ill-fitting. He had no hair on his body and he compensated with a red wig and eyebrows affixed with glue. His ideas were as unorthodox as his appearance. He was called "radical" by many of his acquaintances; "too brilliant for his own good" by others; and "anti-everything" by still others.

But he was not without talent. He described himself in the telephone directory as a psychologist. He practiced hypnosis and was apparently fascinated by it. He had a library on this subject, as he did on human anatomy, about which he often exhibited amazingly detailed knowledge. He kept white mice and claimed to be working on a cure for cancer. He was an accomplished pianist and an unsuccessful candidate for the priesthood of the "Orthodox Old Catholic Church of North America."

By all accounts, he was a restless, driven, tormented nonconformist, an outcast from "respectable society," bitter and distrustful of all authority. He was an adventurer and a seeker of causes or unorthodox ideas in which to immerse himself and find outlets for his hyperactive mind. He was to attain neither success nor apparently any solid achievement.

In 1958, while still with Eastern Airlines, he became Senior Executive Officer of the Cadet Squadron at the New Orleans Lakefront Airport, one of two Civil Air Patrol Units located in the New Orleans area. Lee Harvey Oswald served for a few weeks in the summer of 1955 or 1956 in one of the two squadrons; no one has been able to prove with certainty whether in Ferrie's or in the other, located at Moisant International Airport.

In early 1961 Ferrie became associated with a group of Cuban expatriates whose purpose was counterrevolution in Cuba. There were several organizations of these refugees from Castro at this time and membership frequently overlapped. One group known as the Crusade to Free Cuba was headed by one Sergio Arcacha Smith. It had been formed in early 1961 by Smith with the assistance of a New Orleans public relations man, Ronnie Caire. Caire was successful in recruiting as financial supporters many prominent and affluent New Orleanians of conservative persuasion. They included William Reily, the owner of a thriving coffee import company; William Monteleone, major owner of one of the city's principal hotels; Jim McMahon, funeral parlor director; and Dr. Alton Ochsner, a surgeon of international fame and founder of Ochsner Foundation Hospital in New Orleans. The nucleus of the group was about a dozen or so Cubans who were allowed to frequent the office of Guy Bannister and to use his telephone and other office services. Bannister was never a member.

Another organization active in 1961 was the Cuban Revolutionary Democratic Front. Locally, the group was not as well organized or financed as the Crusade; however, it was but part of a larger apparatus operating in several cities, including Miami. Smith apparently exercised leadership in this group, also.

In early 1961 Ferrie persuaded Smith that he, Ferrie, could render valuable service to the cause. The two became friends, and Ferrie was active, probably in both groups, but certainly in the Democratic Front. His sojourn with the Cubans was brief, but interesting. Early that year he conceived and worked on a contraption similar to a midget submarine at his home, located at the time in Jefferson Parish adjoining New Orleans proper. It was a one-man gadget supposedly designed for attaching explosives to warships. Both the plan and the contraption were ultimately junked.

Ferrie boasted of having taken part in a commando-type raid on the coast of Cuba and having suffered a wound in the abdomen as a result. Autopsy photographs of Ferrie following his sudden death in February, 1967, supposedly show a fourteen-inch scar across the abdomen.

Ferrie also assisted in making a haul of explosives and grenades from a local military installation, probably the Algiers Naval Ammunition Storage Base. The grenades and explosives were placed in an eight-foot by ten-foot U-Haul truck and destined for the Democratic Front in Miami. When officers of the Front arrived to receive the truck of explosives, they examined and rejected much of it as unusable.

Sometime in early 1961 a number of the group journeyed to Houma, Louisiana, about 60 miles south of New Orleans to an ammunition bunker of a company known as Schlumberger Well, a surveying corporation with home offices in Texas. The group met in Ferrie's home in Jefferson Parish and proceeded to Houma in two cars and a laundry truck. The purpose of the journey was to pick up a quantity of explosives and deliver them to New Orleans for further transportation to Miami for use in the Bay of Pigs invasion. The invasion itself commenced April 17th, 1961.

Among the group journeying to Houma with Sergio Arcacha Smith and Ferrie were a twenty-six-year-old electronics expert specializing in bugging equipment, a sometime bar operator named Gordon Novel, his fiancee, Marlene Mancuso, to whom he was later married and divorced, two young men, Rancier Ehlinger and Andrew Blackmann, and a younger man, then only nineteen, unknown to most of the others, who seemed to wander around Ferrie's home as though lost while the balance of the group made plans. He was Layton Martens, a music student who had become acquainted with Ferrie while serving as a member of his Civil Air Patrol Unit. Although the intricacies of the operation are still somewhat shrouded, it appears clear that the Schlumberger Well's bunker was serving that night as a transfer point for explosives with the acquiescence of its management, either here or in Texas and with officials of the United States Government, including, presumably, the Central Intelligence Agency.

In fact, Smith's party had a key to the bunker. There was no forced entry, nor was there any report of theft by the company's employees.

In the summer of 1961 Ferrie was arrested, though never convicted, for attempted crime against nature with a juvenile. Arrested with him was Martens. Apparently, the basis of Martens's arrest was nothing more serious than his presence in Ferrie's company. In September, Martens moved to Lafayette to continue his music studies at the University of Southwest Louisiana.

In October, 1961, Ferrie's brief Cuban adventure ended. Carlos Bringuier, a Cuban expatriate and attorney, asked Smith if he might meet with Ferrie; for from the things he had heard, said Bringuier, he did not think that association with Ferrie would do Smith or the Cuban cause any good. Shortly thereafter, Smith took Bringuier to Ferrie's house. Smith, Bringuier, Ferrie, and two young boys were present. Smith and Bringuier stayed but five minutes. Bringuier came away convinced that Arcacha Smith should have nothing more to do with Ferrie and he so advised Smith. Ferrie's association with the group ended.

In February, 1962, the Crusade to Free Cuba disbanded. Undoubtedly, a major contributing factor was the dismal failure of the Bay of Pigs invasion. Whatever the cause, the group had accomplished little, fell to bickering, and the small group of prominent New Orleans conservatives left in disgust.

Shortly after the group disbanded, Smith, in considerable disfavor with the Cuban community, left New Orleans for Texas, settling first in Houston and ultimately in Dallas.

The activities of the Cuban community in New Orleans, if there were any, through the balance of 1962 and early 1963 apparently have left little impression on the memories of those close to the scene. There remains no evidence of any activity of significance, and such conjecture as has been forthcoming has made no mention of specific ventures. Through 1962 and 1963, Ferrie was frequently to be seen at the New Orleans Lakefront Airport and remained active in the Civil Air Patrol Unit through the beginning of 1963. He also performed investigative work for Bannister. Though Ferrie may have retained a friendship with some of the Cubans, he was distrusted and disliked by others.

In the fall of 1963, Layton Martens had returned to New Orleans because of a serious illness suffered by his mother. Upon her discharge from the hospital in mid-November, 1963, he stayed for two weeks with

Ferrie, who now resided in an upper apartment on Louisiana Avenue Parkway in New Orleans. Martens was employed by a blueprint company at the time and recalls vividly, as does almost every other American, hearing the news of the assassination on the afternoon of the 22nd of November. He recalls, also, that Ferrie was not around that weekend.

Following Marcello's acquittal, Ferrie had attended a victory party at the Royal Orleans Hotel. Immediately thereafter, about 9:00 P.M., he and two companions drove first to Vinton, Louisiana, to attend to certain business for Gill, then to Houston and Galveston for a short vacation. The purpose? To go ice skating and hunting. The trip had been planned for some time and was to take place when the trial ended. Prediction of the precise length of any complex trial is impossible even for the most experienced. Martens did not find it at all unusual that Ferrie was gone that night. It was his habit to come and go as he pleased and he accounted to no one.

Ferrie's companions were Alvin Beauboeuf, a young man of nineteen whom he first met as a cadet in his Civil Air Patrol Unit, and Melvin Coffee, an engineer employed at the National Aeronautics and Space Administration Facility at Michoud on the outskirts of New Orleans. The first night Ferrie took care of his business in Vinton, Louisiana, then drove to Houston where he and his companions registered at the Alamotel about 4:30 A.M. on Saturday, the 23rd. Late that afternoon they went to the indoor Winterland Skating Rink, one of the few in this part of the country. Three and one-half years later, Garrison was to claim that Ferrie did not even put on a pair of skates, but that he stood waiting for several hours by a telephone. This was obviously the "communications center," Garrison was to claim. According to Beauboeuf and Coffee, however, Ferrie went ice skating, then talked to the manager about the possibility of opening a rink in Baton Rouge, Louisiana. Ferrie had recently received a substantial sum of money from Eastern Airlines as a result of his severance in 1961 and he was seeking a venture in which to invest. The night of the 23rd was spent at the Driftwood Motor Hotel in Galveston. The three went out looking for some "night life" and found that "the only thing you could buy was beer." "By our standards, it was dead," said Ferrie. "It couldn't get deader. So far, the vacation had been falling on its head."

According to Ferrie, they went hunting the next morning, which was Sunday. They boarded a ferry across a channel along the south shore. "We did, in fact, get to where the geese were and there were thousands, but you couldn't approach them," Ferrie claimed. "They were a wise bunch of birds."

At about this time came Jack Martin's telephone call. The information was passed on to the First Assistant D.A., Frank Klein, who thereafter conducted the operations. Five investigators were assigned to watch the Louisiana Avenue Parkway apartment. Garrison left two telephone numbers, one for the New Orleans Athletic Club and the other for the local Playboy club, with instructions that he should be called if anything developed.

The investigators went to Ferrie's apartment. No one was there. Martens himself spent very little time at home that weekend. Finally, the investigators called G. Wray Gill, Marcello's attorney and Ferrie's employer. Their interest was aroused considerably upon being informed that Ferrie had gone to Texas for the weekend.

Later that day Ferrie and his companions decided to go to Alexandria, Louisiana, where Beauboeuf had relatives. After arriving, they decided to stay two or three days, but Ferrie thought it wise to call Gill and advise him of his whereabouts. Gill told Ferrie that he had better get back at once as the D.A.'s men were looking for him.

"For what?" asked Ferrie.

"It has something to do with the assassination of the President," responded Gill. Gill narrated the information that Jack Martin had passed on to the D.A.'s office concerning Ferrie's supposed acquaintance with Oswald.

Ferrie decided that he was not yet ready to be arrested. Upon arriving in New Orleans, shortly after midnight on the 24th, he dropped Beauboeuf at his, Ferrie's, apartment with instructions to remove certain items that had best not be there if the apartment was raided—specifically, certain lewd photographs and a number of hypodermic needles that he might need. Ferrie, as far as is known, did not use narcotics, but injected himself with various drugs for numerous ailments with which he was constantly plagued.

Ferrie was to wait in the car around the block. Martens was in the apartment, an upstairs duplex, when Beauboeuf entered. After removing the photographs and needles, Beauboeuf left. He was greeted at the bottom of the stairs by the D.A.'s men. "Let's go upstairs, son," said one. Beauboeuf and Martens were arrested. They were booked with being "fugitives from Texas." The D.A.'s men confiscated numerous items, including a number of weapons and a flare gun, several voluminous abstracts on posthypnotic suggestion, as well as a library on hypnotism and three U.S. passports without pictures or descriptions.

Also confiscated from Beauboeuf were a number of obscene photographs, including several of Beauboeuf himself. Martens and Beauboeuf were confined for twenty-four hours. They were questioned extensively about David Ferrie and the details of the trip to Texas, about which Martens, of course, knew nothing.

In the meantime, when Ferrie realized what had happened, he dropped Coffee at his home and fled to Hammond, about sixty miles north of New Orleans, where he stayed the night with a friend. He returned the following day and, accompanied by his attorney, surrendered to the District Attorney's Office. He was asked if he knew Oswald. Ferrie replied that he did not. The D.A.'s aides decided this was a lie and booked him with being a fugitive from Texas. He underwent questioning for several days.

On Monday night, Martens and Beauboeuf were released to the Federal Bureau of Investigation. The F.B.I. had been contacted by Garrison's office and advised of possible implications by the two men, as well as Ferrie. His ownership of a plane was mentioned to the Bureau. The agents asked Beauboeuf and Martens if they wanted to answer the questions or speak to an attorney first. Beauboeuf said he was tired and wanted to talk to a lawyer. Martens gave a written statement. Both men were released. The F.B.I. as well as the Secret Service questioned Ferrie following his release by the District Attorney. Separate investigations were conducted by each agency and Ferrie's movements and whereabouts in Texas were corroborated fully. Satisfied with Ferrie's story, the Bureau did not thereafter contact Beauboeuf or Martens. The conclusion of the Secret Service: Martin was apparently an alcoholic and was totally unreliable.

Two New Orleans police detectives went to the New Orleans Lakefront Airport and checked Ferrie's single engine plane even before his return to New Orleans. They noticed two flat tires, instruments missing, and a general deteriorated condition, and determined that it wasn't flyable. In fact, it had not been airworthy since the spring of 1962.

After his release, Ferrie proceeded to conduct his own investigation to determine how and when he was alleged to have known Oswald. He went to Oswald's former residence on Magazine Street to speak to his ex-landlady, found the place swarming with Federal investigators, and could obtain no information.

Three months prior to the assassination, Oswald had been in the news as a result of a scuffle on August 9th with Carlos Bringuier, the anti-Castro Cuban refugee. Ferrie went to see Bringuier at his place of business. He apparently did not recall the Cuban from their short meeting at Ferrie's apartment two years earlier. Bringuier was cool to Ferrie. He said any information he had about Oswald would be given to Federal authorities and only to them.

Ferrie went through old albums, scrapbooks, and papers of his Civil

Air Patrol activities, but could find no reference to Oswald. Nor could anyone else glean anything of significance from the Civil Air Patrol records, except for the bare association of Oswald with that organization for a few weeks in 1955–56.

Martens had now been arrested twice, both times apparently for no other reason than being associated with David Ferrie. He decided that twice was enough and broke off his acquaintanceship. Beauboeuf continued to see Ferrie regularly over the next three years.

The purpose of the trip, the ice skating, the hunting, the business in Vinton, the gloomy sojourn to Galveston, all were later to be characterized by Garrison as clever fabrications to cover a major involvement in a plot to assassinate the President. The repeated protestations and minute accountings by Ferrie, Beauboeuf, and Coffee were dismissed as lies, or perhaps, in the case of Beauboeuf and Coffee, as naïve interpretations of the events by men intended to be pawns in the sinister affair. Indeed, Garrison would ultimately claim that "the thread that unraveled this whole case was the trip that Ferrie made to Houston the day after Kennedy was killed."

But that was to come later. Public clamor for the "truth" behind the assassination still lay in the future. This was the fall of 1963, and Garrison turned to more important things.

For the time being, the matter was closed.

7

THE EXACT TIME OF THE REBIRTH
of Garrison's interest in the assassination is hard to determine with any
degree of precision. Much has been made of a conversation alleged to
have occurred in November, 1966, between Garrison, United States
Senator Russell Long of Louisiana, and a wealthy New Orleans businessman named Joseph Rault. Supposedly, while en route to Washington,
the trio, fellow passengers by chance, discussed the Warren Report. All
three were skeptical. It is practically certain that by November Garrison
had already begun to take note of the mounting vocal public dissatisfaction with the Report's conclusion and with the by now popular cliché
that "one man could not have done it alone."

Using a species of logic which Garrison himself had mastered so well,
Rault concluded that if three such people as himself and his two
companions harbored serious doubts as to the Commission's findings,
there must be some sound basis for these doubts. Long was to go on
record as stating that Oswald was not a good enough marksman to
accomplish the deed; that the proper investigative procedure would be

to ascertain the hundred best marksmen in the world and to find out which one was in Dallas the day of the assassination. He has never informed the world as to the next step, should it be determined that none of them was there.

Undoubtedly, the conversation, which has been reported by Garrison himself, merely heightened the D.A.'s determination to discover the plot that virtually everyone knew to have existed. Certainly by November he had already taken note of the fact that Oswald had been in Dallas less than two months at the time of the assassination. For the previous five months, Oswald had been in New Orleans and Garrison meant to inquire into the activities of Oswald while in "my jurisdiction." Garrison set out to determine whether there was a conspiracy hatched during that period. To many who know him, it is not surprising that he found that there was.

He first immersed himself in the growing body of literature on the subject, not only the Warren Report, but also the volumes of the critics:

There was Harold Weisberg, author of *Whitewash*. Weisberg agreed with the Warren Commission conclusion that Kennedy was assassinated in Dallas on November 22nd, 1963—and with nothing else in the report.

There was Mark Lane, the glib, publicity-oriented New York attorney, author of *Rush to Judgment*, the most popular of the offerings of the critics.

There were the scholars. Richard H. Popkin, author of *The Second Oswald*, apparently considered the evidence gathered by the Commission as an unusually interesting jigsaw puzzle. Because all of the pieces did not fit precisely, he determined that the Commission had found the wrong answer. And there was Edward J. Epstein, author of *Inquest*, whose orderly mind likewise rebelled at the untidiness of unexplained facts and the existence of others whose place in the puzzle has not been found by the Commission.

It is curious that among the career critics of the Commission there are few who qualify by training or experience as investigators, and fewer yet whose lives have been spent in the evaluation of evidence. The Warren Report and the assassination itself seem to hold a strange fascination for those who dwell in ivory towers.

Garrison concluded that the Commission was wrong; that Lane, Weisberg, Epstein, and Popkin were right. Garrison was to borrow heavily from all of them. Thoroughly saturated with the works of these critics, and like Don Quixote de la Mancha, Miguel Cervantes's demented student of knighthood, Garrison felt it was time for action.

Before he was through, he was to tilt at windmills in such realistic fashion that Sancho Panza himself would have taken them for giants.

He had a starting point. Ferrie had driven to Houston the day of the assassination—and Houston is in Texas—and had offered the totally unsatisfactory explanation that he had gone ice skating and hunting. As further proof of the sinister nature of the trip, Ferrie and his companions had traveled through a "driving rainstorm." So often was Garrison to ridicule the avowed purpose of the trip by reference to the "drive through a thunderstorm to go ice skating" that one might legitimately wonder whether the explanation would have sufficed had the weather been clear.

Garrison quickly concluded that Ferrie was a key factor in the assassination. What other purpose for this trip through a thunderstorm? Obviously, he knew Oswald and had plotted the assassination with him. The true purpose of his trip, namely, some planned participation in the assassination, would have to be established, and the identity of those who knew this purpose and knew the exact nature of Ferrie's role in the plot were in turn known to the D.A. It was now a matter of extracting the truth.

In late November or early December, Alvin Beauboeuf was asked to come into the D.A.'s office where he was again questioned about the details of the trip to Texas. His statement was needed to complete an old file that was about to be closed out, he was told. Beauboeuf obliged. They had gone ice skating and hunting, he repeated. Nothing strange or sinister had occurred as far as Beauboeuf knew. He knew nothing about the assassination or any other involvement of David Ferrie. Beauboeuf was questioned repeatedly by the D.A.'s office thereafter until he tired of going in. Then the investigators started coming to his home. Obviously, Beauboeuf was either lying or was simply naïve and did not understand some of the strange activities of Ferrie or the fact that the trip was a cover for Ferrie's true purpose.

Martens, too, was called back into the office to "complete the file." He was asked again about Ferrie, his acquaintances and his activities, and about Martens own involvement in them. He responded freely. A number of things he told the D.A. made no sense. Despite a close friendship with Ferrie in the fall of 1963, he did not know Oswald and had never seen him in the company of Ferrie. He was asked to take a lie detector test and readily agreed. It was administered by the New Orleans Police Department polygraph operator who advised the D.A.'s office that he found no evidence of deception. It didn't matter. Obviously, Martens was lying.

Melvin Coffee had by now been transferred to the Space facility at

Cape Kennedy and escaped questioning for several months. In February, a discreet, well-worded letter invited him to come to New Orleans in connection with an investigation of "the utmost importance." The D.A. suggested that if Coffee felt that his employment would prevent his appearance, that the D.A. would be happy to discuss the matter with Coffee's superiors. Coffee appeared voluntarily. He recounted the details of the trip to Texas, and told the D.A. he was with Ferrie at all times "except when he went to the bathroom." He then returned to Cape Kennedy.

In the meantime, there was another starting point—a short, rotund, black-haired, jovial, wise-cracking, 44-year-old lawyer. His name was Dean Andrews.

*   *   *

Andrews loves words. When not talking, which is seldom, he is usually wearing a broad, boyish grin, or laughing lustily, for he appears to see the world as a huge joke. Almost as perpetual as the grin is a pair of dark glasses which are his virtual trademark. Lawyers as a group have often been accused of dullness and of lacking imagination or originality, all caused, it is said, by overly cautious use of words to convey information logically. Attempts at preciseness of communication have stifled the creativity of most lawyers, say the profession's critics. Not in the slightest degree do these criticisms apply to Dean Andrews.

One quickly concludes that often his words are designed to create effect, or to entertain, or to amuse rather than to communicate facts. His flights of fancy are enlivened with a flowery extravagance of language. His accent is an aural caricature of Brooklynese. Few realize that the accent native to parts of New Orleans is almost identical to the better known Brooklyn variety.

The spontaneous outpouring of Andrews's colorful language is sometimes remarkable. One is often awed by an apparently limitless flow of baffling originations. Most discerning listeners have little trouble in recognizing his soaring adventures in imagination for precisely that. It would be a mistake, however, to conclude that his narratives are totally or perpetually illusory. They are not. None who has truly known him would accuse him of stupidity. Prior to 1967 he had successfully practiced law for fifteen years and was serving as a part-time assistant D.A. in Jefferson Parish. His practice, while perhaps not qualifying him for service with Wall Street firms, has been interesting and colorful—and useful and honorable.

If many people do not take Dean Andrews quite seriously, it is also true that practically none would wish him harm. If he often has little regard for fact, it is equally clear that he has little expectation that his prevarications will be relied on by others to their detriment. It is doubtful that he has ever intentionally caused harm to anyone. Cruelty and malice are alien to his nature.

In May of 1963, Lee Harvey Oswald, according to Andrews, appeared in Andrews's office. He was with some "gay" kids. They were "Mexicanos," says Andrews. He declares he saw Oswald three to five times thereafter over the next few months and that Oswald usually had one particular "Mexicano" with him, a "gay" kid with a "butch" haircut. Oswald, Andrews continues, sought his assistance in a variety of matters —citizenship problems for himself and his wife and correction of a less than honorable discharge from the service. Andrews avers that Oswald couldn't pay, and says he did little for him. He says that he assumed that Oswald had been sent by a French Quarter bar owner of many years acquaintance who frequently referred "gay" kids to him for legal services. The name of the bar owner was Eugene Davis. Circumstances strongly suggest that Andrews may never really have laid eyes on Oswald.

The day after the assassination, Andrews was confined in a New Orleans hospital, Hotel Dieu, under sedation undergoing treatment for pneumonia. He thought of the fame and glory that would be his if he could represent the man charged with committing the crime of the century—thoughts similar to those undoubtedly being entertained at the time by Mark Lane. He received a call from his friend, Eugene Davis. He certainly would like to represent Oswald, said Andrews. Andrews is not certain Davis replied at all. If he did, it was with a vague and offhand remark to the effect that he would see what he could do.

The following day, still hospitalized, Andrews called an attorney friend, Sam "Monk" Zelden. "I may get to represent Oswald," said Andrews. "If I'm not able to handle it, would you take it?" Later in the conversation, Zelden asked Andrews to hold the phone while he investigated the cause of a disturbance at the scene being shown on his television set. A moment later, Zelden advised Andrews that his client Oswald had been shot.

On November 25th, 1963, Andrews advised the local F.B.I. office that Oswald had been in his office that summer. He was interviewed that day by two agents—"feebees," as Andrews calls all F.B.I. agents. In the course of explaining his relationship with Oswald, Andrews could not resist informing the agents that he had been "asked" to defend him in Dallas. The inevitable next question had somehow not occurred to Andrews.

"Who asked you?" inquired the agent.

In fact, no one had asked him. He had asked Davis. Once, several years previously, an acquaintance had introduced Davis to Andrews at an affair that Andrews termed a "fag wedding reception," unaware that the two were longtime friends. Davis was introduced to Andrews as "Clay Bertrand." People in "gay" circles frequently hide their true identity to outsiders, as well as to each other. The friend was simply being prudent. Andrews had laughed and said, "That's not Clay Bertrand. That's Gene Davis."

Now Andrews had no desire to direct the F.B.I. to Davis.

"His name is Clay Bertrand," said Andrews.

No, Andrews could not say where Bertrand lived. He saw him only once or twice, said Andrews. He referred clients sometimes, though. Could Andrews describe him? Yes, he was approximately 6′ 1″ to 6′ 2″ in height, had brown hair and was well dressed—most assuredly not an accurate description of Davis.

Not long thereafter, F.B.I. agents were combing the French Quarter looking for Clay Bertrand. Finally, Andrews decided to tell the F.B.I. that Bertrand did not exist. As Andrews was later to explain to the Warren Commission, for whom he re-created the legend of Clay Bertrand, he did finally tell the F.B.I. that Bertrand was a figment of his imagination:

> . . . I knew that the two feebees are going to put these people on the street looking, and I can't find the guy, and I am not going to tie up other agents on something that isn't that solid. I told them, "Write what you want, that I am nuts. I don't care."

> They were running on the time factor and the hills were shook up plenty to get it. Get it. I couldn't give it to them. I have been playing cops and robbers with them. You can tell when the steam is on. They are on you like the plague. They never leave. They are like cancer. Eternal.

Said Andrews:

> It was my decision if they were to stay there. If I decide yes, they stay. If I decide no, they go. So I told them, "Close your file and go someplace else." That's the real reason why it was done. I don't know what they wrote in the report, but that's the real reason.

It was in July, 1964, that Andrews was served at his office with a subpoena to appear before Wesley J. Liebeler, an Assistant Counsel to the Warren Commission. He was to appear at the Federal Court Building in New Orleans to give a deposition. Andrews played cat and mouse for awhile, but finally made an appearance. Said he to Liebeler: "I don't know anything about this. What I told the F.B.I. was all a bunch of lies." Liebeler, apparently somewhat at a loss, did not know how to take Dean Andrews. "Would you repeat the lies under oath?" said Liebeler. "Be my guest," said Andrews. "I'll swear to anything."

Apparently, Andrews took Liebeler at his word. He revived the Bertrand story, only the new Bertrand was "5′ 8″ with sandy hair, blue eyes, ruddy complexion, must weigh 165, 170, 175."

Liebeler, more bewildered than ever, asked his perplexing witness to explain the discrepancy between this description, particularly with regard to height, and that furnished the F.B.I. Said Andrews:

> But you know I don't play Boy Scouts and measure them. I have only seen this fella twice in my life. I don't think there is that much in the description. There may be some to some artist, but to me, there isn't that much difference. Might be for you all.

"Is this fellow a homosexual, do you say?" asked Liebeler. "Bisexual," said Andrews. "What they call a swinging cat."

Otherwise, Andrews's story of the telephone call from Clay Bertrand was substantially the same to Liebeler as it had been to the F.B.I. Said Andrews to Liebeler:

> I was in Hotel Dieu and the phone rang and a voice I recognized as Clay Bertrand asked me if I would go to Dallas and Houston—I think Dallas, I guess, wherever it was that this boy was being held—and defend him. I told him I was sick in the hospital. If I couldn't go, I would find somebody that could go. . . . I had seen Clay Bertrand once some time ago, probably a couple of years. He's the one who calls in behalf of gay kids normally, either to obtain bond or parole for them. I would assume that he is the one that originally sent Oswald and the gay kids, these Mexicanos, to the office, because I had never seen those people before at all. They were just walk-ins. . . . He is mostly a voice on the phone. . . . This is my impression for whatever it is worth of Clay Bertrand: His connection with Oswald I don't know at all. I think he is a lawyer without a briefcase. That's my opinion. He sends the kids different places. Whether this boy is associated with Lee Oswald or not, I don't know, but I would say when I met him about six weeks ago, when I ran

up on him and he ran away from me, he could be running because he owes me money, or could be running because they have been squeezing the Quarter pretty good looking for him while I was in the hospital, and somebody might have passed the word he was hot. . . .

The Warren Commission dismissed Andrews's testimony as being of little significance and he is barely mentioned. It would be hard to fault the Commission for this.

One afternoon in the fall of 1966—Andrews places the date at October 27th—Andrews received a call from his longtime friend, Jim Garrison. Garrison asked Andrews to meet him at Broussards, one of the better French Quarter restaurants. They were to meet at 1:30. "I knew him," said Andrews, "so I went at 3:00 o'clock. He still wasn't there." When Garrison finally arrived he displayed to Andrews a copy of *Whitewash*. "I didn't know you were in the Warren Commission Report," said Garrison. The two chatted about Andrews's testimony and the conclusions of the Warren Report, in which neither of the two had confidence.

"I had a chance to solve the assassination right after it happened," said Garrison. "But I blew it."

Andrews says that he suggested to Garrison that he try and obtain the cooperation of the *Life* magazine staff. *Life* had the original movie film taken of the assassination by the amateur photographer, Abraham Zapruder, Andrews pointed out, and maintained a continuing interest in research and investigation into the assassination. Garrison ultimately did work in cooperation with representatives of *Life* magazine, at least for awhile, though the details of any agreement have never been made known.

By and large, Garrison received little information from Andrews that was not contained in the Commission Report. Garrison was primarily interested in the names of some of the "Mexicanos" or other Latins who were seen by Andrews in the company of Oswald.

The two men met on a number of occasions at the same restaurant or in Garrison's office throughout November and into December. Andrews could furnish Garrison with no more information concerning the mysterious Clay Bertrand than was available in the Commission Report. Finally, however, pressed by Garrison for names of the Latin companions of Oswald, Andrews reached into the blue and replied: "Manuel Garcia Gonzales." Why had he made up the fictional character with the most popular of Latin names? As Andrews was later to explain to a national television audience: "He [Garrison] wanted to shuck me like corn, pluck me like a chicken, stew me like an oyster. I wanted to see if this cat was kosher."

Garrison promptly charged one Manuel Garcia Gonzales with selling narcotics, an extremely serious offense under Louisiana law. Of course, there was no evidence of any offense, and not the slightest conception as to who Manuel Garcia Gonzales might be. Shortly thereafter, the two men, Garrison and Andrews, again met and Garrison informed his friend that Manuel Garcia Gonzales had been arrested in Miami. As Andrews was further to explain to the same television audience, he didn't know which Manuel Garcia Gonzales had been arrested in Miami, but if it was the same one that he, Andrews, had mentioned to Garrison, then Garrison "Had the right ha ha, but the wrong ho ho."

Garrison was to become convinced that Manuel Garcia Gonzales was one of the assassins in Dallas and, apparently, for a time believed that he was the leader of the group and the prime culprit. Writing for *Tempo* magazine, an Italian publication, in April, 1967, Garrison stated he would gladly give up Clay Shaw if he could but get hold of the true assassin—Manuel Garcia Gonzales.

But who was Clay Bertrand? The question intrigued Garrison. Bertrand must be located. There were certain clues. He lived in the French Quarter. He spoke Spanish. He was well known to many deviates. Who, Garrison asked his staff, was known by many homosexuals, lived in the French Quarter, and spoke Spanish? He would, perhaps, be someone well known, for he seemed to be a leader in "gay" circles. "Clay Shaw," said one of Garrison's assistants. The assistant was joking; Garrison was deadly serious.

Clay Shaw not only had the same first name as the mysterious Bertrand, but he did, indeed, speak Spanish. He did have a fine house in the New Orleans French Quarter and the nature of the acquaintances of the fifty-four-year-old bachelor had, at times, been the subject of idle gossip by those who manage to find gratification in such speculation.

But there were other things about Clay Shaw that were also true, that apparently, to Garrison, bore no relevance.

Clay Shaw was born in Kentwood, Louisiana, a small town near the Mississippi border. He moved with his parents to New Orleans at age five where he attended the public schools. Like many other successful businessmen, Shaw quit before graduation. He went to work as local manager for Western Union. Later, he moved to New York City where he took courses at Columbia University, then went to work in New York as manager of Western Union's mid-city area.

Sometime in the late 1930's Shaw quit his job with Western Union and went into public relations and advertising on a free-lance basis. In 1942 at the age of twenty-nine, he joined the Army and was placed in the Medical Corps as a private. Shortly thereafter he went to Medical Administration Officers' Candidate School and was commissioned as a second lieutenant. He was assigned to England as Administrative Officer with a general hospital unit and subsequently transferred to the Supply Corps and made aide de camp to General Charles Thrasher, Commanding Officer of the United States Forces in the southern half of England. Shaw was subsequently assigned as Deputy Chief to General Thrasher when the latter commanded United States Forces in northern France and Belgium. Prior to his discharge in 1946, Shaw had reached the rank of major and received decorations from both countries—he was named Chevalier of the Order of the Crown of Belgium, was the recipient of the title of Chevalier de l'Ordre du Merite Commercial from the French Government. He was also decorated with the Bronze Star and Legion of Merit by the United States.

After his discharge from the Army, Shaw devoted his life to the arts, to restoration of property in the New Orleans French Quarter, and to the New Orleans International Trade Mart. The Trade Mart, organized in 1947, is a nonprofit organization designed to promote world trade with emphasis on Latin America and, more particularly, to increase foreign commerce through the port of New Orleans. He is given credit for making a success of the Trade Mart venture by most of the New Orleans business community and for realization of a new International Trade Mart complex recently constructed at the foot of Canal Street.

When Shaw resigned in September of 1965 as Director of the Trade Mart, a post he had held since its inception in 1947, he was the recipient of numerous accolades from many leading citizens. Architect Edward Durrell Stone, who designed the new Trade Mart building, described Shaw as "one of the greatest, if not the greatest client I ever had." Trade Mart President, Lloyd Cobb, described Shaw's life as a "noteworthy contribution to the City of New Orleans." The City of New Orleans awarded Shaw its International Order of Merit Medal.

Shaw resigned, he said, because his work had been done. He now wanted to devote his life to his primary interest, the arts—particularly playwriting—and to restoration of French Quarter property. Shaw is the author of a number of published plays, including The Idol's Eye and Submerged, both one-act plays, the latter still being performed by amateur groups. He wrote a full-length play produced in New Orleans in 1948, entitled In Memoriam. In early 1967, he was working on a drama concerning Antonio Ulloa, the first Spanish Governor of Louisiana. Shortly after his retirement from the Trade Mart, he journeyed to

Spain to obtain the permission of the widow of the Spanish playwright, Alejandro Casona, to translate one of Casona's plays, *The Trees Die Standing*, into English. He was almost certain to be seen on any opening night of any cultural attraction in New Orleans, whether symphony, opera, or drama.

Shaw's house in the French Quarter is located at 1313 Dauphine Street. It is a two-story white carriage house with a red door. It is elegantly appointed and furnished. He has restored some sixteen houses in the French Quarter since returning to New Orleans following World War II. His activities in this area were generally considered to be an incentive for other investors at a time when the Quarter was at its lowest ebb. Restoration of French Quarter property has since become widespread and it has, of late, become a "high rent" district.

Shaw is widely liked and respected. He has served on numerous civic boards or agencies. He was a close friend of the late Mayor de Lesseps S. Morrison. Those close to him state that he is liberal in view with regard to politics and an admirer of the late President Kennedy.

Like Garrison, he is tall, 6 feet 4 inches, dignified, and distinguished in appearance. Like Garrison, it is hard to mistake the sharp-featured, silver-haired Shaw for anyone else. The comparison ends there. Shaw is quiet, modest, unassuming.

In December, Shaw was asked to come into Garrison's office and was thereupon questioned extensively. He had assumed initially that the basis for the questioning was the distribution by Oswald on August 16th, 1963, of pro-Castro leaflets in front of the Trade Mart Building at Camp and Common Streets. Oswald and his companion had left before Shaw arrived on the scene and he did not see Oswald at all. Garrison became convinced beyond per adventure that the companion was Manuel Garcia Gonzales and he scoffed at aides who suggested further inquiry.

Shaw was advised by his interrogators that Oswald knew a "Clay" who lived in the French Quarter. Could it have been he? Shaw replied, as he was many times to state thereafter, that he did not know Oswald, had never seen him, and to his knowledge, did not know anyone who did.

Garrison again spoke to Dean Andrews. He had discovered Bertrand's identity. It was Clay Shaw. Could he, Andrews, identify Clay Shaw as the Clay Bertrand he knew? No, said Andrews, he could not. Garrison didn't believe him. He tried to inspire his reluctant friend. According to Andrews, he said, "We will ride to glory together." Andrews still balked. "We have other witnesses who can identify him," said Garrison.

"Do whatever you want," replied Andrews, "but leave me out of it. Everybody knows I don't even know Clay Shaw."

Andrews's version of his subsequent conversations with the D.A. is that he agreed with Garrison that while he would not identify Clay Shaw as Bertrand, that he would not say that he was *not* Bertrand. "In other words," said Andrews, "I won't say he is and I won't say he ain't." As Andrews was later to tell it to me: "I never believed that Jim would go through with a frame-up." Garrison has never publicly commented on this understanding as alleged by Andrews. It may be assumed that he would deny it. It is, to those who know both men, almost impossible that the two could come away from any conversation with the same impression. In the months to come, Andrews was to make a gallant attempt to stick by his understanding of his agreement with Garrison.

*   *   *

In the meantime, however, there was much work to be done. Obviously, Oswald, Ferrie, and Shaw, alias Bertrand, were coconspirators. Necessarily, there must have been many clandestine meetings among them. Certainly, they must have been seen by acquaintances in each other's company. Some evidence must exist of Shaw's use of the name "Bertrand." Garrison would need investigative help and he turned to William Gurvich, one of three Gurvich brothers making up the Gurvich Detective Agency, an established and reputable firm. Gurvich spoke with Garrison at length and learned firsthand from the D.A. that he was in the process of solving the mystery of the assassination. But there was much that must be done in the way of gathering proof, said Garrison. Would Gurvich like to help? No investigator worth his salt was going to turn his back on the opportunity to assist in gathering evidence that would convict the murderers of President Kennedy. And if Garrison said that he was solving the assassination, who was Gurvich to doubt it. Garrison was, after all, the District Attorney and would not make such statements unless some proof existed. Gurvich agreed to help. It was a challenge he could hardly refuse.

And Garrison was indeed well on his way to "solving the assassination." He noted that the Warren Commission Report related that the first pamphlets handed out by Oswald on August 9th bore the imprint, "FPCC, 544 Camp St., New Orleans, Louisiana." This was the same building that was used by the right-winger Guy Bannister, and frequented by the anti-Castro Cubans, such as Arcacha Smith! The facts were falling into place. Garrison was later to claim repeatedly that it was not at all hard to solve the assassination. "It really wasn't that difficult," he related in a television interview in June of 1967 over a local station. To a journalist he had boasted in March: "What it took to solve this puzzle was imagination and evaluation. It was like a chess game—and I once played an expert eight hours to a draw."

And the solution?

The pro-Castro activity of Oswald was a sham as was his entire purported Marxist orientation. This was simply a cover. He was, in truth, working with the anti-Castro Cubans, deliberately trying to disguise himself as a Marxist so that the Marxists and Communists would receive the blame for the deed that was plotted by his right-wing friends.

The motive for the assassination? The Cubans, who, according to Garrison, were actively and vigorously training throughout 1962 and 1963 for an invasion of their homeland, felt themselves betrayed by Kennedy's avowed peaceful intentions toward Cuba and his détente with world Communism, including Premier Castro. According to Garrison, Kennedy had killed all hope of liberation. Thereafter, according to the D.A., their wrath was turned toward Kennedy and his doom was sealed.

There were, to be sure, several problems. One was the question of dates. The activity of the Cubans and their frequency of the building at 544 Camp, according to the evidence at hand, had occurred in 1961 and had terminated by February, 1962. Arcacha Smith left New Orleans about eight months later, and it had never been established that he ever returned. Oswald was not in New Orleans at all in 1961 or 1962. He had been in Russia since 1959. Upon his return to the United States in June, 1962, he lived in Forth Worth and Dallas until his move to New Orleans in late April, 1963. The Warren Commission, after an exhaustive investigation, could find nothing to connect Oswald to the Camp Street address even in 1963. The building, however, it should be noted, is but two blocks from the William B. Reily Company at 640 Magazine Street where Oswald worked for a little more than two months as a greaser of coffee-processing machinery. And Oswald apparently had need for some address. He had written V. T. Lee, National Director of the Fair Play for Cuba Committee, on August 1st, 1963, claiming that an office he had rented for F.P.C.C. activities had been "promptly closed three days later by renters, they said something about remodeling, etc." The use of that address was undoubtedly fraudulent as was most information forwarded by Oswald to V. T. Lee, including his boast of having distributed "thousands of circulars," and, in truth, his very claim to Lee of the existence of a local organization of the F.P.C.C. Oswald was the organization.

However, Garrison had sources of information that the Warren

Commission did not. There was Jack Martin and there was an acquaintance of Martin's, a twenty-six-year-old freight agent and former private investigator named David F. Lewis. Prior to working for Continental Trailways in his capacity as freight agent, Lewis had held about five jobs during a three-year period beginning in 1962. During the months of January, 1961, through January, 1962, he had been employed by Guy Bannister Associates. A previous short stint in the Navy was terminated with a discharge for psychiatric reasons. In the summer of 1963 he had no steady employment and used to stop by Bannister's office from time to time to see if "there was any leg work to be done." He has been described as being as talkative as Jack Martin, but not quite as reliable.

Martin and Lewis were questioned with increasing frequency and their presence in and around the District Attorney's office was quite prominent. They seemed to enjoy thoroughly their roles as key informants. As early as mid-December, Garrison's investigators and assistants had extracted "information" from Martin and Lewis establishing Oswald's presence, usually in the company of Cubans, in the Newman Building at 544 Camp Street in the summer of 1963. Garrison has consistently alleged his version of the plot to assassinate Kennedy to be supported by "credible witnesses." It appears certain that the "credible witnesses" include Martin and Lewis.

According to Lewis in a statement given the District Attorney on December 15th, he had been introduced in the summer of 1963 to a man named "Lee Harvey" in Mancuso's Restaurant located on the ground floor of the Newman Building. Present at the time were Sergio Arcacha Smith and a fellow named "Carlos." Said Lewis to the D.A.: "It has now been determined by me through photographs that this man was Lee Harvey Oswald." Carlos was later identified as Carlos Quiroga, a Cuban refugee who has been living in New Orleans since September of 1961.

Jack Martin also claimed to have seen Oswald at various times in the summer of 1963 in the Newman Building. According to Martin, he saw Oswald once in the office of Guy Bannister in the presence of David Ferrie who was wearing an Army-type fatigue suit. Present with Ferrie was one Morris Brownlee, godson of David Ferrie. On still another occasion, Martin claimed to have seen Oswald with Sergio Arcacha Smith and Quiroga in Mancuso's Restaurant.

Garrison has claimed Oswald's associations here were "exclusively—not merely frequently, but exclusively—with persons whose political orientation was anti-Castro."

Garrison may be somewhat straining the point. As already mentioned, his informants have had troubles with dates. First statements of Martin and Lewis to Garrison were that they had seen Oswald with Quiroga in

Mancuso's Restaurant in the summer of 1962. But Oswald was in Russia, Fort Worth, and Dallas in 1962 and the date was later corrected to 1963. But the presence of any of the anti-Castro group in the Newman Building in 1963 has never been established by anyone but Martin or Lewis and has been denied consistently by those with first-hand knowledge, including the Cubans themselves.

The time element was not the only problem. What of Oswald's leftist and pro-Castro activities? How could his widely known Marxist leanings be reconciled with exclusive association with known rightists? Again, Garrison's explanation of this activity as a sham and a cover for right-wing convictions may be somewhat strained. The Warren Commission Report quotes one William E. Wulf, formerly President of the New Orleans Amateur Astronomy Association, an organization of high school students. Oswald applied for membership at the tender age of fifteen. Wulf told the Commission that he remembered an occasion when Oswald

> started expounding the Communist doctrine and saying that he was highly interested in communism, that communism was the only way of life for the worker, et cetera, and then came out with a statement that he was looking for a Communist cell in town to join but he couldn't find any. He was a little dismayed at this, and he said that he couldn't find any that would show any interest in him as a Communist, and subsequently, after this conversation, my father came in and we were kind of arguing back and forth about the situation, and my father came in the room, heard what we were arguing on communism, and that this boy was loudmouthed, boisterous, and my father asked him to leave the house and politely put him out of the house, and that is the last I have seen or spoken with Oswald.

Further, while only sixteen years of age, he had written a letter to the Socialist Party of America professing his belief in Marxism.

Oswald's avowed pro-Marxist statements throughout his military career and later, and his defection to Russia are well known. If it was a cover, it was extremely elaborate and beautifully concealed over a period of many years. Apparently it was effective with all of his contacts in New Orleans, Dallas, and elsewhere in the United States, as well as in the United States Marine Corps and Soviet Russia. That the cloak was assumed while Oswald was yet in high school, however, must certainly have strained somewhat the credulity of even Garrison's most devoted followers.

It is, and must remain, a matter of conjecture as to how much of the fine web of a plot being woven in Garrison's mind was the result of "information" from Martin or Lewis, how much the contrivances of witnesses such as Andrews, and how much the result of Garrison's own deductive logic.

*   *   *

But there was yet one other starting point to the D.A.'s probe. Garrison had learned that in the summer of 1963 there was a training camp for Cuban exiles in St. Tammany Parish, north of Lake Pontchartrain, New Orleans's northern boundary. Also, in July of 1963, the Federal Bureau of Investigation had discovered a cache of arms located in a rural area in St. Tammany Parish which had belonged to a group of Minute Men, the militant right-wing organization. The connection of the Minute Men hideaway and the cache of arms with the Cuban training camp was not immediately clear to Garrison, nor was any conclusive evidence of any connection ever developed. It didn't matter. Garrison did not believe in coincidences.

Obviously, the camp was where the assassins, including Lee Harvey Oswald, trained for their big day in Dallas on November 22nd. The Cubans who trained here must be identified and located. They were part of the guerrilla team that Garrison determined had fired at the President from three different directions in Dallas.

Again, the bare facts were less sensational:

In early 1963 one Laureano Batista headed an anti-Castro organization in Miami known as the Christian Democratic Association. Batista planned an undercover fishing fleet based in Nicaragua to engage in operations against Cuba. Contact was made between Batista and one Rudolph Richard Davis who had resided off and on in Cuba since early childhood, having most recently returned to the United States on January 12th, 1961. Shortly thereafter, Davis became active in the Christian Democratic Movement.

Davis agreed to try to set up a training camp in the vicinity of New Orleans and thereupon spoke to members of the De la Barre family of New Orleans about the possibility of locating such a camp on certain property owned by the De la Barres in St. Tammany Parish on the north side of Lake Pontchartrain. Apparently Davis told neither the De la Barres, nor subsequently, the F.B.I., the true purpose of the camp. Instead, Davis sold the De la Barres on the idea of forming a corporation known as "The Guatemala Lumber & Mineral Corporation." Cuban refugees were to be trained at the camp, according to his cover story, for the purpose of cutting lumber in Davis's mahogany forests in Guatemala. The Guatemala Lumber & Mineral Corporation, so went the story, had a contract with the Guatemalan Government to take mahogany out of that country. The consideration to the De la Barres for permitting the use of their land as a training area is not clear. However, it appears that a camp was set up on the De la Barre property near Lacombe in St. Tammany Parish. The house and grounds were completely run-down and the task of the first Cuban refugees who arrived the end of June in 1963 was to refurbish the area. There was a swimming pool located on the grounds which was fed by an underground spring. The camp was served by a dirt road well off the main highway.

Approximately a dozen Cubans arrived at the camp during the next five weeks. At no time did any of the men stray further than about 200 yards from the house. No shooting whatever took place at the camp, nor was there much to shoot with. One trainee reported that they had a total of two or three old Springfield rifles and one M-1 carbine. They were used to demonstrate assembly and disassembly of the weapons, but were never fired. During the course of many of the exercises, the men carried small logs to simulate weapons.

The camp was beset by problems during its short existence. On one occasion, a pro-Castro spy was discovered. The local Cuban community was much chagrined to learn that there was no crime for which a pro-Castro sympathizer could be punished for spying operations in the midst of an anti-Castro group. An additional group of about ten Cubans arriving from Miami were the subject of an inquiry by the Federal Bureau of Investigation when the automobiles in which they were traveling had broken down on one of the highways leading out of New Orleans. Upon hearing Davis's story to the F.B.I. of the purpose of their venture, the Cubans were furious. They had been told that they were to train to liberate their homeland. They had never been told of any cover story and were not interested in cutting timber. As a final straw, at the end of July the Federal Bureau of Investigation discovered the cache of explosives at another location in St. Tammany Parish. Neighbors of the De la Barre property, already jittery due to the presence of the Cubans, suspected a connection between the cache of explosives and the strange operations on the De la Barre property and caused further inquiry. By August 1st every one of the Cubans had been sent back to Miami by bus. Thus ended the abortive attempt to locate a Cuban training camp near New Orleans.

Three and a half years later, Garrison's imagination was fired by the bits and fragments of the story that came to him. Through one of his "credible" witnesses, he became convinced that Lee Harvey Oswald had trained at this camp. First, the camp must be located. Then, it must be investigated thoroughly for telltale signs of the conspiracy that ripened at the camp and, particularly, for the ominous presence of Lee Harvey Oswald. The campsite itself was soon discovered by Garrison's assistants, but the evidence indicated that no firing had occurred there. Obviously, however, target practice had taken place somewhere. The place where the target practice occurred was obviously, Garrison was to claim, the "covert" camp, the De la Barre farm the "overt" camp—in other words, a subterfuge. The real camp had yet to be found.

Garrison wondered if perhaps the deactivated United States Army Camp Villere, located near Slidell, Louisiana, about thirty miles away, might be the place. One of Garrison's most competent and experienced trial assistants was assigned new duties. He was sent to the old Camp Villere area with hip boots and a sack with instructions to salvage spent cartridges that could be found on the target range.

Bill Gurvich was surprised one morning to see the assistant, Alvin Oser, his face covered with mosquito bites, tramping through the D.A.'s office with hip boots.

"Where have you been?" asked Gurvich.

"In the g– d--- swamp," replied Oser.

"Doing what?" asked the bewildered Gurvich.

"Looking for bullets," responded Oser, showing a sack full of spent cartridges.

"What bullets?" queried Gurvich.

"Oswald's," responded Oser.

Gurvich was not at all sure he understood. He determined from Garrison that Oser's report was, indeed, accurate, and the D.A. patiently explained to Gurvich that he was looking for a 6.5 Mannlicher-Carcano bullet, one that would have been fired from a weapon of the type used by Oswald in the assassination of Kennedy.

Gurvich was incredulous. "What are you going to do with it when you find it, Jim?" asked the investigator. "That stuff was Army surplus and plenty of people have 6.5 Mannlicher-Carcano rifles and ammunition. Even if you find one," said Gurvich, "what do you have to compare it with? You don't have Oswald's gun."

"You just let me find one," said Garrison. Several members of his staff patiently examined each of the spent cartridges under magnifying glasses for marks which would identify it as coming from a rifle similar to Oswald's.

Shortly after this incident, Garrison approached Gurvich and advised that if a cartridge from a 6.5 Mannlicher-Carcano could not be found on the ground, that perhaps one might be buried under the ground.

"Can you get a metal detector for us?" asked Garrison.

"Of course," responded Gurvich.

"You can?" asked the delighted and admiring Garrison. "How long will it take you?"

"About twenty minutes," said the investigator as he thumbed through the yellow pages of the New Orleans Telephone Directory to the listing of rental businesses.

"Can you show us how to work it?" asked Garrison.

"Sure," responded Gurvich. "You turn on the switch and start walking."

No 6.5 Mannlicher-Carcano cartridge was ever found.

Garrison was determined that the "covert" camp must have been somewhere. Gurvich, a licensed pilot, was sent to scour the area from the air for telltale signs while Oser took photographs. Oser had been designated as the training camp specialist in the office. Much of the area was photographed and the results given to Garrison for scrutiny.

Finally, one day Garrison exclaimed excitedly that he had found the camp. A dirt road led to the apparent entrance from the main highway. A large blowup of the photograph was prepared and representatives of Life magazine were invited to inspect it. They duly appeared and were much impressed by Garrison's finding.

Gurvich, however, was more skeptical. He went with Oser by car to locate on the ground what had been revealed by the aerial photographs. This is not always a simple task. Gurvich and Oser went up one dirt road and another, only to come to dead ends. Finally, after considerable trial and error and restudy of the aerial photographs, they found the road in question and followed it to the end. A large sign greeted the two men and informed them without the necessity of further inquiry what had been discovered. This was the location of the Tulane Primate Center maintained by the Tulane University Medical School. Gurvich and the assistant decided to see for themselves despite the "no trespassing" signs. As they wandered into the area, Gurvich pointed to the chimpanzees located within.

"Do these look like Cubans to you, Al?"

"I have to admit they don't look very Latin to me, Bill," responded Oser.

Garrison was not defeated. In fact, he was only starting, and his work was cut out for him. Carlos Quiroga must be found and questioned about his acquaintanceship with Oswald. Acquaintances, business associates, friends, and employees of Bannister, Ferrie, and their close associates must be checked out. All leads must be followed through. This would involve investigation in such divergent places as Miami, Dallas, Houston, and anywhere else the trail of witnesses might lead.

8

VERY EARLY IN HIS PROBE, GARRI-
son became convinced of the involvement in the assassination plot of
Cuban exiles interested in the overthrow of Castro. However, this theory
was not always a matter of public knowledge. Garrison's known interest
in the Cubans was widely assumed to indicate involvement of a pro-
Castro group—a natural assumption in view of Oswald's supposed ties
to the Fair Play for Cuba Committee. It failed to take into account,
however, that such a simple and obvious conclusion could hardly appeal
to Jim Garrison. Hence, the early enthusiasm of the anti-Castro exiles
for the D.A.'s probe was of short duration.

On December 28th, 1966, a newsman friendly to Garrison was
introduced to Carlos Quiroga at the Moisant Airport as Quiroga and his
friend, Carlos Bringuier, awaited the landing of certain Cuban Americans
recently arrived in this country via Miami. There was much that could
be learned from Quiroga if indeed he was not one of the conspirators.
Garrison wanted to know about his association with Oswald and why he
was with him in Mancuso's Restaurant in the summer of 1962 (as

Martin and Lewis had first placed the time) and he could further shed considerable light perhaps on the activities of the training camp, including the location of the "covert" camp and the activities of Lee Harvey Oswald there. Perhaps, he could also shed some light on the whereabouts of the true assassin, Manuel Garcia Gonzales.

On January 8th, 1967, Frank Klein, who had been engaged by Garrison to do special investigative work in connection with his assassination probe, called Quiroga into the office and questioned him extensively as to various Cubans with whom he might have been acquainted, including Arcacha Smith and Manuel Garcia Gonzales. Klein also questioned Quiroga about his knowledge of Ronnie Caire and his "Crusade to Free Cuba," about David Ferrie, and about Guy Bannister. Quiroga was also questioned about Lee Harvey Oswald.

Quiroga did, in fact, know Lee Harvey Oswald. On August 16th, 1963, he had gone to Oswald's residence to try and infiltrate the Fair Play for Cuba group. Quiroga's friend, Carlos Bringuier, had been considerably upset by the fact that some time prior to August 9th, the date on which he had scuffled with Oswald as the latter passed out pro-Castro pamphlets, Oswald had tried to infiltrate the anti-Castro group in New Orleans. It was, in fact, Bringuier's chagrin at suddenly discovering that Oswald was, in truth, an enemy of the anti-Castro group and had attempted to spy upon them that precipitated Bringuier's attack. Bringuier determined to fight fire with fire and quickly agreed to Quiroga's suggestion that he, Quiroga, infiltrate Oswald's group. Quiroga had a lengthy discussion with Oswald and came away without any doubt whatever that he was a confirmed Marxist. Oswald gave Quiroga certain literature and an application blank to the Fair Play for Cuba Committee.

On January 12th, David Lewis reported to Jim Garrison that while standing by the Royal Orleans Hotel he was shot at by a Cuban in a passing auto. The Cuban "could have been Quiroga," but there was no identity of the man or the car by Lewis. D.A. assistants were sent to the scene to scour the area for the spent pellet—without success. Garrison ordered Quiroga and "anyone with him" arrested on sight. Gurvich urged caution—and a lie detector test for Lewis. Garrison shrugged, but did not object. Following the test, Lewis was asked by the investigator why he had lied. Lewis explained that he thought the story would please the boss. Told of these developments, Garrison shrugged again.

On January 20th, Quiroga was subpoenaed to appear in Garrison's office. Garrison was now armed with a revised Code of Criminal Procedure effective January 1st, 1967, which permitted him to subpoena witnesses to his office rather than to the Grand Jury, and to compel their testimony to Garrison privately. Quiroga was one of the first to be so subpoenaed. He brought with him on January 20th a scrapbook on the Crusade to Free Cuba, the organization which had disbanded in February, 1962. Quiroga, unlike Dean Andrews, did not know Garrison, arrived on time, and consequently was obliged to wait in one of the outer offices approximately four hours. On the wall of the room in which he was placed Quiroga noticed a large glass which had no apparent reason for being there. He continually heard footsteps from an adjacent room beyond the glass and correctly guessed that the glass was a one-way mirror. Among those who were being asked to view Quiroga through the one-way mirror were Jack Martin and David F. Lewis.

Finally, after being searched for weapons, Quiroga was ushered into the office of Jim Garrison. Without Quiroga's knowledge, the conversation between him and Garrison was recorded and transcribed. Garrison asked Quiroga about Oswald's presence in the camp across the lake. Quiroga replied that Oswald had no connection whatever with the camp across the lake. Garrison became angry and demanded the truth on pain of subpoena before the Grand Jury. He announced that his office had discovered that Lee Harvey Oswald was not at all a Marxist but was a dedicated anti-Castroite. Quiroga found this ludicrous and so told the D.A. Garrison asked Quiroga if he would take a lie detector test. The Cuban agreed and Garrison said that he would be contacted the following day, which was a Sunday. Quiroga remained at home Sunday waiting to receive a call from Garrison's office. He heard nothing. On Monday an investigator called and Quiroga, angered by the delay, replied that he would have to discuss the polygraph test further with Garrison before submitting himself to it.

On January 24th an investigator called and asked Quiroga again to come into the office. Quiroga appeared and found that Garrison's hostility had apparently vanished. Garrison now confided in Quiroga, among other things, that he had proof that Manuel Garcia Gonzales, the true assassin, was in Dallas on November 22nd, 1963. Among other information received by Quiroga was the fact that Garrison had now determined that it was William Reily who had brought Oswald to New Orleans and that Reily, McMahon, Ochsner, and Monteleone were members of the plot. All of this Garrison had determined by reading Quiroga's own scrapbook. The D.A. not only repeated this suspicion on later occasions, but announced to associates his intention of arresting the four men as accessories.

Obviously, said the D.A., Reily had brought Oswald to New Orleans, for it was Reily's business at 640 Camp Street where Oswald worked for two months before being fired for inefficiency on July 19th, 1963.

Garrison also told Quiroga of a training camp conducted by Smith in 1961 and of credible reports of the presence of himself, Oswald, and Smith in the Newman Building in 1962 and 1963.

Quiroga knew the Crusade had disbanded in February, 1962. He also knew the facts about the camp across the lake. He knew that Arcacha Smith had never conducted a training camp in 1961 or at any other time. He knew also that Lee Harvey Oswald could not have been with Sergio Arcacha Smith or with himself in 1962, for Oswald was in Russia till June, then in Fort Worth and Dallas. Finally, he knew that no one could have seen him with Oswald or anyone else in Mancuso's Restaurant, or anywhere in the Newman Building in 1963 as he, Quiroga, had not been in the building at all since early 1962.

Quiroga told Garrison that he should investigate the people who were giving him this completely false information. Jack Martin was revealed as the source of much of this intelligence, and Quiroga asked to be confronted with him. Martin was in the office at the time and the confrontation was permitted. Quiroga quickly established Martin's considerable difficulty with dates by asking him in what year the assassination took place. Martin replied that it had occurred in 1962. The investigator present immediately stopped any further interrogation by Quiroga and a few minutes later told the Cuban that "if Martin changes his mind now about testimony he has given us before, I'll break his head."

Garrison also turned his attentions to Carlos Bringuier. Bringuier was first questioned by assistant district attorneys and later expressed the feeling that he had been treated like a defendant, although he had appeared voluntarily. He quickly concluded that the District Attorney's Office was on the wrong track completely in its investigation and called Garrison on February 13th to ask if he might talk to Garrison personally. A meeting was arranged on February 14th. During this meeting, Garrison explained to Bringuier in detail his theory that anti-Castro Cubans were responsible for the assassination of Kennedy. Replied Bringuier: "You are the District Attorney and you should know, but I think that is stupid."

Garrison pressed Bringuier closely on the "two" training camps in St. Tammany Parish—the "covert" and "overt" camps. Bringuier stated emphatically that he had no knowledge of a second camp in St. Tammany Parish or elsewhere, and did not know of any connection between the training camp and the place where the cache of arms had been found.

Garrison was angered. He asked if it was not possible that perhaps Bringuier might have been fooled by the Cubans. "Maybe I have been fooled and maybe you have been fooled," replied Bringuier. "We will have to see which one of us is the fool."

*   *   *

The investigation was by no means limited to interrogation of witnesses in New Orleans. Beginning in early January an intensive systematic operation was instituted. Assistants and investigators were sent far and wide to run down all possible leads. An elaborate code system was set up. David Ferrie was "Blackstone." Guy Bannister, who had died July 1st, 1964, was "Barney." Morris Brownlee, Ferrie's godson, was "Brown." Lee Harvey Oswald was "Patsy." Other Cuban suspects, including the dangerous Manuel Garcia Gonzales, were dubbed with their own code names. Included were such covers as "Bugs Bunny," "El Toro," and "El Bravo." Terse instructions were issued. One assistant was dispatched to Houston to check out a visit to that city by Morris Brownlee in October of 1963. Another was sent to Dallas to check out suspected temporary residences of certain Cuban suspects and also to make his own examination of the grassy knoll area and the adjacent picket fence which have figured so prominently in the theories of the critics. Other assistants and investigators were assigned to investigate all possible contacts of Bannister and Oswald in New Orleans.

Particularly, Garrison was interested in detailed descriptions of all guns owned by Bannister, and in determining who had taken possession of voluminous files he was known to keep. Names and all relevant information concerning all Cuban organizations in New Orleans since January, 1961, were to be obtained. The printing company that had printed Oswald's F.P.C.C. pamphlets was to be queried concerning previous use of that company by Ferrie. Several barrooms frequented principally by Latins were to be checked nightly for the presence of any of Garrison's suspect Cubans.

An intensive surveillance of Ferrie was ordered. "Be prepared on shortest possible notice to increase surveillance on Blackstone to include picking him up in the A.M. and putting him to bed at night," read the Garrison directive to his investigators.

All assistants on assignments in other cities were instructed to call in daily at precise times. Law enforcement agencies in other cities were not to be given the true nature of the investigation. All information sought was for the purpose of developing a "narcotics case." Secrecy was the key to success.

Soon the information started coming in. Unfortunately, it did not, by and large, seem to be sufficiently accurate or specific. Garrison complained to his staff that many of the statements were "vague and insufficiently developed in the area of primary concern." In truth, he had drawn a complete blank thus far.

Typical of the reports received was one from Houston advising the D.A. that Brownlee had, indeed, been to Pasadena, Texas, on October 28th, 1963. The report contained the highly significant information that "Pasadena, Texas, is a suburb of Houston with a large Latin-American population." The D.A. was further enlightened by the fact that the "Brownlee party on both nights spent at the motel had the motel place in their room a baby bed." "This could well indicate that this party was a family unit," concluded the Garrison sleuths.

*   *   *

Meanwhile, Ferrie was becoming increasingly beset by rumors of impending arrest. He was perpetually besieged by messages from acquaintances that they had been questioned by the District Attorney's Office. The hounding continued without letup. On December 15th, Ferrie had gone to the District Attorney's office upon the D.A.'s request and had again given them a complete detailed statement about his activities during the sojourn in Texas, beginning the night of the assassination. Upon leaving the D.A.'s office, Ferrie went to the place of business of Carlos Bringuier and asked his help in trying to identify Oswald or to place him through his acquaintances. He asked Bringuier again, as he had three years before, for any information that would help him determine whether or not he had, in fact, been acquainted with Oswald as the D.A. had claimed. Ferrie was frightened. The D.A. was trying to advance himself politically and it appeared as though he was going to be framed, he told the Cuban. Ferrie was increasingly embittered. "All lawyers and judges should be hanged!" he exclaimed. "I am a lawyer and my father was a judge," replied the placid Cuban, "so I don't necessarily agree with you." Bringuier again offered little assistance.

On February 5th arrangements were made with a resident across the street from Ferrie's Louisiana Avenue Parkway upper apartment to conduct a continuous surveillance. Ferrie's front door contained glass panels with no curtain and the officers using binoculars had a clear view into the apartment. They noted that Ferrie seemed to be an extremely nervous person who continuously paced from one side of the room to the other. They noted that, from time to time, he would lie on a mattress on the floor, or sit on a pillow, then stand for a few minutes and walk around. He was followed during the day when out. He was constantly under surveillance while home. His every movement was reported to Garrison. His acquaintances and former acquaintances were besieged for information. Garrison was patient. Sooner or later Ferrie would break and tell the true story.

About a year previously, his godson, Morris Brownlee, had been arrested on a narcotics charge, but prosecution was declined by the District Attorney on grounds of insufficient evidence. Now the matter was reopened and Brownlee was arrested and jailed. Now, not only could he be available for questioning about Ferrie, but, explained Garrison to his aides, it might also accelerate the process of breaking Ferrie's obstinacy.

Later that month, Ferrie lost his position with the flying service at the New Orleans Lakefront Airport. He apparently was involved with the law in some way and the continual checking on his activities and the surveillance conducted by the District Attorney's Office was not at all welcomed by his airport associates.

*   *   *

On February 17th, 1967, the story of the Garrison probe broke with large headlines in the local press. Two reporters, long aware with many others of Garrison's investigation, learned of his cooperation with Life magazine and suspected a scoop by the national publication. Expense vouchers for the numerous trips by the assistants and investigators were checked at City Hall and published in the story. They revealed a total of over $8,000 spent in a little over three months.

Garrison first refused to comment at all on the investigation or its prospects. First Assistant D.A. Charles Ward was quoted as having stated that he had little hopes that the investigation would uncover any new information. Ward simply stressed that even the most routine leads must be checked out in a matter as important as a Presidential murder.

Garrison broke his silence the following day. He claimed that the premature publicity had hurt his probe and that the lives of his witnesses were now endangered. Both reporters who authored the copyrighted story of the 17th, however, claimed that Garrison was shown the story in advance and told of its imminent publication. Garrison termed them liars. Garrison assured his public, however, that not only was he in fact conducting an investigation, but that there would be arrests and convictions.

Undoubtedly, the D.A. was not prepared for the glare of international publicity that was immediately focused on him. Two days later, he felt obliged to hold a press conference for the horde of newsmen who were dispatched to New Orleans. Representatives of the local press were excluded and thus punished for their audacity. He chose the Fountaine-bleau Motel as the scene for the conference to avoid legal ramifications in excluding them from a news conference in a public building.

The full impact of the sensation he had created with his promise of arrests had not fully been brought home to him until he approached the assembled mass of newsmen and cameramen. He was heard to mumble, "My God." The conference added little to the public's store of knowl-edge. He could not reveal much, said Garrison repeatedly, as it could cause further harm to the progress of his investigation.

If the publication of the story of Garrison's probe increased pressure on the D.A., it had an even greater effect on David Ferrie. To the newsmen who descended on New Orleans from all parts of the world, it was no secret that Ferrie was the pivotal point of Garrison's inquiry. He was besieged night and day with telephone calls and with personal visits from newsmen. Ferrie found such calls no less vexatious than those of the D.A.'s investigators. On February 18th, a Saturday, Ferrie was inter-viewed by an assistant D.A. accompanied by an investigator. Ferrie was feeling increasingly ill. He had already remarked to an associate that he did not expect to live long. According to the assistant D.A., Ferrie moaned and groaned with each step he took up the stairs to his upper apartment. Garrison's men found Ferrie depressed and bitter. He ex-pressed his cynicism to them as he had to others concerning the law and everyone connected with it.

On Tuesday, February 21st, Carlos Bringuier was again in Garrison's office by Garrison's request. He was asked to serve as interpreter during an interrogation of one Emilio Santanna, another of Garrison's suspect Cubans. Santanna asked what the interrogation was all about. The assistant D.A. advised Bringuier not to tell Santanna anything; that it was not important that he know what it was about. His presence actually resulted from his having been once convicted of burglary with one Miguel Torres. Garrison had learned from a city directory that Torres once lived near Oswald. Garrison was interested in knowing, among other things, if Santanna was one of two Cubans who had deserted the 1963 Cuban training camp. He was not. He had never been there.

In the course of the interrogation, Santanna stated that Arcacha Smith had been present in New Orleans in 1964 recruiting for a Cuban organization known as "Alpha 66." Bringuier corrected him by identify-ing the Cuban who was, in fact, doing this recruiting in 1964 and reminded Santanna that Smith had not been in New Orleans since 1962. Santanna soon acknowledged that Bringuier was right and ad-mitted that he had been mistaken in his statement to the District Attorney's Office. The D.A. interrogators were much chagrined, for they had counted heavily on Santanna's statement as corroboration of Martin's and Lewis's stories as to Smith's presence in New Orleans in 1963.

On the same day Garrison issued another angry blast at the premature exposure of his probe by the press. It would now be months, he said, before arrests could be made.

Shortly after Bringuier returned to his place of business from Garrison's office, he was approached again by David Ferrie who pleaded for help. He needed information about Oswald to help clear himself. The two men walked to a nearby restaurant for coffee. Bringuier found that Ferrie was falling behind. Ferrie complained he could not walk fast as he was suffering internal pains.

*   *   *

There were other events occurring on February 21st. Garrison had become increasingly convinced of massive attempts by the F.B.I. and other components of the Federal apparatus to monitor his office. He was, and remains, suspicious that telephone taps and other forms of bugs are everywhere. He needed someone proficient in bugging and anti-bugging equipment to assist. He turned to Willard Robertson, a multi-millionaire businessman, owner of the exclusive distributorship for Volkswagen automobiles in the southeastern part of the United States. Robertson had long been a friend and political backer of Garrison. He did, indeed, know a man, the owner of The Jamaican Inn, a French Quarter bar, who possessed certain talents that could be of benefit to Garrison. He was an electronics expert who specialized in bugging and anti-bugging equipment. This was exactly what the D.A. needed. On February 21st Robertson introduced him to Garrison and the two men struck up a friendship that was to come to an abrupt end a month later. The name of the electronics expert was Gordon Novel.

Garrison spoke to Novel that day at length. He quickly learned to his delight that Novel had been quite close to Garrison's No. 1 suspect, David Ferrie. Like Andrews and others who figured prominently in the Garrison probe, Novel had a passion for words and in Garrison he had a receptive audience. Garrison listened with fascination to the tales of the loquacious Novel. Here was a man who knew something of David Ferrie, his background, his activities, his associates. From Novel, Garrison heard of Cubans, of Sergio Arcacha Smith, and of a trip to Houma in 1961 to gather explosives. Among the vehicles used, Garrison learned, was a laundry truck.

Now, no less a person than Mark Lane had theorized that a green Ford pickup truck parked at the right curb on Elm Street near the triple underpass in Dallas had been used to transport the assassins to the grassy knoll at Dealy Plaza from where, as everyone but the members of the Warren Commission knows, the fatal shots were fired. Undoubtedly, the same truck was used by the Cuban conspirators and their American friends in Dallas as was used in their jaunt to Houma. Novel drew a picture of the truck, dated it, and gave it to Garrison. Garrison had his staff take pictures of various laundry trucks around the city that appeared similar to that used in the Houma escapade. Unknown to a number of local launderers, including Sam Wing Laundry & Cleaners, Naborhud Washwoman, and Wee Washit, their trucks were photographed by Garrison's men. As Gurvich was later to remark: "The truck used for the Houma trip was apparently similar to the one identified by Lane to this extent: They both had four wheels."

A key subject, of course, of Garrison's queries to Novel was David Ferrie. Some way had to be found to break down the preposterous story of the ice skating and hunting trip to Texas following the assassination. Garrison seriously discussed with Novel the latter's suggestion that Ferrie be immobilized by the use of atropine darts or rubber bodyhammers so that the hapless pilot might be kidnapped and administered truth serum.

Garrison had suggestions of his own. He wanted Novel to plant electronic equipment in Garrison's home and office. Upon "discovery" of the equipment, Novel, as an expert in electronics, was to declare that such equipment was available only to agencies of the Federal Government, such as the F.B.I. He also suggested that Novel state that he knew Andrews to be acquainted with Clay Shaw. Novel balked at the suggestion.

In the weeks that followed, Novel was a ready and apparently limitless source of information. Very little that Garrison required by way of information could not be furnished by Novel in short order. Novel's fertile imagination worked overtime, supplying Garrison with many of the details he requested and, to compound the charade, Novel was in contact with the mischievous Andrews, who had once done legal work for him. The rotund lawyer, likewise, was never at a loss for suggestions as to information that should be fed to the D.A.

Garrison was to have the last laugh, however. Both men, Novel and Andrews, were later to become targets of the D.A.'s wrath and would pay heavily for their short period of merriment at Garrison's expense.

*   *   *

On the night of February 21st, Ferrie sat alone in his room staring into space as he had done on many other occasions. Later he was interviewed by George Lardner, a columnist for the *Washington Post*, who arrived about midnight. As Lardner was to remark to reporters, "Once you get him talking, it's hard to shut him off." The columnist remained until about 4:00 A.M. Sometime later that morning the tormented Ferrie found peace.

At about 11:40 A.M. his lifeless body was found in a bed, a sheet pulled over his head. On the dining room table in the apartment was an unsigned note which read in part: "To leave this life is for me a sweet prospect. I find nothing in it that is desirable and on the other hand, everything that is loathsome." A wide assortment of drugs was found. The apartment itself was filthy and disheveled as though it had not been cleaned or straightened in months.

Garrison immediately pegged the death as suicide: "The apparent suicide of David Ferrie ends the life of a man who, in my judgment, was one of history's most important individuals."

Said the D.A.: "Evidence developed by our office has long since confirmed he was involved in events culminating in the assassination of President Kennedy." Garrison informed the press that earlier that morning a decision had been reached to arrest Ferrie early the following week. "Apparently, we waited too long," said Garrison.

When asked if he had any reason to believe anybody but Lee Harvey Oswald took part in the actual assassination, Garrison replied: "I have no reason to believe at this point that Lee Harvey Oswald killed anybody in Dallas on that day." He would, he said further, give no evidence to any other agency, specifically to agencies of the Federal Government. "The Federal Government," said Garrison, "has as much jurisdiction over a murder conspiracy in New Orleans as has the S.P.C.A."

Garrison was roundly criticized by the American Civil Liberties Union and several national figures for his bombastic remarks.

Several of Garrison's assistants met with him. They suggested that it might be the better part of discretion to now announce his regret at the death of Ferrie and to explain that the investigation had centered around this eccentric and, further, that while Garrison had expected to establish his involvement in the assassination, that his sudden death was, at least temporarily, impeding any further progress in the probe. It was further suggested to Garrison that he might now let the matter die quietly while he was ahead. Garrison agreed. He announced that he would decline further comment because of what he termed the adverse effect of publicity on his investigation. As usual, his resolve lasted until his next exposure to the press.

This exposure was not long in coming. On February 24th Garrison, returning from lunch in the Shell Oil Building with several of his wealthy businessmen friends, including Joseph Rault, was swamped in the corridors with a massive display of television cameras and legions of newsmen.

Had Garrison solved the assassination?

> Why, we did this weeks ago. We're working out details of evidence which will probably take months. We know that we are going to be able to arrest every person involved—at least every person who is still living.

The newsmen hung on every word Garrison uttered. Titillated by the adoration, Garrison was unstoppable:

> The key to the whole case is through the looking glass. Black is white and white is black. I don't want to be cryptic, but that's the way it is.

Garrison entered the elevator of the Shell Oil Building with the press at his heels like so many hunting dogs. Another thundering horde of newsmen awaited him in the lobby. Garrison was on stage again:

> My staff and I solved the case weeks ago. I wouldn't say this if I didn't have evidence beyond a shadow of a doubt. We know the key individuals, the cities involved and how it was done. . . . There were several plots, but that's more than I wanted to say. . . . Ferrie might not at all be the last suicide in the case. The only way they are going to get away from us is to kill themselves.

No more significant insight into Garrison's mental processes could be wished for than the sequence described in this oft-quoted remark delivered extemporaneously on the same day:

> We know what cities were involved, we know how it was done in the essential respects, we know the key individuals involved and *we are in the process of developing evidence now* [emphasis supplied].

He had the knowledge. He would now get the evidence. Continued Garrison:

. . . That does not mean arrests are imminent. There are some individuals that I would like to arrest now, some that I know . . . will be around to arrest later. I have to take the risk that they will stay around because you can develop a better case if you prolong arrests until you can have the whole group of key individuals.

A most interesting pronouncement in view of the events to come.

Arrests were not imminent, said Garrison because "We're now building a case and I might add, it's a case we will not lose and anybody that wants to bet against us is invited to. But they will be disappointed."

Garrison also took the occasion to announce the formation of a group consisting of approximately fifty wealthy backers and admirers called "Truth and Consequences." The purpose was to furnish the D.A. with private funds for which there need be no accounting, thereby eliminating a source of interference by the press. The group was "proud of our D.A.," as a spokesman said and felt that he should be permitted to carry out his probe in secrecy. Three principal members were Joseph Rault, Willard Robertson, and Cecile Shilstone, owner of a chemical firm. The identities of other members of the group were not revealed.

The sudden focus of world attention on Garrison's activities brought undreamed of attention to David Lewis and Jack Martin, both before and after the death of Ferrie. To the local press, the day before Ferrie died, Lewis warned that "the people involved in this plot are very vicious and capable of anything. If they are capable of assassinating the United States President, they would not hesitate in getting rid of the witnesses. Garrison's got himself a case, I'm convinced of that. . . . There was a plot. I know about it and I know the people who were involved," said Lewis.

Martin, too, was afraid for his life. At the time of Ferrie's death, he left town and wandered around to points as distant as Lower California. Newsmen were curious about the financing for such a trip, but Garrison deemed any query about his own part in underwriting Martin's wanderings to be unmeritorious and unworthy of an answer.

Shortly after the death of Ferrie, Lewis took a flyer at converting some of the fame into cash and offered United Press International a tape "naming names" for $1,000. U.P.I. was not buying.

Little noted amidst the press reports of Garrison's pronouncements was an item published on February 25th to the effect that his investigators were questioning a twenty-five-year-old insurance salesman from Baton Rouge, Louisiana. His name was Perry Raymond Russo.

Meanwhile, Orleans Parish Coroner, Nicholas Chetta, who conducted exhaustive tests in conjunction with the autopsy on David

Ferrie, concluded that Ferrie had died of natural causes, a cerebral aneurysm. Garrison persisted, Chetta's tests notwithstanding, that Ferrie was a suicide.

During the three days following Garrison's startling revelations about having solved the assassination, little was forthcoming from the District Attorney. The press waited impatiently for every morsel of information. He well realized that the world was "chomping at the bit" to see what would come of his investigation, said Garrison, but arrests may not come for months.

About noon on March 1st as Clay Shaw was leaving his Dauphine Street home, he was served with a subpoena to appear at once in Garrison's office. He apparently saw no need at all for an attorney and he accompanied the Deputy Sheriff. He then spent most of the afternoon being shunted from one office to another.

Two other individuals were questioned during the day. One, James R. Lewallen, a thirty-eight-year-old former associate of David Ferrie, appeared with his attorney at 11:00 A.M. Lewallen had once lived with David Ferrie and, in fact, spent considerable time in the Louisiana Avenue Parkway apartment during September, 1963, a month that was to become of crucial importance in Garrison's case.

The other witness was not subpoenaed. He appeared voluntarily. This was the Baton Rouge insurance salesman, Perry Raymond Russo.

Shaw remained in the D.A.'s office for several hours. He had assumed that the questioning would be routine as it had been on other occasions. Garrison had not been in his office and was rumored to be sick. However, he arrived at the building a few minutes after 4:00 P.M. As usual, he was besieged by reporters and peppered with questions.

Was the investigation proceeding on schedule? "Of course," responded the D.A., "we see no problems."

Why was Shaw subpoenaed? "Mr. Shaw? That's a familiar name," he responded straight-faced. Sometime after Garrison's arrival in the afternoon, Shaw realized that he was in need of legal assistance. A longtime friend and attorney, Edward F. Wegmann, was called. He was out of the city, but due to return momentarily. Another attorney, Salvadore Panzeca, was dispatched to meet with Shaw. They were allowed to consult in private. Panzeca passed a note to Shaw advising that they communicate in writing. Panzeca felt the room was bugged.

Finally Garrison demanded that Shaw submit to a lie detector test. Panzeca agreed, but the test could not, he said, be conducted that day. Shaw had been questioned extensively; he would need to rest before submitting to the polygraph. Garrison was adamant. He did not have to submit to any conditions.

Bill Gurvich, who had been in Houston on an assignment, had returned to New Orleans earlier in the afternoon. He was astonished to hear Garrison suddenly order the arrest of Clay Shaw. Gurvich suggested that some statement had best be prepared for the waiting packs of newsmen. It was Gurvich's birthday, and the D.A. decided, as he put it, to give his chief investigator a birthday present. Gurvich would make the announcement.

At approximately 5:30 P.M. Gurvich called the newsmen, who literally jammed the vast corridor of the Criminal Court Building, for a press conference. He read from a printed statement bearing Garrison's name:

> The first arrest has been made in the investigation of the New Orleans District Attorney's Office into the assassination of President John F. Kennedy.
> Arrested this evening in the District Attorney's office was Clay Shaw, age 54, of 1313 Dauphine Street, New Orleans, Louisiana.
> Mr. Shaw will be charged with participating in a conspiracy to murder John F. Kennedy.
> It should be pointed out, however, that the nature of this case is not conducive to an immediate succession of arrests at this time. However, other arrests will be made at a later date.

Shaw was led from Garrison's office in handcuffs. He was taken to the detention facility behind the Criminal Court Building, known as Central Lockup.

That night, thousands of stunned New Orleanians watched Shaw being led by a host of D.A. investigators and assistants down the Criminal Court hallways. Shaw's twitching jaw was his only betrayal of tension. He bore the humiliation with dignity.

Many said that they would not believe Shaw's participation in a conspiracy to kill President Kennedy unless he admitted it himself. Others said that they would not believe Shaw guilty of such a deed, even were he to admit it. But most felt that Garrison would not charge an individual of such substance as Clay Shaw unless he had conclusive evidence indeed.

At the time of Shaw's arrest on March 1st, 1967, Garrison had the testimony of Perry Raymond Russo—and nothing else.

9

ABOUT A MONTH PRIOR TO THE
March 1st arrest of Shaw, the First Assistant D.A., Charles Ward, told
reporters he doubted that Garrison's investigation would turn up anything new. On February 26th, three days before the arrest, Garrison told
reporters that arrests were months away. What had happened between
February 26th and March 1st? What had happened was the appearance
on the scene of a dark-haired, dapper, well-spoken twenty-five-year-old
man named Perry Raymond Russo.

At the time he became embroiled in the Garrison investigation, Russo
was employed as a salesman by Equitable Life Insurance Company in
Baton Rouge. He had attended public school in New Orleans until his
graduation in 1959 and thereafter he attended Tulane, then Loyola
University, graduating from the latter institution with a bachelor's
degree in social science in 1964. After graduation he attended Loyola
Law School for one year.

In 1962 Russo made the acquaintance of David Ferrie. His introduction to Ferrie, like that of many other young men, was through the Civil

Air Patrol Unit. He had visited Ferrie's apartment in Jefferson Parish to attend a meeting of the group. One of his companions at the time was "Lefty" Peterson, a twenty-five-year-old blond-haired cab driver. Later, Russo was given an open invitation by Ferrie to visit the latter's new residence on Louisiana Avenue Parkway in New Orleans. This Russo did quite frequently. Ferrie also visited Russo's apartment on Elysian Fields Avenue, well across town from Ferrie's home.

Russo has always had an avid interest in baseball and was a member of the Professional Umpires Association. He has also been interested in politics and for several years was a member of the Young Republicans. According to some of Russo's acquaintances, he had an intense craving for publicity and had ambitions to run for high political office. Like other Garrison witnesses, Russo was no stranger to psychiatry. He was treated for about a year and a half in 1959 and 1960.

In early 1963, Russo was seated in his apartment with two companions. He appeared depressed. He told his companons that his psychiatrist had advised him that he had a "split personality." Suddenly Russo jumped up, relates one of those present, and ran to the bathroom and sliced the underpart of his forearm with a razor blade. His two companions immediately stopped him. One, frightened, quickly left. The other remained and took Russo to a hospital. Another of Russo's acquaintances described a much earlier attempt of Russo to fling himself from a second-story window of the high school he attended.

Like Ferrie's apartment, the quarters of Perry Russo were apparently the scene of considerable social activity of a less than conventional nature. Hypnotism, for one thing, seemed to hold the interest of Russo and his many visitors, including Ferrie. In one of the experiments Ferrie hypnotized Al Landry, a young man for whom Ferrie apparently held a strong fascination. At other sessions, Russo hypnotized a young girl named Sandra Moffett. He once demonstrated his powers at posthypnotic suggestion by telling Sandra that after he removed her from the hypnotic spell, she would still be unable to arise from her chair. The suggestion was effective, and the girl found herself unable to move until released by Russo. On another occasion, he burned her arm after first successfully convincing her that she would feel nothing. On still another occasion, he had stuck a pin in her arm and on yet another, is reported to have used a nail on a different individual who apparently experienced no pain.

Russo had other diversions. Photography was one, with particular interest in pornography. He took pictures of men and women in various sex acts. Photographic art, however, was not his only interest in pornography. The sale of the film for profit was another. On one particular occasion, he sold a pornographic movie film for $150.

Sometime in 1962 while David Ferrie and the youth, Al Landry, were out of the country on one of several trips the two had taken together, Landry's mother asked Russo's help in alienating her son from Ferrie who, she said, possessed some strange power over him. Russo agreed. He was ultimately successful and Ferrie threatened to kill Russo for having encouraged the youth to break off the relationship.

But Ferrie also held a strong fascination for Russo, who in turn held the older man somewhat in awe. They continued to see each other, usually in Ferrie's apartment, until Russo moved to Baton Rouge sometime in the spring of 1966. He first worked in Baton Rouge as a part-time credit manager for General Electric Company, then as a salesman for Equitable Life.

On February 22nd, 1967, Russo was seated at a drugstore in Baton Rouge discussing the death of David Ferrie with two companions. He told them that Ferrie had been a very smart man; that he was a psychologist and had many other talents. He also said that he had heard Ferrie say that it would be easy to kill President Kennedy. On one occasion, said Russo, he even heard Ferrie say, "We are going to get him."

A day or so thereafter Russo wrote the Orleans Parish D.A. and said that "I had occasion to meet Ferrie and some of his friends and I am willing to tell you what I know about them." He mentioned nothing about having met anyone named "Bertrand." Nor did he mention having met anyone named "Oswald," nor any plot to assassinate the President.

Russo's name first appeared in the press as a prospective witness about February 24th. On that date he outlined in detail his knowledge of the case to Bill Bankston of the *Baton Rouge Times*. He spoke to the reporter for about an hour as, he said, he wanted to "get the whole story down with somebody." He told Bankston nothing at all about Bertrand, Shaw, Oswald, or an assassination plot.

Later that night Russo was interviewed by three newsmen from Baton Rouge and New Orleans radio and television stations. To none of them did he say that he knew Bertrand, Shaw, or Oswald, nor anything of an assassination plot. On the contrary, asked if he knew Oswald, he replied without equivocation that he did not. He had never heard of Oswald, said Russo, until he heard the name on television immediately after the assassination.

The following day, February 25th, Russo was interviewed for approximately three hours by Anthony Sciambra, one of Garrison's assistants.

Sciambra prepared for the District Attorney a 3,500-word summary of the interview. It was written with great care and contained considerable detail. To all appearances, it purports to set forth Russo's association and experience with Ferrie and the acquaintances he met through him, all in chronological order.

The memorandum describes at length Russo's recitation of his attempt to alienate Landry from Ferrie; of Ferrie's threat against Russo; and of meeting Ferrie at a service station sometime later in Jefferson Parish, one that Ferrie appeared to manage or own, according to Russo. It then describes Ferrie's relation to Russo, and, his, Ferrie's, use of drugs as a sexual stimulant. The memorandum described at length Russo's introduction to various Cubans from time to time at Ferrie's apartment, and told of Ferrie's obsession with the idea that an assassination could be carried out with the proper planning. Ferrie, according to the memorandum, spoke about the "availability of exit" after such a deed. According to Russo, said the memorandum, in September and October, 1963, Ferrie became worse in his speeches and harangues about an assassination. For the first time, according to Russo, he began making direct references to the assassination of Kennedy, whereas previously he had mentioned "assassination" in the abstract without mention of any particular victim. On several occasions, according to Russo, Ferrie stated: "We'll get him" and "It won't be long."

There then appears in Sciambra's memorandum this perplexing statement: "Russo said he hasn't spoken with Ferrie since the assassination." This may give some insight into Russo's orientation as to time. Ferrie's operation of the service station in Jefferson Parish was from January, 1964, almost two months after the assassination, to November, 1964. More importantly, it is in direct conflict with testimony later given in open court.

The memorandum then recites that Russo was asked to identify photographs. He was shown a picture of a Cuban and he stated the Cuban resembled the subject in a pornographic film that he, Russo, had once sold.

Then he was shown a picture of Clay Shaw, whereupon there followed the memorandum's most significant passage:

> He said that he saw this man twice [emphasis supplied]. The first time was when he pulled into Ferrie's service station to get his car fixed. Shaw was the person who was sitting in the compact car talking with Ferrie. He remembers seeing him again at the Nashville Avenue wharf when he went to see J.F.K. speak.

The latter occasion referred to by Russo was a visit of John F. Kennedy to New Orleans in May of 1962, some twenty months before Ferrie's business venture with the Jefferson Parish service station.

Nowhere in the entire memorandum is there any material expanding on the passage quoted above, wherein Russo specified that he had seen Shaw *twice*. Nowhere in the memorandum is there any mention of the name Clay Bertrand or any indication by Russo that he knew Clay Shaw by any name whatever.

Russo also mentioned a roommate of Ferrie whom he had seen at Ferrie's apartment two or three times between May and October, 1963. The exact words of Sciambra's memo in this connection are interesting:

> He said that Ferrie introduced him to someone he called his roommate. He said Ferrie mentioned his name, but he can't remember it right now. He said the roommate had a sort of dirty blond hair and a husky beard which appeared to be a little darker than his hair. He said the guy was a typical beatnik, extremely dirty, with his hair all messed up, his beard unkempt, a dirty T-shirt on, and either blue jeans or khaki pants on. He said he wore white tennis shoes which were cruddy and had on no socks. He said the roommate appeared to be in his middle twenties. Russo said that he went to Ferrie's apartment about five or six times and he can remember seeing the roommate about two or three times.

Russo's description of the roommate indicates that he was extremely introverted and apparently had little interest in talking to anybody. According to the memorandum, whenever Russo would come into Ferrie's apartment the roommate would get up and leave and go into another room by himself. Russo related that one day he tried to make conversation with the roommate by asking him where he was from and the roommate replied "everywhere" and that Russo never tried to talk to him any more because to him the roommate appeared to be a real "punk."

After viewing the photograph of Shaw, Russo was next shown a picture of Lee Harvey Oswald. According to Sciambra, Russo

> began shaking his head and said that he doesn't know if he should say what he's thinking. I told him to go on and tell me what was on his mind and that we would accept this in relationship to all the information we had, and it may not be as wild as he thinks it is. He then said that the picture of Lee Harvey Oswald was the person that Ferrie had introduced to

him as his roommate. He said the only thing that doesn't make him stand up and say that he is sure beyond a shadow of any doubt is the fact that the roommate was always so cruddy and had a bushy beard. He then drew a beard on the picture of Oswald and said that this was Ferrie's roommate.

Russo persisted in his description of the roommate as "cruddy" and wearing a "bushy beard" throughout his later questioning under hypnosis and in testimony given in open court. The roommate, none other than Lee Harvey Oswald according to Russo, was repeatedly described by Russo as bearded, disheveled, unkempt, and dirty. His descriptions perplexed those who had known Oswald during his five months stay in New Orleans in 1963. A state employment interviewer who had seen him twice during that period describes him as being neat in appearance and dress. The owner of a garage located next door to Reily's Coffee Company on Magazine Street had seen Oswald almost daily for a month and a half prior to Oswald's discharge from that employment in mid-July. He, too, described Oswald as very neat in appearance and dress. To a local reporter he said that "he (Oswald) had such a light growth of hair on his face I don't honestly think he could grow a heavy beard."

Oswald's landlady, Mrs. J. J. Garner, saw Oswald several times during September and described him to the local press as always clean-shaven and neatly dressed. "I never remember him needing a shave. He was always neat, certainly not sloppy," she was quoted as saying.

Other close acquaintances of Ferrie during September, including Beauboeuf and Martens, denied ever seeing Oswald at all and do not specifically recall any roommate of Ferrie's during September, 1963. The individual who apparently spent the greatest amount of time during this period at Ferrie's Louisiana Avenue Parkway apartment was one James Lewallen, a mechanic employed at Michoud, a NASA space facility on the outskirts of the city.

Lewallen was not a "double" of Oswald, nor could the resemblance between them be described as remarkable. However, their general build and features were similar. Lewallen, as befitted his occupation, generally wore blue jeans or khaki pants, and these were often grease-stained and dirty. He was himself often described as being sometimes dirty and unshaven. According to some acquaintances he usually had a stubble of a beard.

Further, he was often referred to as "Lou" or "Lee."

Garrison's men had questioned Lewallen primarily about Ferrie's activities over the period of several years of acquaintanceship with him, and about Clay Shaw. Lewallen once lived near Shaw, and the D.A.'s men pressed him on the possibility of his having known Shaw as Bertrand. He did not. Further, he informed the D.A. that as far as he knew, Ferrie and Shaw did not know each other, nor had he ever heard either man mention the other. Somehow the interrogators scarcely brushed on his association with Ferrie in September, 1963.

Russo had two suggestions for Sciambra with regard to the Oswald photograph. The first suggestion was that if Sciambra were to draw a beard on the picture of Oswald and show it to certain acquaintances of Ferrie's they would undoubtedly identify the picture of Oswald as Ferrie's roommate. Weeks later this was done. None could make the identification. "Lefty" Peterson, for one, denied recognizing the photograph of Oswald despite Russo's statement that he, Peterson, had seen the roommate several times.

The second suggestion was that if he were to be hypnotized he might have total recall on names, places, and dates. He had been hypnotized before, said Russo, and he was certain that it would help him to recall.

Garrison was extremely impressed with Sciambra's memorandum. Here was a witness, and a very cooperative one, who knew Ferrie during the time when Ferrie was obviously plotting the assassination of the President. Here was proof that Ferrie's roommate was none other than Lee Harvey Oswald and, above all, Clay Shaw, a living, breathing conspirator, had been seen in the company of Ferrie. Garrison was discouraged not at all by the fact that the new witness had said nothing about plans to assassinate the President having been mentioned in the presence of the shy and retiring roommate, or that Shaw had not been identified as Bertrand, or that his witness apparently did not know the tall, white-haired man to be either Bertrand or Shaw, or that the tall, white-haired man had never been present when the "plan" of the assassination was discussed. Obviously, all of these things were true, and had occurred, and the truth could be developed with patience.

*   *   *

For many months after Russo's courtroom testimony during the Clay Shaw preliminary hearing beginning March 14th, Garrison was to react with characteristic outrage at assaults on Russo's credibility. He demurred that never before had a District Attorney gone so far to be fair. He had not been content merely to rely upon Russo's own unsupported testimony, Garrison protested, but had used on his witness certain "objectifying tests." Thus, a new adjective was born.

Russo was not a difficult subject to "objectify." As he explained to

James Phelan of the *Saturday Evening Post* two and one-half months later, he "picked up a lot of information from Garrison's people just from the way they asked questions." "I'm a pretty preceptive guy," added Russo, "and besides when they get through asking me questions, I asked them a lot of questions—like 'Why is this man important' and so on. I also read every scrap of paper printed about the case before the Shaw hearing."

The "objectifying" tests began on February 27th at the Mercy Hospital in New Orleans. Present with Russo were Sciambra, Al Oser, Dr. Nicholas Chetta (the Parish Coroner), and two other doctors. The group gathered in the operating room, and Russo was administered a saline solution, then sodium pentothal, commonly known as truth serum. According to Chetta, the purpose of the drug is to "remove any mental block" to divulgence of the truth. According to testimony Chetta was later to give at Shaw's preliminary hearing in mid-March, fantasies do sometimes appear in the mind of persons placed under sodium pentothal. "It is," said Chetta, "up to the man doing the test to tell whether the person is lying or speaking fantasy." The doctor acknowledged that the occasion of the February 27th test was the first time that he had seen Russo. He spent but an hour with Russo before administration of the drug.

Under the influence of the drug, Russo was again questioned by Sciambra, as he had been on February 25th without the benefit of the sodium pentothal. Now Russo repeated the story of his initial meeting with Ferrie and his part in breaking up the relationship between Ferrie and Al Landry. He also repeated his account of Ferrie's prowess in the art of hypnosis. Russo further informed those present that he had met a number of Cubans with Ferrie but that they did not speak any English and that he could not remember their names. He described them as being very strong and rough looking. Russo was then asked about Ferrie's roommate. Russo replied that he had seen the roommate on three different occasions in Ferrie's apartment and that Ferrie at first told Russo that his roommate's name was Leon. Leon seemed to be around twenty-five years old and what Russo noticed most about the roommate was that he was very dirty and a "beatnik-type guy." "He appeared to be a little nuts and would never talk to anyone," said Russo. Ferrie also told Russo that Leon was "a little nuts about guns," and Russo recalled one occasion at Ferrie's apartment when he saw Leon sitting on a chair, his leg up, cleaning a rifle. According to Russo, the rifle was bolt action and had a telescopic sight. Russo also recalls that Leon had a pistol.

When asked about the time that he saw the roommate with Ferrie, Russo replied that it was "September 20th until around September 25th, 1963." Russo said that he was "pretty sure" that the dates were correct and that he knew that it had to be in September.

Earlier in the day Russo had been in the District Attorney's office while beards of all shapes and thicknesses were drawn on innumerable photographs of Lee Harvey Oswald. After many such sketches, Russo finally identified a number of the photographs of Oswald as being the roommate of Ferrie introduced to him as Leon. Sciambra now asked the drugged witness if the pictures drawn in the District Attorney's office earlier in the day resembled Leon, and Russo replied that they did. The roommate had a bushy beard and his hair was all messed up and he was extremely dirty, said Russo. The picture that had been drawn in the morning was "very, very close to Ferrie's roommate, except maybe the guy was a little dirtier." In a memorandum to District Attorney Garrison containing the account of the sodium pentothal interview, Sciambra included this paragraph:

> He also said another thing that he remembered about the roommate was that Oswald wore a wedding band on his left hand and it appeared to be gold or brass. I then pointed out to him that he referred to the roommate as Oswald and asked him if there was any particular reason why he now referred to Ferrie's roommate as Oswald. He said that he didn't know—that seems to be what he was called or what somebody said his name was.

Sciambra then asked Russo if he knew Clay Shaw. Russo replied that he did not. Sciambra inquired if the witness knew Clay Bertrand. Russo now replied that he did know Clay Bertrand and "he is a queer." He had been introduced to Bertrand by Ferrie while visiting Ferrie's apartment on Louisiana Avenue Parkway. Bertrand was described to Sciambra by Russo as being a tall man with white kinky hair, sort of slender.

Had Russo ever seen Bertrand before? Yes, he had seen Bertrand on two other occasions. One occasion when his car had trouble and he pulled into Ferrie's service station on the Veterans Highway and on another occasion when he went to see President Kennedy speak at the Nashville Avenue wharf. Russo could remember Bertrand well because Bertrand was "hawking some kid who was not too far from him at Kennedy's speech." Then came a series of questions between Sciambra and Russo which were summarized in Sciambra's memorandum to Garrison in the following manner:

I then asked him if he could remember any of the details about Clay Bertrand being up in Ferrie's apartment and he told me he was in Ferrie's apartment with Clay Bertrand and Ferrie and the roommate. He remembers Ferrie telling him that "we are going to kill John F. Kennedy" and that "it won't be long." He said Ferrie again repeated his earlier statement that he could plan the perfect assassination of the President because he could fly anything that had wings on it and the perfect availability of exits out of the country. When I asked him who Ferrie was referring to when he said, "we," he said, "I guess he was referring to the people in the room." He said this was not the first time Ferrie had talked to him about how easy it would be to assassinate the President. He said that Ferrie in September and October of 1963 became obsessed with the idea that he could pull off a perfect assassination.

The remainder of the sodium pentothal interview was perfunctory in nature. But "Bertrand" had now been placed in Ferrie's presence when the latter spoke of assassination! The following day, February 28th, the memorandum was submitted to Garrison.

Later that day Russo was sent with several D.A. investigators and assistants to keep a surveillance on the Dauphine Street house of Clay Shaw to enable Russo to make a positive identification of Shaw as the Clay Bertrand he described. After a ninety-minute wait, Shaw appeared for a few seconds. Russo identified him to the D.A.'s men as Bertrand.

They waited an additional two hours or so, however, to get a better look. Then it was decided that Russo should knock at Shaw's door pretending to be selling insurance. He did. Shaw answered the knock. After a brief conversation, Russo returned to his companions and identified Shaw as Bertrand.

It was the following morning, March 1st, that the instanter subpoena was issued for Clay Shaw. At 5:30 that evening, Shaw was arrested.

Sometime later the night of March 1st, Russo was taken to the office of the Coroner at Tulane and Broad where he underwent yet another objectifying process. Dr. Esmond A. Fatter, a private medical practitioner, Dr. Chetta, Mr. Sciambra, and a cousin of Russo's were present. Russo was to be hypnotized by Dr. Fatter.

*   *   *

The use of suggestion during hypnosis and the phenomenon of posthypnotic suggestion are matters well known to laymen. Less widely understood is the basic nature of the hypnotic state itself as one of dramatically increased suggestibility.

G. H. Estabrooks, a Doctor of Philosophy in the field of educational psychology, states in his volume *Hypnotism* that

> the first concept we get of hypnotism is that curious picture of an unconscious mind controlled by the conscious mind of the operator. The subject will accept any suggestion the operator gives, within certain limits. . . . In fact, suggestion appears to be the key of hypnotism. It is the method by which the hypnotist first gains control and unseats the normal conscious mind. After this, he finds that his only way of controlling the subject is again through suggestion, for the subject, left to himself, will generally do nothing at all. . . .

A similar view is expressed by Dr. Jerome M. Schneck, a Clinical Associate of Psychiatry at the State University of New York, in a treatise entitled *Hypnosis in Modern Medicine:*

> In our everyday clinical practice there is no doubt that the increased suggestibility is the most conspicuous feature of the hypnotized patient. We offer the suggestion; the patient carries it out . . .

According to Schneck, the wide acceptance of this statement by medical men is easily demonstrated. Asked "what is hypnosis," says Schneck, the majority will answer that it is "a state of increased suggestibility."

And according to Estabrooks, ". . . the subject in hypnotism is never deaf, is always on the alert for any suggestions."

"The suggestion," adds Estabrooks ". . . leaves an indelible impression and provokes [the subject] to acts which are quite apart from any intellectual processes the individual may use."

Dr. Fatter had been briefed by the District Attorney's Office on the "facts" of the conspiracy to assassinate President Kennedy. He spoke with Russo about his background and asked Russo had he ever been hypnotized before. Russo replied that he had. He was asked by the doctor the means used to hypnotize him and he replied it was by use of a silver coin. Fatter took a coin from his pocket and placed it in front of his face. Russo said, "The last time I was hypnotized I saw two coins." Fatter held the coin close to Russo's face. Russo told the doctor he might resist the hypnotism. Fatter replied that he had a right to do this.

Dr. Fatter later explained at the preliminary hearing that on this occasion he used what he termed the "trans-induction technique." Said Fatter, "I used the doctor-patient relationship . . . I cannot make anybody do anything. I can only help him use his constitutional endowment. Who does it benefit? It benefits Mr. Russo."

Dr. Fatter described this as a "teacher-pupil relationship," explaining that he was teaching Russo to use his (Russo's) trance-state and he said this was done for Russo's benefit, "not mine." According to the doctor, Russo reached a "moderately deep trance-state." The doctor described the tone of the muscles of Russo's face as one indication of the success of the hypnosis. The condition of his arms was described by the doctor as "though he were inanimate, just like the arms of a doll. You picked them up and they dropped to his side. His eyelids were closed. The levitation of movement was elicited," said the doctor. "You lift up one finger on one hand or any other part of the body and the limb would just drop, Russo was able to regress very beautifully," he continued, "and he was able to verbalize, like talking in his sleep."

Then the questioning began.

DR. FATTER: Perry, I am going to ask you a date, as you see that date on the television screen, lift your right index finger. . . . All right, I wonder what date you see?

RUSSO: September 16th.

DR. FATTER: I wonder what year, Perry?

RUSSO: No year.

DR. FATTER: Look at the television and a picture will come on and when the picture becomes very vivid to you, and the program begins, lift your right index finger and if you care to, you can tell me about that picture.

This was the format that Dr. Fatter was to use throughout the hypnotic interview. Russo was told to view past events as though looking at an imaginary television screen. After a few preliminary matters concerning his acquaintanceship with David Ferrie, Dr. Fatter told Russo:

Continue looking at that television picture and notice the newscast . . . the President, President Kennedy, is coming to New Orleans and as you look, describe it to us.

Russo then described his presence at the Nashville Avenue wharf where Kennedy spoke. Then followed this exchange:

DR. FATTER: Who is that white-haired gentleman who is over there, looking at President Kennedy?

Russo had not yet mentioned the white-haired gentleman in the hypnotic session.

RUSSO: He is either with the New Orleans Police Department or government because my friend remarked about it. He said that he was the only man not looking at the President—he was looking at us. . . .

DR. FATTER: How about this white-haired gentleman?

RUSSO: That was him.

Then on the first of several occasions during the interview, Russo was asked the name of the "white-haired gentleman."

DR. FATTER: Do you know his name?

RUSSO: No.

Following this, Dr. Fatter then turned his attention to the incident that Russo had previously recounted to Sciambra concerning his having seen a tall, white-haired individual in Ferrie's service station:

DR. FATTER: We are looking at the television screen again and when it is clear again, your finger will lift up. Study the picture and you are in an automobile driving into a service station. Tell me about that program on the television.

RUSSO: I had trouble with the car because it wouldn't start at a red light and I didn't have any money except four or five dollars, and I just drove in and an old friend of mine came up and he said, "You remember me," and I said, "Yes." These boys fixed the tire, took the battery out, charged the battery and I had to pay $2.50 and I left.

DR. FATTER: Tell me about the white-haired man sitting in that automobile over there.

Again the subject of the white-haired gentleman had been broached by Fatter.

RUSSO: He is talking with Dave and they are just talking and I interrupted their conversation and he thought it was

> rude and he left. He was sitting next to Dave and I
> yelled to Dave about getting the boys to hustle. I had
> to go because he was very ill at ease because Dave and
> I were suspicious of each other.

DR. FATTER: About what?

RUSSO: He told me he was going to kill me.

DR. FATTER: Why, Perry?

RUSSO: Because I broke up he and Al.

DR. FATTER: Isn't there a calendar in the service station somewhere,
              Perry?

RUSSO: No.

DR. FATTER: I wonder what is the day . . .

RUSSO: 1964.

DR. FATTER: What is the month, Perry?

RUSSO: March.

DR. FATTER: I wonder what day it is in March?

RUSSO: I don't know.

For the first time Russo had placed the service station incident in
1964. Previously, he had told Sciambra that this was the first time he
had seen the person whom he identified from a photograph as Clay
Shaw. Now, under hypnosis, the incident was placed in March, 1964—
after the President spoke at the Nashville Avenue wharf and *after* the
assassination of President Kennedy. Dr. Fatter continued his questioning of Russo:

DR. FATTER: Take a look at the white-haired man again in the auto-
              mobile and when you see him, lift your finger up. . . .
              Did you ever see that man before?

RUSSO: Yes—he was a friend of Dave's.

DR. FATTER: Where did you see him before?

RUSSO: At the Nashville wharf!

There is no mention whatever of having seen Shaw (or Bertrand) at
Ferrie's or at any place whatever on any other occasion.

Fatter then asked Russo about Cubans he had met with Ferrie. Russo had previously been unable to recall the names of any Cubans for Sciambra. In response to a question of Dr. Fatter: "And how did he introduce the others?" Russo responded, "Manuel." Manuel Garcia Gonzales, perhaps?

Russo also mentioned in the hypnotic session a Cuban to whom he had been introduced by the name of "Juliana" or, as Russo said, "Julia—Jules—They talked in Spanish and Ferrie talked in Spanish." Julian Buznedo, perhaps? Another of Garrison's suspect Cubans.

Dr. Fatter continued his probe into the recesses of Russo's mind. He now turned his attention to the heart of Garrison's theory.

> DR. FATTER: Continue to go deeper and deeper to sleep. You are comfortable and blank . . . look at the television screen again, picture and visualize and your finger will lift again when it is clear. That is right. A picture is going to come on when you were in Ferrie's apartment on Louisiana Avenue Parkway. Would you look at that picture and tell us the story that you see?

> RUSSO: He introduced me to his roommate who was a kook!

Russo then described the roommate "Leon Oswald," as he had before, as having sandy brown hair, dirty white shirt, and "dirty, dirty, dirty, dirty."

Upon Dr. Fatter's admonition to continue looking at the picture and to state who else was in the apartment, Russo said: "Nobody, just me and him." "Just you and—Ferrie?" asked Dr. Fatter. "And Oswald," replied Russo.

On this occasion, according to Russo, nothing of note happened.

Fatter thereupon set the stage for the next meeting at Ferrie's apartment, and this time he would not wait for Russo to volunteer the presence of the white-haired man. He had had more success by broaching the matter himself and he decided to do so again.

> DR. FATTER: That's right. Continue to go deeper and deeper—now, picture that television screen again, Perry, and it is a picture of Ferrie's apartment and there are several people in there and *there is a white-haired man* [emphasis supplied]. Tell me about it.

> RUSSO: We are having a party and I came in and everybody is drinking beer. There are about ten of us and I am there, the roommate, Dave, some young boys and some other friends of Dave's and I was with Sandra.

DR. FATTER: And what month is it?

RUSSO: September, September 16th.

DR. FATTER: And what year, Perry?

RUSSO: 1963.

Russo said that there was a record player in the middle of the room and that the recording was of someone making a speech in Spanish and that everybody laughed. Then Dr. Fatter returned to his favorite subject.

DR. FATTER: And how about the white-haired man. . . .

RUSSO: That is a friend of Dave's.

DR. FATTER: His name?

RUSSO: Clem Bertrand.

This is the first time during any of the "objectifying" processes that Clem Bertrand had been mentioned.

DR. FATTER: Had you seen him before?

RUSSO: Yes. I saw him at the Nashville wharf.

It will be recalled that earlier in the hypnotic session he had stated he did not know the name of the man seen at the Nashville Avenue wharf.

DR. FATTER: I wonder where else?

RUSSO: Nowhere.

Dr. Fatter became more specific.

DR. FATTER: Is that the same white-haired gentleman in the service station?

RUSSO: I don't remember the service station.

Dr. Fatter dropped the subject of the service station until later in the interview. He turned Russo's attention back to Oswald with the query: "I wonder who that is sitting on the sofa with the rifle?" "Leon," Russo replied. In response to Fatter's questions, he then described the rifle as being similar to a .22 caliber rifle owned by Russo. According to Russo, it had a wooden or plastic stock and a barrel-type eight-inch long telescopic sight. After the description of the rifle, Fatter returned to the subject of Bertrand:

> DR. FATTER: Continue looking at the television program and Clay [emphasis supplied], the white-haired man, is going to come into the room. You are at Ferrie's apartment. There are many people. Who did he introduce Clay to?

Russo had never mentioned the name Clay. Russo now replied unresponsively that Ferrie was introduced to everybody; that there were four Cubans there, including Juliana and Manuel. At Fatter's request, Russo described where each was sitting. It is noteworthy that when asking about Juliana, Dr. Fatter referred to him as "Julian." Immediately thereafter in speaking of this Cuban, Russo also referred to him as "Julian," the first time he was to do so.

When asked by Fatter to describe what "Leon" was doing, Russo stated that he was deprecating Russo and, apparently, did not like Russo. According to Russo, he told Ferrie that he wanted to go home.

Fatter tried again:

> DR. FATTER: Let your mind go completely blank, Perry. . . . See that television screen again, it is very vivid. . . . Now notice the picture on the screen. There will be Bertrand, Ferrie, and Oswald and they are going to discuss a very important matter and there is another man and girl there and *they are talking about assassinating somebody* [emphasis supplied]. Look at it and describe it to me.

Russo had said nothing at all about any plan to assassinate anyone. This was the first time in the hypnotic session that either party had interjected any mention of assassination, and the party was Dr. Fatter.

> RUSSO: We are sitting around on the sofas and I came in late. Dave offered me a drink and I said no, I didn't want anything and I sat down and played like I belonged. I didn't know what was going on. Dave went and got drinks for everybody—all the drinks were coffee—and they resumed the conversation and I was just sitting. They planned to assassinate President Kennedy.

Fatter then asked Russo to relate what everyone said. According to Russo, Ferrie paced the floor as he talked and told the others that "if they were to get the President, they would fly to Mexico or Cuba or to Brazil." Then Russo, again referring to Bertrand as "Clem," quotes him as finding fault with Ferrie's plan, which prompted "Leon" to speak sharply to Bertrand.

Dr. Fatter asked Russo what the group had discussed about Dallas, and Russo replied that no mention had been made of Dallas. There then followed this exchange between Fatter and Russo:

DR. FATTER: Is Clay Bertrand the same person that you saw in the District Attorney's office and the same person you went to sell insurance to yesterday, Perry?

RUSSO: Dave never took me to his house.

DR. FATTER: You went to his house yesterday to sell insurance with somebody from the District Attorney's Office, Perry. Is that the same man that was in with Ferrie and Oswald and the same man that was at the wharf?

RUSSO: I don't understand—Dave never showed me any places like that.

Fatter persisted:

DR. FATTER: Now go to sleep, Perry . . . and now, Perry, I want you to see that television screen again and when you visualize it, and it is clear, you will see the face of a white-haired man. You met him yesterday when you went to his apartment. This is yesterday, the last day of February. Picture him in your mind. Have you seen him before? Have you seen him on several occasions and what were these occasions, Perry?

RUSSO: He was Dave's friend and I saw him at Dave's house.

Fatter was persistent, but so was Russo. During the entire hypnotic session, there was never any identification of Clay Shaw, who had been seen by Russo the day before at Shaw's apartment, and again a few hours before the hypnotic session in the D.A.'s office, as the man who had been present at the party in September of 1963.

The questioning continued:

DR. FATTER: Where else did you see him, Perry?

RUSSO: I saw him at the Nashville Avenue wharf.

DR. FATTER: Where else, Perry?

RUSSO: I saw him at the Nashville Avenue wharf.

DR. FATTER: What is his name, Perry?

RUSSO: Clay Bertrand.

Apparently, Russo switched with ease from "Clem" to "Clay." Dr. Fatter then set the stage for the next and last meeting between Russo and "Leon Oswald."

DR. FATTER: Perry, see the television screen again . . . a picture is going to flip up and this is the last time you saw Oswald and Ferrie together. . . . Describe the scene to me.

RUSSO: I came over to Dave's house and we just talked about the usual stuff and the roommate had to leave. He brought out two bags, all beat up. The suitcases were like a canvas bag with extra pouches and real heavy canvas and he has a little smaller bag and he is just leaving. I guess Dave is kicking him out.

DR. FATTER: And Dave, I wonder where he is going?

RUSSO: Houston.

DR. FATTER: Look up at the top of the television screen and you will see the date that film came on . . . what date?

RUSSO: October 7, 1963.

Russo was quite specific in his designation of this date and was to persist in his recollection of a departure date of October 7th, 1963.

The Warren Report quotes the testimony of a neighbor who reports observing Oswald leave his Magazine Street apartment on September 24th carrying two pieces of luggage and hurriedly board a bus. Oswald was delinquent in his rent by about fifteen days as of this time. The landlord found Oswald's apartment vacant on September 25th.

Also, according to the Warren Commission, Oswald departed New Orleans by Continental Trailways Bus No. 5121, bound for Houston, at 12:20 P.M. on September 25th. The wife of a member of the Socialist Labor Party in Houston received a telephone call from Oswald that night which she believes was a local call. On September 26th, Oswald boarded Continental Trailways Bus No. 5133 in Houston and departed at 2:35 A.M. for Laredo, Texas. He is further confirmed to have crossed the border from Laredo to Nueva Laredo, Mexico, between 1:30 and 2:00 P.M. and from there to have traveled to Mexico City.

His activities and travels have been continuously documented thereafter throughout his abortive attempts to obtain permission to enter Cuba through the Cuban Embassy in Mexico City until about October 1st. He thereupon went to Dallas, where he resided at the rooming house of one Mary Bledsoe until mid-October. His activities thereafter until November 22nd were the subject of detailed scrutiny by the Warren Commission. He never returned to New Orleans.

DR. FATTER:	Is this the same roommate that is called Lee Oswald?
RUSSO:	Leon.
DR. FATTER:	Perry, I imagine you know Leon Oswald. Was he married?
RUSSO:	Yes.
DR. FATTER:	What was his wife's name?
RUSSO:	Margaret.

Oswald's wife was not named Margaret. Her name was Marina. Oswald's mother was Margaret.

In further questioning Russo finally pinpointed the date of his first meeting with Oswald as September 13th. At the doctor's direction Russo envisioned a serial picture on a television screen. Each time he saw Leon Oswald, and the date was to be in the upper right-hand corner. Said Russo first: "September 13th."

DR. FATTER:	Another picture flips.
RUSSO:	September 16th at Dave's.
DR. FATTER:	The picture flips again.
RUSSO:	October 7th at Dave's.

In response to further questioning, Russo replied that he did not know whom Oswald was going to visit in Houston. Dr. Fatter then interjected a new name to the hypnotic session. "I wonder, Perry, who is Brett Wall?"

Who indeed? For many months Garrison considered one "Breck

Wall" to be a conspirator in the assassination. The reason? Wall, an officer in the Entertainers' Union in Dallas, was a friend of Jack Ruby, the murderer of Lee Harvey Oswald. It appeared that Wall left Dallas the day after the assassination and went to Galveston passing en route through Houston. The day after the Kennedy assassination Ruby called Wall in Galveston. Garrison found the entire matter highly suspicious. In early March he told James Phelan, the *Saturday Evening Post* correspondent: "Wall is a homosexual, a friend of Ruby, and passes through Houston while Ferrie was there, so Wall has got to be in on this thing." In point of fact, Wall had passed through Houston long after David Ferrie had left the Winterland Skating Rink, the supposed "communications center," and Wall has consistently denied knowing either Ferrie, Oswald, or Shaw. The subject of the telephone call has been stated by both Ruby and Wall to be a complaint by Ruby to Wall, as an officer of the Entertainers' Union, that strip joint competitors of Ruby's stayed open after the assassination.

Now, in response to Fatter's question about "Brett Wall," Russo had the following information:

RUSSO:	A friend of Leon, he was supposed to help Leon.
DR. FATTER:	How, Perry?
RUSSO:	He didn't say. Dave asked him about it.
DR. FATTER:	And I wonder—who is Jack Ruby?
RUSSO:	I don't know.
DR. FATTER:	I wonder if Brett Wall knew Jack Ruby?
RUSSO:	I don't know.
DR. FATTER:	And I wonder if Ferrie knew Brett Wall.
RUSSO:	I guess so, it sounded like a mutual acquaintance. Ferrie asked Leon to be there.
DR. FATTER:	I wonder if Ferrie asked Leon if he would be at Brett Wall's place in Houston?
RUSSO:	He just asked Leon if Brett Wall would be there. He said he supposed so.
DR. FATTER:	I wonder where Oswald was to be in Houston, Perry?
RUSSO:	He didn't say.

Again, Dr. Fatter took the initiative and asked what the Winterland

Skating Rink was in Houston. Despite several attempts in this direction, Russo could furnish no more information, nor could he state who was to play any particular role in the assassination. According to Russo, "They don't put people in roles."

Said Fatter: "I wonder, Perry, if they ever talked about anyone shooting a gun from a school window or grassy knoll." "No," replied Russo. The hypnotic session ended with this exchange:

DR. FATTER: I wonder what they talked about as to how they were going to assassinate the President?

RUSSO: Dave said someone had gone up to President Eisenhower some time ago and was able to touch him and this just goes to show you could do the job. He said there would be a cross fire with a mob in between and if everybody was looking at the guy who was the diversionary and made the diversionary shot, the other guy could make the good shot. One would make the diversionary shot and the other would do the job.

DR. FATTER: Who was going to be used for the diversionary shot and who for the actual shot?

RUSSO: They never said.

No less than eight times had the subject of the "white-haired man" been introduced into the hypnotic session. On each occasion, it was by Dr. Fatter. Not once was the subject volunteered by Russo.

This was not the last time Russo was to be hypnotized before the preliminary hearing in mid-March, nor was it the last objectifying process he was to undergo.

A week later Russo was dispatched with an assistant district attorney and an investigator to the office of a qualified polygraph operator. After being alone with Russo in the polygraph room, the operator emerged and informed the D.A.'s men that the machine indicated evidence of deception, and that in his, the operator's, opinion Russo was not telling the truth.

The operator was instructed to stop the test and the D.A.'s men departed with Russo. It is doubtful that the test was of any value in one direction or the other, however, for among the questions asked that indicated evidence of deception was the question: "Did you know David Ferrie?" Clearly, the evidence from all quarters established that Russo did, indeed, know David Ferrie. Such results, according to most qualified polygraph operators, indicate severe emotional instability as highly probable.

On March 2nd, 1967, the local newspapers published a story detailing Shaw's presence in San Francisco the day of the assassination. Shaw had been in that city from November 21st until November 24th, 1963, and was talking to trade people about the new International Trade Mart in New Orleans. He stayed at the St. Francis Hotel, reservations having been made for him by the Executive Director of the San Francisco World Trade Center. At the time of the assassination, Shaw was at the Trade Center discussing respective functions and problems with his San Francisco counterpart. Upon hearing the news of the assassination, Shaw and thirteen other guests stood and offered a silent prayer in memory of the slain President.

On March 9th, one week after the publication of the story concerning Shaw's whereabouts on November 22nd, 1963, Russo underwent a second hypnotic session by Dr. Fatter. The only new "facts" of significance injected into the session by Russo was a claim that "Clem" Bertrand had stated at the party of September 16th that he intended to be "on the Coast" the day Kennedy was assassinated.

Finally, on March 12th, 1967, only two days before the start of the Shaw preliminary hearing, Russo underwent a third hypnotic trance by Dr. Fatter. The trance concluded with this admonition to Russo by the doctor:

> That's right, go back deeper, relaxed. Any time you want to, you can permit yourself to become calm, cool, and collected. . . . You will be amazed at how acute your memory will become in the next few weeks. Things will seem to pop into your mind and it will only be the truth as you saw it. . . . You can permit these starts to come into your mind exactly as you have seen them without fear, without remorsefulness . . . all you will be doing is telling the truth, Perry, as you see it. . . .
>
> Remember, now that you have a task that you, yourself, have elected to perform. You can do it well and you will do it well. And remember, Perry, the truth always wins out.

Fatter told Russo to open his eyes at the count of five. Russo complied.

Russo was now objectified.

10

FOLLOWING THE ARREST OF CLAY
Shaw at about 5:30 P.M. on March 1st, Garrison's office recommended
bond in the amount of $25,000. The bond was set by Judge Thomas
Brahney of the District Court, however, at $10,000, and Shaw was re-
leased later that night.

In the meantime, Garrison's staff had not been idle. While Shaw was
still incarcerated and while Russo was still in his hypnotic trance with
Dr. Fatter, the D.A.'s investigators presented to Judge Matthew Braniff
an application for a search warrant authorizing the search of Shaw's
French Quarter house. The application was based on an affidavit by a
D.A. investigator, which read in part:

> Affiant has evidence that meetings were held in the apart-
> ment of David W. Ferrie at 3330 Louisiana Avenue Parkway
> and the people present were David W. Ferrie, Clay Shaw
> (alias Clay Bertrand), Lee Harvey Oswald, an informant and
> other persons. The meetings were held in September, 1963

and the above individuals were discussing how they would kill John F. Kennedy, President of the United States.

At these meetings, there was an agreement and combination between Clay Shaw (alias Clay Bertrand), Oswald, Ferrie and others to kill John F. Kennedy. At these meetings there was discussion and agreement to carry out this plan.

Then the portion that was heralded most loudly by the press:

One of the sources of information of this affidavit is a confidential informant present at the meeting, who saw the conspirators and heard their plan. This confidential informant saw Ferrie and Shaw and Oswald and the others and heard them agree to kill John F. Kennedy, and heard them discuss means and manner of carrying out the agreement.

The said confidential informant, after giving this statement to affiant, voluntarily submitted to sodium pentothal, a drug known as truth serum, which was administered under the care, control and supervision of the Coroner of the Parish of Orleans, a licensed physician. The confidential informant, while under sodium pentothal, verified and corroborated and reaffirmed his earlier statement.

The search of Shaw's home was conducted that night, and like most events of the Garrison probe, was conducted under the glare of the cameramen's lights. Newsmen and photographers milled about the scene. D.A. assistants and investigators were photographed carting away material from Shaw's house.

The purpose of the search, according to the warrant, was to seize property

which has been used as a means of committing an offense or which may constitute evidence tending to prove the commission of an offense, to-wit: photographs, letters, political propaganda, leaflets, address books, newspapers, telegrams, canceled checks, maps, diagrams, blueprints, time schedules, telephone bills, copies of manuals and manuscripts, recordings, ledgers, canceled airplane tickets, telephone vouchers, tools and implements, guns, rifles, ammunition, telescopic sights, gun cases, miscellaneous gun parts, gun cleaning kits.

The objects actually seized by the D.A.'s men:

A ledger sheet from 1963—a map—three pieces of rope—one chain—five whips—two pieces of leather—one Army cartridge belt—one black hood and cape—one black gown—one black net hat—one shotgun and case—one black leather book cover with numerous papers—one book entitled *A Holiday for Murder*—17 folders containing various papers— one green leather checkbook with odd papers—26 folders containing various papers and documents—three manuscripts—one Underwood typewriter case—one white photo album with pictures—two other photo albums—five green checkbooks—one black account book—one green leather journal—two carbon papers—four paperback books—and twelve hardcover books—one brown leather folder containing personal documents—one copy of the *Wall Street Journal*, Monday February 6, 1961—one letter holder containing various papers—three pocket calendars, 1954, 1966 and 1967 —and one calorie counter.

Some of the more exotic items were taken to Garrison's house and there photographed by representatives of *Life* magazine.

The night of the arrest, Shaw, at the direction of his attorneys, Edward Wegmann, his brother William Wegmann, and Guy Johnson, said nothing. The next morning he appeared before Judge Bernard Bagert, serving that day as Committing Magistrate. The duties of Committing Magistrate are served on successive days by each judge in rotation. The purpose of the arraignment before the Committing Magistrate is to advise arrested persons of their rights to refuse to answer the questions of the police or other representatives of the State, to demand the presence of a lawyer if desired in the event of questioning, and to enable the accused person to request a preliminary hearing if desired.

The "preliminary hearing" is a hearing held in open court for the purpose of determining whether or not the State possesses "probable cause" upon which to hold the accused person. Broadly speaking, "probable cause" means existence of some evidence tending to show commission of a crime by arrested persons. It is something more than suspicion, but something less than proof such as is required in a trial.

The hearing may be demanded of right by any person under a state of arrest, whether incarcerated or free on bond, provided he has not been formally charged by the District Attorney in a bill of information or by the Grand Jury in an indictment. Once the formal charge is filed whether by bill of information or indictment, the accused no longer has a right to demand the preliminary examination. The request for such an examination where a formal charge exists, is almost routinely denied. The purpose of the mandatory preliminary examination is to require that the District Attorney either charge the accused or release him. The preliminary examination may be requested either by the accused or by the District Attorney. It is almost always requested by the accused person, particularly those represented by counsel, and practically never by the State. It should not be surprising that this is so, for it is of no conceivable advantage for the State to reveal its hand. It normally benefits only the accused.

At the arraignment of Clay Shaw on March 2nd, however, it happened. Before any formal motion could be made by the defense, the assistant district attorney representing Garrison's office formally moved for a preliminary hearing. Guy Johnson, one of Shaw's defense attorneys at the time, later remarked to newsmen: "This is crazy. I don't know what the hell they're doing." Later, more controlled, he said, "We do not understand the motivation of Mr. Garrison." The hearing was set by Judge Bagert for March 14th, the next date on which he was to sit as Committing Magistrate, the customary procedure.

That night Shaw made his first public statement following his arrest. Flanked by his attorneys, he said to the press and television:

> I am shocked and dismayed at the charges which have been filed against me. I am completely innocent of any such charges. I have not conspired with anyone at anytime or at any place to murder our late and esteemed President, John F. Kennedy, or any other individual. I have always had only the highest and utmost respect and admiration for Mr. Kennedy.
>
> The charges filed against me have no foundation in fact or in law.
>
> I have not been apprised of the basis of these fantastic charges and assume that in due course I will be furnished with this information and will be afforded an opportunity to prove my innocence.
>
> I did not know Harvey Lee Oswald [sic] nor, to the best of my knowledge, do I know anyone who knew him. I have never seen or spoken to Oswald or anyone who I knew was associated with him. I have received messages of support from persons in this country and abroad who are dismayed and shocked at the accusations that are made against me. These people know me well and know I am incapable of being involved in a plot of this kind. Their expressions of confidence have been gratifying.

This done, the defense now was obliged to turn to the formidable task of preparing for the preliminary examination scheduled for March 14th. The problems confronting the defense were almost nightmarish in quality, even for attorneys accustomed to dealing with the complex and often subtle problems involved in the defense of criminal cases.

*   *   *

Unlike the trial of civil cases, the criminal trial still assumes the aura of a game or contest of skill. Through legislation and judicial fiat throughout the last thirty years the element of surprise has been largely removed from civil proceedings. In civil cases, adversaries are armed with an arsenal of devices enabling "discovery" of virtually everything contained in the opponents' files. In any dispute between private citizens, whether involving alleged civil wrongs, breach of contract, divorce or any one of the infinite variety of subjects that burden the civil dockets, the litigant's attorney is entitled to subpoena the opposing litigant into his office. He may there question him under oath about every conceivable aspect of the dispute. He may subpoena or demand inspection of any object or document intended for use in the trial of the case. He may demand the names and addresses of all witnesses that his opponent intends to call upon during the trial and may then subpoena the witnesses themselves to his office and examine them under oath to determine the nature of the testimony they will give. He may demand in advance a list and description of any documents or physical evidence that will be used. He may submit written questions to his opponent on any matter relating to the litigation and demand written answers.

The civil disputes are tried upon written pleadings which must adequately inform the opponent of the basis and particulars of the claim or the defense to be made. The pleadings, together with the discovery devices available, render the proper preparation of a civil trial laborious and often tedious. But the pertinent facts, all of them, can be properly determined, studied, and marshalled. The extent of the advocate's knowledge of his opponent's case is limited only by the time and funds available for that purpose.

Subject only to those limitations, the advocate will enter the civil courtroom reasonably certain of the case to be presented by his opposition and of any weaknesses and contradictions that are inherent in it.

Surprise, of course, is never entirely eliminated. The human element will not permit it. But given sufficient money and time to prepare, the trial attorney confronted with a major surprise in the midst of a civil trial, can blame himself alone in virtually all instances.

Not so in the criminal arena. It is still a game and its name is surprise. The person accused of crime is entitled by law to know the crime for which he is charged, whether murder, robbery, theft, or gambling, etc., the name of the victim, if any, and the time, date, and place of the offense. With certain minor exceptions peculiar to particular crimes, he is entitled to nothing else. A person charged with theft, for instance, must be informed of the subject of the theft—whether an automobile or a radio, but little else.

He is not entitled to be informed of the witnesses against him or the substance of their testimony. A person charged with burglary is not told, and is not entitled to learn, whether he is suspected by virtue of identification by eyewitnesses, or by discovery of fingerprints at the scene. One charged with murder is not told, nor is he entitled to be informed, as to whether he is alleged to have poisoned his victim or to have done him in with a shotgun.

Nor is the defendant in any case entitled to demand the State's theory as to whether he directly committed the crime, whether he is guilty by virtue of his participation in a plan to commit it, or by virtue of his assistance to another to do so.

The State, too, suffers at times from the virtual nonexistence of effective discovery. The District Attorney does not know in advance whether the defendant charged with murder will claim self-defense or alibi. The possibility of the appearance of hitherto unknown witnesses to establish the defendant's presence in a place far distant on the day of the crime can frequently be quite unsettling even to the most experienced prosecutor.

But the discomfort of the District Attorney is rare in comparison to the constant burden on the defense. The District Attorney has at his beck and call the vast resources of the State—his own investigators, the Police Department, and the cooperation of the numerous city, state and federal investigative agencies. The defendant generally has nothing. Most can ill afford attorneys. Fewer still can afford necessary investigative help. Then, too, most evidence is submitted by the State. It is the State that has the burden of proof. Frequently, the defense produces nothing and must content itself with sniping at prosecution testimony.

The root cause of this vast difference between civil and criminal discovery procedure is the defendant's constitutional right against self-incrimination. The right of discovery in civil procedure is mutual. Each party must respond to his opponent. But the defendant cannot, by prohibition of the Federal and State constitutions, be compelled to furnish any information that can be used against him.

He pays heavily for this protection. It is a handsome price even for the guilty. For the innocent, it is exorbitant. The guilty may know their accusers, or if not their identity, then the substance of their testimony—though often this knowledge will not be imparted to the attorney. Often the attorney must fight back in total darkness, thanks to his guilty client's foolish protestation of innocence.

For those falsely accused of crime, the problem is frequently beyond solution. The plight of the innocent is often truly hopeless. Funds for investigative help are useful, but not always will money suffice. Witnesses cannot be made to speak even if investigators are available to interview them. Though the D.A. generally lists his witnesses in the Office of the Clerk of Court to insure the automatic issuance of subpoenas at trial, he is not compelled to do so. Nor can the defense be sure that one or more surprise witnesses have not purposely been omitted from the witness list.

In the routine cases the defense lawyer will rely on his rapport with the police and with the assistant district attorney in charge of the prosecution. He will expect, and often receive, helpful information that will enable him to determine the course of his defense. Frequently, witnesses, even the victims of crime, will not refuse a tactful approach by the defense lawyer or investigator and will speak freely. This is in the usual routine case. The Shaw case was neither routine nor usual.

Hence, the preliminary hearing, when available, is invaluable to the defense. True, only in a clear and compelling case involving a complete failure of proof, will the court release a defendant on such an examination; for if there is any evidence whatever, what need for the publicity-conscious court to release, on his own determination and responsibility, one whom the police have arrested? That is the job for the jury and in case of doubt, let the jury decide.

But this does not deter the defense counsel in the slightest, for the examination is a means of discovery, a rare opportunity to see the cards held by the State. There is, in the usual case, every advantage and no disadvantage whatever to the defendant in a preliminary hearing. In a sense, no defendant ever loses a preliminary hearing. There is no determination of guilt, only a determination of probable cause to hold him for trial. Nothing at all is lost. This, too, is true in the "usual and ordinary" criminal cases—which the Shaw case was not.

News stories concerning the coming preliminary hearing in the matter of Clay Shaw were trumpeted to a fever pitch almost approaching frenzy. The principals were interviewed, televised, and badgered with questions. Every meaningless word was repeatedly broadcast, printed, and scrutinized for possible significance. Every bit of information, misinformation, speculation, and gossip was repeated in all of its variations in the news media, dissected, analyzed, and squeezed for every bit of possible news value and was not put aside until wrung completely dry.

This was not to be a trial, the press and TV cautioned. Guilt or innocence would not be determined, reiterated the commentators. The public was not concerned about "technicalities," however. No trial in the city's history had created quite this degree of tension. It had all the elements of conflict. There were two sides. There would be a determination by the Court. There would be a winner and a loser.

There was never a preliminary hearing quite like this one. The thus far unnamed witness mentioned in the application for the search warrant would not be revealed merely to the defense. His testimony would be followed with interest around the nation and, more importantly, would be devoured avidly by virtually the entire adult population of New Orleans. His testimony would be printed in the daily press and the power of the printed word is formidable indeed. It would undoubtedly be believed by many.

Thus, one week after Shaw's arrest his attorneys decided that the price of the preliminary hearing was too high. They moved to set aside the order granting the hearing. They also filed with Judge Bagert an "application for particulars," seeking to be informed as to certain specifics concerning the charges against Shaw. What crime did he commit? If a conspiracy was involved, what are the names of the other conspirators? On what date, what time of day, and in which parish did the conspiracy take place? What is the name and address of the confidential informant cited in the application of the search warrant?

There was one other question asked by the defense. Conspiracy is defined as an agreement between two or more persons to commit an offense. However, in order to punish for a conspiracy, it must also be proved by the State that some "overt act" was committed by one or more of the conspirators in furtherance of the plan. Thus, individuals can plot and plan with impunity all manner of crimes, providing nothing is done. There is no prohibition against mere talk. Now the defense asked in their application for particulars: "What action was taken in furtherance of the conspiracy and when did that occur?"

The motion to set aside the order for the preliminary hearing was denied. The requests for information were likewise denied. This was not a trial, ruled the Judge. This was a preliminary hearing and there was no basis for compelling the State to furnish any information whatever. Thus the defense would be obliged to enter the hearing without the vaguest conception as to the time of the supposed conspiracy, not even the year, much less the month or day, would be known. As for the identity of the informant, the defense would learn that, too, at the preliminary hearing.

"We are entitled to be prepared," argued William Wegmann without success, "and not come in here and shoot off the cuff." But the defense was relegated to a close study of news articles and other stray bits of information to determine, if possible, the informant with whose testimony they would soon be faced. To be sure, Russo's name had appeared, albeit inconspicuously, in the press prior to the preliminary hearing. So had many, many other names appeared. Names of witnesses, prospective witnesses, and rumored witnesses were sprinkled like so much spice throughout press reports of the investigation.

Two of the names, of course, that appeared quite frequently in the press were those of Garrison's credible witnesses, Jack Martin and David Lewis. It was not necessary for the press to seek out this pair. Sooner or later many of the reporters were contacted by them. Lewis freely informed one and all that he had seen anti-Castro Cubans in Bannister's office with David Ferrie on many occasions and that he had seen Oswald there several times. Martin promised to divulge "hot leads" to aid in the cause of "sensational journalism." They sometimes appeared to be trying to outdo each other. Martin claimed to at least one reporter that Ferrie had mentioned Clay Shaw to him. He further complained that F.B.I. agents "twisted around what I said . . . because they think I'm a jerk and a bum and an alcoholic." He offered to work on a retainer basis for the *Washington Evening Star*. The *Star* was not interested.

Judge Bernard Bagert decided that he could use the assistance of two of his colleagues and announced that the hearing would be presided over by three judges and that all decisions would be made by a majority vote among the three. The colleagues selected were Judges Malcolm O'Hara and Matthew Braniff. On March 11th Irvin Dymond entered the case as chief defense counsel for Clay Shaw. On the day prior to trial Shaw and the two Wegmann brothers filed several motions with the Court. The motions sought, first, to set aside the order convening the three-judge court on the ground that there was no precedent or basis in law for such a court; second, that the defense be entitled to use its own court reporter so as to be able to have transcripts for their own use prepared by the end of each day's proceedings; third, that Shaw be permitted to inspect and reclaim certain property seized from his home on March 1st, particularly homestead stock valued at $30,000. The retention of the stock, Shaw's lawyers argued, was depriving him of needed funds for his defense. In addition to legal expenses, Shaw was forced to retain a company of private investigators commencing shortly after his arrest and to continue his employment of these investigators for many months thereafter. All of the defense motions were denied.

*   *   *

As the date of the hearing approached, a festive atmosphere prevailed. The inhabitants of Tulane and Broad suddenly found their humble abode in the merciless glare of an international spotlight. Reporters from newspapers the world over, including *Pravda*, mingled in the hallways with the old-timers of the building. Photographers and television cameramen, banned from the building itself by a strict set of guidelines laid down by the Court concerning press coverage, milled about in front of the building on Tulane Avenue waiting eagerly to turn their equipment on anyone possibly connected, however remotely, with the exciting spectacle. Local reporters who had covered the scene at Tulane and Broad for many years agreed that they had seen nothing quite like it.

The excitement was not at all limited to Tulane and Broad. The impending hearing monopolized conversation throughout the city. Thousands sought some means of access to the limited number of seats available in the courtroom. Criminal Sheriff Louis Heyd announced that entrance would be by special pass only and that all spectators would be searched for weapons.

On the morning of March 14th the hearing began as scheduled. It was marked by the fourth courtroom appearance of Jim Garrison. He was flanked by five of his assistants and two investigators. The assistants conducted the examination of a few preliminary witnesses—police photographers—who identified pictures of Ferrie and Oswald and of Ferrie's Louisiana Avenue Parkway apartment.

The State then called its next witness—Perry Raymond Russo. Now the world knew. Russo walked confidently and calmly to the witness stand. He smiled briefly at the entourage at the prosecution table then waited soberly for the questioning by District Attorney Jim Garrison. Seated at the prosecution table with District Attorney Garrison and his assistants, staring directly at Perry Russo, was Dr. Esmond Fatter.

Under questioning by Garrison, Russo related very briefly his background and acquaintance with David Ferrie. He identified a photograph of Ferrie that had been previously introduced through the testimony of police officers. He also identified Ferrie's Louisiana Avenue Parkway apartment. During the summer of 1963, Russo said, he had an arrangement with Ferrie whereby each man was free to come to the other's home at any time.

"Do you remember anything unusual happening in the fall of 1963?"

asked Garrison. Russo then related that around the middle of September he had occasion to go to Ferrie's apartment. "I walked in and there seemed to be some sort of party in progress," said Russo. "There were about ten persons sitting around drinking." After awhile, according to Russo, there were only four persons left in the apartment. He explained that he had waited around because he did not have a ride home. Who were the other three persons in the apartment beside Russo? "Ferrie, a person I had seen several times . . . Leon Oswald, and a third person, Clem Bertrand," responded the witness.

Leon Oswald was identified as being the person depicted in the photographs previously identified as those of Lee Harvey Oswald.

"Do you see the man you know as Bertrand in the courtroom?" asked the D.A.

Russo did, indeed, and he pointed to Shaw.

According to Russo, "David Ferrie began the conversation, pacing back and forth as he talked." According to Ferrie, "An assassination attempt would have to use diversionary tactics," said Russo. And Ferrie stressed "diversification."

Russo then went on to quote the deceased pilot as explaining that "There would have to be a minimum of three people involved. Two of the persons would shoot diversionary shots and the third . . . shoot the 'good' shot." Russo further described how Ferrie emphasized this point by holding up a thumb, and the index and little finger to illustrate the "triangulation of cross fire." One of the three would have to be the "scapegoat," the witness quoted Ferrie.

Judge Bagert suggested a recess for lunch. Garrison urged that Russo be permitted to continue until a more convenient breaking point. The Judge agreed.

In addition to "diversification" and "triangulation of cross fire" and "diversionary tactics," Russo also discoursed about Ferrie's lecture on "availability of exit." According to Russo, Ferrie felt that the sacrificed man would give just enough time for the other two people involved to escape. "Ferrie was a pilot. . . . He said they could either go to Mexico or they could fly directly to Cuba. He talked about the risks of flying to Cuba."

This was not all. In the discussion about escape, it was decided that "Mr. Ferrie, Mr. Oswald, and Mr. Bertrand would be in the public eye . . . Dave Ferrie said something about making a speech at Southeastern." Bertrand, according to Russo, said that "If this is the alternative, he would go on a business trip for his company."

"Did he say where he would go?" Garrison asked.

"He said he would go to the West Coast," replied the witness.

Garrison now directed that Russo step from the witness stand, walk behind the defense table, and place his hand over the head of the man he knew as Clem Bertrand. Without hesitation, Russo complied and placed his hand, palm outstretched, over Shaw's head. In this posture, Russo looked over his right shoulder at Garrison. Garrison now advised the Court that he felt the luncheon recess was in order. The Court agreed, and the reporters raced to the telephone to call their papers.

Following the luncheon recess Russo was shown a rifle with a telescopic sight. The gun had been at the prosecution table throughout the morning session and had precipitated considerable speculation and comment by the spectators. Russo was asked if he could identify the gun and stated that it appeared to be similar to the one he saw in Oswald's hand in Ferrie's apartment. Russo further described his confrontation with Clay Shaw on the day before Shaw's arrest and his pose as an insurance salesman as a means of identifying him. Garrison tendered the witness to the defense for cross-examination.

The defense had prepared subpoenas for records from the employers and schools attended by numerous persons who had been mentioned to the press as witnesses in the Garrison probe. They now filed subpoenas to the Equitable Life Insurance Company and to Loyola and Tulane universities for Russo's records. They asked for and received a delay until the following morning on which to begin their cross-examination.

*   *   *

Cross-examination, according to the popular conception, is a trial by ordeal. Though the truthful witness will stick to his story despite the most persistent badgering or skillful trickery of the opposing counsel, the trial attorney possesses a special skill which will entrap and ensnare the most proficient prevaricator, and will ruthlessly expose the slightest inaccuracy or misconception. No false statement, illusion, or error in memory or observation can withstand the mysterious skill of the competent cross-examiner.

If the witness persists in his testimony, it is obviously truthful and accurate. For otherwise, it would be dramatically exposed. There would be no room for doubt, for the witness would ultimately be obliged to confess his error, or falsehood in the face of the irresistible logic inherent in the method of the cross-examiner. The false or mistaken testimony would be exposed to all and would stand naked, even to the most unsophisticated observer.

It is, of course, a myth and nothing more. Trial lawyers may engage in a lifetime of practice and never observe such a complete collapse of a witness as is depicted in the fictitious trials of movies and television. Nor is the true impact of effective cross-examination always so readily discerned by the casual, the careless, the untrained, or the unsophisticated observer. Even the deliberately untruthful witness will persist in his testimony and there is no magic or mysterious technique of the cross-examiner that can force a confession of perjury. The most accomplished cross-examiners do well to impute perjury or error by compelling increasingly unlikely statements to buttress the witness's false testimony, or by pointing up inherent but latent contradictions in the story.

Most effective by far are those cross-examinations which have been the subject of careful and thorough preparation. But there must be the material with which to prepare. A witness of good character and background who has been basically consistent in his account of the events in question and whose account is, in fact, truthful and reasonably accurate cannot be hurt by cross-examination no matter how skillful and experienced the examiner and no matter how thorough the preparation. The wisest cross-examination of such a witness consists often of two words: "no questions." It is remarkable how difficult it is, particularly for the inexperienced, to utter them.

However, where they exist, prior contradictory statements of the witness or evidence of such prior conduct that would render him unworthy of belief in any event can be used with devastating effect.

* * *

When Dymond prepared on the night of March 14th to begin his cross-examination of Russo at 10:00 A.M. the following morning, he did not, of course, have a copy of Sciambra's memorandum to Garrison, nor of the transcript of Dr. Fatter's hypnotic sessions, nor an account of the sodium pentothal interview of February 27th. Nor could he know of Russo's experience in the field of pornographic photography. The television film clip of the local station wherein Russo denied knowing Oswald was the only available material of significance.

But the problems in this case were more serious than those posed merely by enforced ignorance of the State's witness. The overall approach to the manner of cross-examination must certainly have caused serious consultations between the members of the defense team. Their client had been accused publicly of complicity in a conspiracy to murder the President of the United States. Certain courses of attack on the testimony were obvious. Why had Russo not come forward for three and one-half years following the assassination? Why had his secret been kept from the Warren Commission, the Secret Service, and the Federal

Bureau of Investigation, as well as all other authorities, and revealed only to District Attorney Garrison? How could he have listened calmly to a plot to murder the President and reveal it to no one if it had, indeed, been a serious discussion? How could he have failed to draw a connection between the Lee Harvey Oswald, whose name and New Orleans background were incessantly repeated on news broadcasts and in papers in the New Orleans area, and the Leon Oswald he had met just two months earlier in New Orleans and whom he had supposedly seen as recently as six weeks earlier?

But what of Russo's background and initial contacts with the District Attorney's Office? There was much that could be learned that would be most valuable in preparation for the trial that would probably follow. Generally, a long and tedious "fishing expedition" by the cross-examiner without any clear idea as to what will be found is a dangerous and unwise procedure. The failure to discover or develop anything of sub- stance tending either to disprove or weaken the testimony or to damage materially the character of the witness will serve only to strengthen his testimony in the eyes of the jury. It will most assuredly appear that the examiner has been unable to "shake" the witness, and the impression of truthfulness will be strengthened.

Dymond must certainly have realized that a properly searching and comprehensive examination of Russo, one for discovery purposes, was certain to fail to blunt the dramatic nature of the testimony given by Russo on his direct examination. A briefer, more penetrating and aggressive cross-examination, limited to those areas of obvious weakness, would certainly be more effective to the public—but with what result?

He could not possibly miss the opportunity to learn everything pos- sible about the key state witness. The defense would now be obliged to take advantage of their one and only opportunity to "discover" Russo fully before the day when the chips were down and everything turned on one roll of the dice. For the time being, the public reaction must take second place. There was a job to do and any temptation to play for public approbation was resisted. There could legitimately have been no other way.

*   *   *

The next morning the proceedings started when Dymond called for a return on the subpoenas that had been issued for the records of Perry Russo. Garrison was not present. He had no intention of sitting through a lengthy cross-examination of his witness. Representatives of Loyola and Tulane universities and the Equitable Life Insurance Company identified the documents of their offices. The records contained nothing startling.

Russo was then recalled to the witness stand for cross-examination.

"Do you believe in God?" asked Dymond.

Russo replied that he did. Asked to define God, Russo replied, "God is everything, the entity of the universe, me, you, and everything." Dymond persisted a while longer in questioning Russo on his religious beliefs until, following Russo's demurrer that he did not understand one of Dymond's questions, Judge Bagert interrupted:

> I don't understand it, either. This is not a catechism class, let's move on out of this area.

Dymond had heard a rumor that Russo had once been threatened with expulsion from school for professing atheism. Dymond was fishing and came up with nothing.

He then began to question Russo about his family background and his early years, about his employment and his education, in considerable detail.

The witness was then asked if he had ever received psychiatric treatment. Russo replied that he had, "in 1959 . . . mid-1960, or maybe it was late 1960. It consisted of treatment and consultations and covered a period of one and one-half or two years," said Russo. Russo was then asked about his early acquaintance with David Ferrie. The names of "Lefty" Peterson and Al Landry were introduced and were the subject of more questions. Asked about Layton Martens, Russo stated that he did not know anyone by that name.

Not until the afternoon session did Dymond turn his attention to the subject of Russo's failure to come forward with his story, even following the assassination, until the death of Ferrie. Russo first explained that he did not know how to interpret Ferrie's threat made as late as October, 1963, that "we will get him" and he added, "I don't know now." Further, said Russo, he did not report it because "everyone but Mr. Garrison said Oswald acted alone." Additionally, Russo explained that "I never push myself on anybody" and "from what I read, everybody had something to say" about the assassination.

Didn't he feel that he had something that should be told to the Warren Commission, asked Dymond? "No, I really didn't think about it," answered the witness. Didn't he have a duty as an American citizen to report the incident to which he testified, asked Dymond? "No, because at the time there was involvement in school," he responded and further, "I am sure the F.B.I. knew what it was doing."

Questioned about the taped interview on February 24th, 1967, when Russo denied that Ferrie had ever mentioned the name Lee Harvey Oswald, or that he knew the name Lee Harvey Oswald, Russo explained:

> I knew Leon Oswald, who was whiskered, dirty and had rumpled hair. I did not know a Lee Harvey Oswald.

Russo was excused from the witness stand while Dymond placed in evidence and played to the court the taped television interview.

In response to Dymond's questions, Russo acknowledged that it would be no exaggeration to say that he had seen at least a hundred pictures of Oswald following the assassination.

Why had Russo not been able to identify Oswald at that time as being the same "Leon" Oswald that he had met in New Orleans? Said Russo, "That face stayed in my mind, but the F.B.I. said that they had got the man who shot President Kennedy. They said that Ruby had shot him. I read the Warren Commission was to investigate. The F.B.I. said they had the man who shot the President and I'm not going to argue with the F.B.I., but I told several of my friends 'I might know that man.' "

Pressed by Dymond as to why he had not gone to the Warren Commission, Russo explained: "I don't know about the Warren Commission. I'm no authority. At that time the F.B.I. said they arrested Oswald and that he was the man. I was twenty-three then, a voice in the wilderness. I wasn't going to fight with the government."

What had finally demonstrated to Russo that Lee Harvey Oswald and Leon Oswald were the same person? It was the whiskers and patches of messed hair drawn on the pictures he was shown by the District Attorney's Office. Who put the whiskers on? "One of the artists in the District Attorney's office," said Russo.

How many times altogether had Russo seen Oswald? asked Dymond. Four times, stated Russo.

Asked who else had attended the party preceding the assassination plot that he had overheard, Russo named Sandra Moffett. He had escorted her to the house, said Russo. Many of the other eight or ten persons present were Spanish-speaking people, possibly Cubans. They wore dark green clothing and some wore khaki outfits.

Russo was questioned about the date on which he had last seen Oswald. He repeated to Dymond, as he had to Dr. Fatter, that he had last seen him on October 7th, 1963. Asked if he were sure that he had

seen Oswald in New Orleans in October in the apartment of David
Ferrie, Russo replied that he was.

"Are you aware that Oswald left New Orleans on September 25th,
1963, on his way to Houston and Mexico and that he never returned?"
asked Dymond as he picked up a copy of the Warren Commission
Report. The State objected that the Warren Report had "never been
proven as a fact in this Court."

Judge Bagert looked down at Dymond who held the Commission
Report in his hand. Said the Judge:

"You're going to introduce the Warren Report?"

Dymond responded that he was. Said Bagert: "You must be kidding."

Dymond cited a State statute providing for the admissibility of all
official reports of United States Commissions created by Executive
Order and further providing for "prima facie" proof of the contents by
virtue of the admission of such reports in evidence. Judge Bagert was
adamant:

> That's your interpretation. You're wrong and you're over-
> ruled.

When Dymond persisted, Judge Bagert repeated: "We told you you
were overruled." Dymond noted that the inside cover of the Report
indicated it was an official copy promulgated by the United States
Government Printing Office. "Does that give it authenticity?" responded the Judge. The three members of the bench consulted. Judge
Braniff later expressed his opinion that the Report was "fraught with
hearsay," and Judge Bagert interjected that the hearsay was "five and six
times removed." O'Hara stated that while he did not necessarily agree
with the Report he felt that under the law it should be admitted. Hence,
by a two to one vote the offer was rejected.

Dymond continued his cross-examination.

Did Russo see Ferrie after the assassination? "Yes, sir," said Russo.
He had seen him about eight or ten months after the assassination when
he drove into the filling station on Metairie Road. How many times
altogether had he seen Ferrie between the assassination and Ferrie's
death? "Maybe four, five, or six times during the summer months."
". . . You didn't know that he had been picked up by the D.A.'s
Office?" asked Dymond, referring to the arrest immediately following the
assassination. "No, sir," said Russo.

"Did Ferrie state to you his plan to kill Kennedy had succeeded?"
asked Dymond. "No, sir," said Russo. Russo didn't question Ferrie
about it because "you didn't question him, he gave you all the answers

before a question was necessary. You got out of the habit of asking questions."

"Your testimony is that you were present when Dave Ferrie entered into a plan to kill the President and you never saw fit to ask him about it?" repeated Dymond. "Yes, sir," responded Russo.

Russo was then questioned about his contacts with the District Attorney's Office following the February 22nd death of Ferrie. Dymond now learned for the first time of the hypnotic interviews and of the other "objectifying processes."

"Are you under hypnosis now?" asked Dymond. No, he wasn't, said Russo.

Turning once again to the subject of Russo's inability to correctly identify Oswald following the assassination as a result of his being clean-shaven, Dymond asked if he had ever seen "Leon" Oswald clean-shaven. "Once," responded Russo.

"When?" asked Dymond.

"When he was leaving for Houston during the first week of October," replied Russo.

"He was cleanly shaven?" repeated Dymond.

"Yes, sir," said Russo.

"Why after having seen him cleanly shaven couldn't you identify him in a picture?" asked Dymond.

"I was only there eight or ten minutes and I didn't take great notice of him," was Russo's explanation.

Russo denied ever having attempted to jump from a window while in high school.

"At any time did you attempt to commit suicide . . . take your own life?" asked Dymond.

"Absolutely not," said Russo.

There were few other matters of consequence developed.

The press and television referred to the two and one-half day cross-examination as "tedious." It was not, however, designed for public consumption. The major purpose of the examination had been to "discover" Russo and from that point of view it was quite successful. The popular point of view in the city was that Dymond had not "shaken" Russo, but "shaking" Russo would have to wait for another day.

Following Russo's testimony Dr. Fatter and Dr. Chetta described the sodium pentothal and hypnotic sessions. Chetta was asked his opinion as to Russo's sanity. To Dymond's objection, Judge Braniff snapped: "You made the implication that this witness was crazy. You inferred that he was testifying under hypnosis and also that he tried to kill himself. Where do you get off objecting now?" The objection was overruled.

The surprises were not yet over. On the second day of the hearing, a twenty-nine-year-old Negro narcotic addict named Vernon Bundy, confined in the Parish Prison for parole violation, sent a letter to the presiding Judge, Bernard Bagert, advising that he, too, knew something about the conspiracy. Bagert referred the letter to the District Attorney's Office. On March 16th, 1967, Bundy was interviewed by investigators of Garrison's staff. He related that in the summer of 1963 he had journeyed to the lakefront in New Orleans for the purpose of "doing up," that is, injecting himself with heroin. As he was preparing to do so, said Bundy, a black sedan pulled up near him and parked in a parking area. The sole occupant of the sedan appeared to be a tall, gray-haired white man. Presently, this man was joined by a much younger man and the two engaged in conversation. The younger, according to Bundy, was wearing a white T-shirt, light tan jeans, and was in need of a shave. Bundy described him as looking like a "junkie" himself. The conversation that ensued between the two men occurred about fifteen to twenty feet away from Bundy, who was preparing for his "fix." Bundy overheard the younger man ask, "What am I going to tell her?" Replied the older man, "I'll take care of that." Thereupon the older man gave a quantity of currency to the other who put it in his right rear pocket. In doing this, some paper fell from the pocket of the younger man. Both he and his older companion thereupon went their separate ways. Bundy noticed that the paper which had fallen to the ground was yellow with black print and that it was approximately four-by-seven-inches. He remembers that the word "Cuba" was printed on it.

Bundy was given a polygraph test by the New Orleans Police Department. The polygraph operator thereupon reported to Garrison that the test revealed clear evidence of deception. It didn't matter. Obviously Bundy was telling the truth. Several of Garrison's assistants recommended against putting Bundy on the stand. Garrison decided otherwise.

So, late in the afternoon of the fourth day of the hearing Bundy took the witness stand. He was questioned by Garrison, who had returned to the courtroom for the first time following the conclusion of Russo's direct testimony on the first day of the hearing. Garrison led Bundy through his testimony and Bundy, through photographs, identified the younger man as Lee Harvey Oswald and the older man as Clay Shaw.

"Are either of the men you saw in court today?" asked Garrison.

"Yes, the gray-headed fellow," replied Bundy.

Garrison asked Bundy, as he had asked Russo previously, to step behind the defense table and place his hand over the man he recognized. Bundy complied and walked to the defense table and held his hand above the head of Shaw.

For the second time in the hearing, Dymond was faced with the task of cross-examination of a witness whose identity was hitherto unknown. Unlike Russo, however, who was at least regarded as a possible witness, Bundy was not known at all to the defense, nor was the existence of a second witness even suspected.

Dymond directed his examination primarily to Bundy's narcotic habit. In response to questioning, the witness stated that his habit was "three or four caps a day" at a cost of $5.00 each. How was he able to raise that much money? Bundy stated he worked on occasion and on other occasions stole in order to support his habit. He began shooting drugs when he was 13 years old, said Bundy, but did not become a "real every day addict" until age 22.

At the time of the incident in the summer of 1963 described by Bundy, the effects of the previous day's injections had worn off, but Bundy was not yet suffering from any of the symptoms of withdrawal. His ability to accurately observe or to recall the events that had occurred two and one-half years previously came under attack by Dymond.

It is doubtful that Bundy's testimony was believed by many, even Garrison's most avid supporters or admirers. The judgment and discretion of the man who had placed him on the witness stand and vouched for his credibility, however, somehow escaped public comment.

Following Bundy's testimony, both sides rested.

*   *   *

Following arguments by counsel the Court retired for a little over half an hour and announced its decision:

> This Court finds sufficient evidence has been presented to establish probable cause that a crime has been committed and, further, that sufficient evidence has been presented to justify bringing into play the further steps of the criminal process against the arrestee, Clay L. Shaw. The defendant is released on his present bond.

Russo had not in the popular vernacular been "shaken." He had testified that in mid-September he had seen a man named Leon Oswald holding a rifle with a telescopic sight. He was plotting to assassinate President Kennedy. About ten weeks later he had seen and heard on television and in the press that a Lee Harvey Oswald, who had previously lived in New Orleans, had been accused of assassinating the President in Dallas with a rifle with a telescopic sight.

Somehow it had never occurred to Russo to connect him with the Leon Oswald he knew. His interest in school was one explanation. The beard was another, though he had seen "Leon" clean-shaven for almost ten minutes when he left New Orleans in October. The impact of these bare facts had been largely lost in the mass of discovery testimony that had been elicited.

On March 20th Judge Bagert was quoted by Leslie H. Whitten of the New York World Journal Tribune:

> This wasn't a question of guilty or not guilty. It was a question of probable cause. I believe there is probable cause . . . given what we got in there, I had no choice. Russo stood up. There were some minor discrepancies, but you tend to doubt, you have to doubt it, when there is a 100% story every time. . . . Just think for one minute about the alternative, that is, if we cut him loose. . . . With the defense depending on cross-examination and not putting on a real case of its own, the nation and the world would have charged a fix.

Russo's testimony had "stood up." Whether it could do so in a trial now that his identity was known and now that his story was committed to record and subject to investigation and verification was another matter, but that would be far in the future. To the public the matter was much simpler. The D.A. had won and the defense had lost. It was doubtful if anyone more fully comprehended the reaction of the public than Jim Garrison.

On March 22nd Russo appeared before the Grand Jury, which thereupon formally indicted Shaw for conspiring "between September 1st and October 10th, 1963" to murder John F. Kennedy. Why the indictment when a bill of information would have sufficed? Said Judge Braniff in response to a newsman's question: "Gee, I don't know; perhaps because of the seriousness of the situation. It's a public affair. The President of the United States is involved." Said an assistant D.A.: "This is the way Mr. Garrison wanted it." It seemed that the same could be said of practically everything that had transpired to date.

11

GARRISON HAD SCORED A VICTORY
in the battle for public opinion, at least on his home ground in New
Orleans. Much of the national press had been less than impressed,
however, and Russo's testimony came under close scrutiny by a number
of experienced and tough-minded reporters.

On March 21st Russo was interviewed in Baton Rouge by James
Phelan of the *Saturday Evening Post*. In 1962 Phelan had done a laudatory article on Garrison for the *Post* in connection with his drive against
vice. He had interviewed Garrison after Shaw's arrest, but before the
preliminary hearing, and Garrison had freely furnished Phelan with a
number of documents, including Sciambra's memorandum of February
25th and a transcript of the first hypnotic session with Dr. Fatter.

Now, in the course of his interview with Russo, witnessed by a reporter for a Baton Rouge newspaper, Phelan handed Russo his own
copy of the Sciambra memorandum and asked him to read it for accuracy. Russo made four minor corrections, none of which pertained to
matters that were the subject of testimony he had given against Shaw at

the preliminary hearing. Russo noted that Phelan had underlined the notation in Sciambra's memorandum that "he stated he has seen this man twice," the importance of which, of course, was readily apparent to Phelan. Somewhat embarrassed upon noting this underscoring, Russo stated: "I should have said three times, counting the party. I am usually careful about what I say, but," and Russo shrugged, "maybe I only said twice." "You first mentioned the assassination plot when?" asked Phelan. "Down in New Orleans," said Russo.

This confirmed to Phelan that Russo had told Sciambra nothing about any assassination plot when first interviewed in Baton Rouge.

About a month later, Phelan returned to Louisiana, this time to New Orleans as Russo had now been transferred by Equitable to New Orleans, and he again interviewed Russo. Phelan's work on this occasion was on behalf of the National Broadcasting Company, which organization was preparing a one-hour special on the Garrison probe. Russo was interviewed daily for six days by Phelan. During the first conversation, Russo exclaimed: "If Garrison knew what I told my priest in Baton Rouge after the Shaw hearing, he would go through the ceiling!"

What had he told his priest? According to Russo, he had told the cleric he wanted to sit down alone with Shaw in a room, listen to him "breathe and talk" and ask him some questions so that he, Russo, could resolve certain doubts he had of his identification of Shaw.

Phelan pursued the subject. At Russo's suggestion, Phelan arranged a tentative meeting between Shaw and Russo with only Phelan present. Before the meeting could transpire, however, Russo withdrew. The reason? Russo first explained to Phelan that news of the meeting would leak back to Garrison, but he later explained: "I lied to you about why I didn't want to meet with Shaw. I was afraid that if I talked to him, I'd know he wasn't the man. What could I do then? I could go on the run to Mexico or to California and become a beatnik, but I couldn't run from myself."

But during his interview with Phelan, Russo revealed on several occasions that he did indeed fear the volatile D.A. He stated repeatedly to Phelan that if he changed his story about Shaw, or even compromised to any degree on the positive nature of his identification, Garrison would "clobber me." He'll charge me with perjury or something," said Russo, "and clunk, there goes my job with Equitable."

Russo volunteered to Phelan that he "did not know the difference between reality and fantasy" and further acknowledged that he had told as much to his roommate, a boy named Steve, and that he had brooded about it considerably. "Everything you have commented on about my testimony has been bouncing around inside my head," he declared. "I'm much more critical of myself than you are," said Russo.

Russo was also concerned about the threat from the other direction. He volunteered that Dymond "could destroy me as a witness with five questions." All Dymond had to do, said Russo, was to study the transcript of the hypnotic session. "It's all right there before him," he moaned.

Apparently Russo's doubts had been made known to the D.A. He had, he said, demanded of Garrison's office "proof" that there was other evidence or testimony supporting the case against Shaw. According to Russo, "They brought out some stuff," to Russo's house and he read it, but wasn't very impressed. In a short-lived moment of determination, Russo told Phelan that he was going to "have a showdown" with Garrison's office and that if the D.A. could not convince him, Russo, that there was a good case against Shaw, Russo would not repeat his accusation against Shaw at the trial.

Phelan talked to Russo again the end of May. Russo was still brooding about his unhappy plight. The journalist reviewed with him the various inconsistencies in his testimony, beginning with his first appearance in Garrison's probe. Said Russo, "I'm not arguing with anything you have said, but I can't see any way I can go without getting clobbered." Russo expressed fear that if he stuck to his story, Shaw and his lawyers would "get" him and that if he changed it, he would be destroyed by Garrison.

Phelan suggested that he simply tell the objective truth. Russo responded that he did not know what the truth was.

*   *   *

Phelan was not the only one to whom Russo confided that he was unable to tell truth from fantasy. He was also interviewed in May by a highly skilled, tenacious investigator for the National Broadasting Company named Walter Sheridan. To Sheridan, as the newsman was later to relate in a nationwide telecast, Russo stated that his testimony had consisted of part truth, part fantasy, and part lies. He expressed the fear that he was unable to determine truth from fantasy.

But Russo was scared. He sought help in his attempt to extricate himself from the trap in which he felt himself held fast.

To George Lardner of the *Washington Post*, shortly before the NBC telecast on June 19th, Russo acknowledged that there were certain "weaknesses" or "holes" in his testimony. "Garrison doesn't know what they are," he said. "I know what they are." But Russo explained to

Lardner as he had to Sheridan and others that he had to "look out for myself." According to the columnist, Russo said he had no intention of disclosing the weaknesses in his testimony to any newsmen without getting something in return. He expressed dissatisfaction with the $3,000 that he claimed he had received from Garrison's office for expenses. Further, he might decide to supply Shaw's attorneys with an opportunity to demolish his testimony, said Russo.

"But," he added to Lardner, "if you say anything about this, I'm going to have to call you a liar."

Among the matters mentioned in the National Broadcasting Company telecast on the Garrison investigation on the night of June 19th was the fact that Perry Russo failed to "pass" the polygraph test administered at the direction of Garrison's office. Garrison, who had been keeping his own watch on Sheridan, knew of the impending claim in advance and set about to make an immediate and dramatic response.

On June 16th, 1967, Police Detective Edward O'Donnell, one of the most experienced polygraph operators in the New Orleans Police Department, was contacted by the District Attorney's Office and asked to administer a polygraph test to Russo. It was explained to him by one of Garrison's assistants that the operator who had given the previous test had antagonized the witness and that therefore the results were not satisfactory. The assistant explained that Russo would like to meet O'Donnell before the test was given as Russo wanted "to see what kind of person" O'Donnell was. O'Donnell agreed.

About 3:00 P.M. Russo appeared in O'Donnell's office. He told the officer that he would like to see how the polygraph operated and that he had prepared a list of twenty questions which he suggested be asked him. He would, he explained, answer some truthfully and others untruthfully and in this way he could determine the effectiveness of the polygraph.

O'Donnell had another suggestion. He asked Russo to pick a number from 1 to 10 and to write it on a piece of paper. O'Donnell would then ask the witness first if the number was 1, then if the number was 2, etc., through number 10. Russo was to reply no to each question and O'Donnell would thereupon state by reading the polygraph the number that had been selected. The test was performed, and to Russo's amazement O'Donnell was able to correctly identify the selected number.

O'Donnell then attempted to determine a pattern by asking routine questions of Russo. This pattern, or test, referred to as a pneumogram, was impossible, however, as the reading obtained when the machine was affixed to Russo was entirely too erratic. By agreement, Russo returned three days later on June 19th in the early afternoon. The NBC program was scheduled that night. On this occasion, O'Donnell again attempted to administer a test, but was forced to stop due to erratic readings. At this time the officer suggested to Russo that he relax and that the two of them discuss the entire matter informally. The crucial questions to be asked, explained O'Donnell, involved the subject of Clay Shaw's presence at the party at Dave Ferrie's home.

Russo spoke freely to O'Donnell as he had to others. He had, he said, been under considerable pressure from all sides, including from Garrison and from the press. O'Donnell told Russo that he did not care about either Garrison or the press; that he worked for neither; that he was interested only in the truth. Russo replied that he was confused.

O'Donnell patiently explained to Russo that he simply wanted to know whether or not Clay Shaw was present at the party that he had testified about at the preliminary hearing. Russo first stated that he wasn't sure if Shaw had been present or had not been. O'Donnell was not satisfied. "It should be simple to be able to state if Shaw was or was not at the party," he explained, and Russo agreed that Shaw was a person whose face and appearance were not easily forgotten. O'Donnell then asked Russo if he was sure that he had seen him previously at all and Russo replied, "Yes, at one place, at the Nashville Avenue wharf during President Kennedy's visit to New Orleans." O'Donnell expressed the opinion that if he were sure of that, he should also be able to state whether Shaw had been present at the party or not.

Russo then told the officer that if he were forced to say yes or no, that he would be obliged to say no.

O'Donnell also wanted to know from his subject whether the discussion at this party had been a serious conspiracy or simply a bull session.

Russo responded candidly that in his opinion it had just been a bull session. Half the time, said Russo, he did not know what was being discussed at Ferrie's house as often when he would visit there he would simply sit in the corner or at one side while others talked about a weird assortment of topics. Among the subjects that he had heard discussed from time to time were how to commit a perfect murder, how to commit a perfect fraud of an insurance company, or how to assassinate a head of state.

Russo also told O'Donnell, as he had Phelan, that he would like a meeting to be arranged with Shaw so that he could see if Shaw were the type of person who could get involved in something such as was being discussed at Ferrie's. He explained to O'Donnell, as he had to Phelan, that he would like to know what else Garrison had against Shaw so that he, Russo, might come to some conclusion as to whether or not Shaw was the guilty party. O'Donnell advised Russo to make up his own mind from his own recollection and not to be guided by other evidence.

Russo left. O'Donnell immediately went to Garrison's office, spoke to the D.A., and advised him of everything that had transpired. Garrison became enraged and fumed that "they" had gotten to Russo. O'Donnell returned to his office and shortly thereafter received word through a D.A. investigator that he, O'Donnell, should "keep his mouth shut."

O'Donnell had been on the police force sixteen years and did not take kindly to such advice. He immediately typed a full report of everything that had transpired and forwarded a copy to Garrison. There the matter rested for approximately one month.

In mid-July O'Donnell was told that Russo was coming for the polygraph test and the officer was asked to come to Garrison's office. Upon arriving he was asked to enter a room where Russo was waiting alone. O'Donnell strongly suspected that the room was "bugged" and had no desire to participate in any contrived meeting with Russo. He waited outside. Finally, a number of other assistant D.A.'s were called into the room. He noticed several of them carrying briefcases, and O'Donnell wondered about the presence of recording equipment in them. Finally he entered the room with the assistants and Russo. Also present were Garrison and one of the D.A.'s secretaries who transcribed the meeting that ensued.

Garrison gave a copy of O'Donnell's report to Russo and asked him to examine it and determine if it were correct. Russo read the report, and in the presence of Garrison, the three assistants, Officer O'Donnell, and the D.A.'s secretary stated that the report was correct except for one small item. The item? His inability to identify Clay Shaw.

During the course of the discussion that followed reference was made to Russo's statement that he did not know what had been discussed at the party he had described at the preliminary hearing. Replied Russo to the assembled group: "I have been telling you all along I don't know what was said at that party." The remark was ignored by Garrison and his assistants.

The balance of the meeting was largely spent in a concerted effort on the part of Garrison and his assistants to convince O'Donnell that a supplemental report should be rendered clearing up the one small error in the original report. O'Donnell declined to argue and patiently listened. When they had finally concluded, O'Donnell advised the group that his original report was quite correct; that he knew what he had heard and that there were no errors in the report. He further advised that he saw no need for a report in any event as he felt the entire conversation had been "bugged" in addition to having been transcribed by Garrison's secretary. He then left.

Russo never submitted to the polygraph examination. The entire matter was dropped.

*   *   *

Russo's almost pathetic quest for an audience to whom he could unburden himself, however, did not end. Approximately a month later, during the evening of August 15th, while driving down Bourbon Street in the French Quarter, Russo spotted a face he recognized from newspaper photographs and television. It was another unhappy former acquaintance of Ferrie's—Layton Martens. Russo "wanted someone to talk to." Martens was a ready listener and the two men drove around the city approximately an hour.

Lamented Russo to his newfound friend: "This is the most blown-up and confused situation I have ever seen . . . I don't think any of these people involved should be convicted of anything because they didn't do anything." Pointed exceptions to this last remark were Walter Sheridan, the NBC newsman whom Garrison now charged with having bribed Russo, and Richard Townley, a news reporter for NBC's local affiliate, WDSU-TV. Townley was likewise charged with bribery and also with intimidation of Gordon Novel's ex-wife, Marlene Mancuso. Russo felt bitterness toward the two newsmen for having "double-crossed" him.

Two days later the two met again. Russo confided in Martens, as he had to Sheridan, Phelan, and O'Donnell previously, that he was not 100 percent certain of his identification of Shaw and that he would like to meet Shaw personally so that he might become absolutely convinced. He was somewhat concerned, said Russo, because he had made his identification to date on the basis of photographs alone. He feared that the person he had identified as Shaw may in truth have been Guy Bannister. He wondered also if the party he identified as Oswald might not have been Lewallen. The possibility of misidentification in both instances had been bandied about considerably by the press and the Oswald-Lewallen similarity had been the subject of discussion on the National Broadcasting Company telecast of June 19th.

Further, related Russo to Martens, he was not at all sure if the discussion of an assassination was directed against Castro or against Kennedy.

Undoubtedly, Russo's conduct caused the D.A. serious concern. The various attempts by what Garrison termed the "eastern establishment" to sabotage his case with pretrial publicity was bad enough without Russo's own self-doubts.

But Russo was only one witness. He was certainly not the only witness —merely one of the few cooperative ones. There were others who could certainly furnish invaluable assistance to the State if only they could be persuaded in the interest of justice to speak the truth. There were, for example, Layton Martens and Alvin Beauboeuf, the two men arrested at Ferrie's apartment the weekend of the assassination.

And there was Dean Andrews.

12

ON MARCH 2ND, THE DAY FOLLOW-
ing Clay Shaw's arrest, Dean Andrews was ordered to appear in the
D.A.'s office. With his attorney, Sam "Monk" Zelden, he answered the
questions of Garrison's assistant for approximately three hours.

He was asked to identify the Mexican with the "butch" haircut from
several photographs furnished by the interrogators. But he could not,
said Andrews, because the photographs did not show the necks of the
subjects and this Mexican had an unusually strong-looking neck, he
explained.

He was asked if he remembered the Warren Commission asking him
about Clay Bertrand. "Where is that?" asked Andrews. A copy of the
report refreshed his memory.

Had Andrews ever had financial dealings with Bertrand? No, he said,
because "the kids always came back and paid." Bertrand never owed
him any money. Andrews was then shown his testimony in the Commission Report to the effect that Bertrand owed him money. He was

"vague" then, said Andrews, because he was being pushed then just as he was being pushed now by the D.A.'s men.

Asked to describe Bertrand as he appeared on the one and only occasion he now claimed to have seen him, Andrews asked for a break to refresh his memory. After "refreshing his memory," he informed his interrogators that he didn't carry a tape measure with him. Andrews finally described Bertrand as having gray hair, a ruddy complexion, and let it go at that.

Did Andrews know Clay Shaw? He had seen pictures of him, but had never met him, said Andrews. Was Shaw similar in physical appearance to Bertrand? Andrews replied that he didn't know and that he "could care less."

In all probability, it was following this private conference that Garrison became painfully aware of the fact that Andrews really knew nothing at all. But it did not temper in the slightest his efforts to obtain Andrews's identification of Shaw as Bertrand.

Andrews's appearance in the building on that day was the first of many during the next few months. He was colorful, good copy, a "character," and the press gave him no rest. He was comic relief, the buffoon, and a willing performer.

His lawyer, "Monk" Zelden, was good copy in his own right. He is a former athlete and looks it. The low-pitched rasping voice seems perfectly in place in his stocky frame. It is sometimes difficult to tell whether Zelden is joking or serious. The safer assumption is that he is joking.

Following their appearance before Garrison on March 2nd, the duo took part in a question and answer session before television interviewers. Zelden was seldom at a loss for a clever retort to the newsmen's queries, and Andrews was his lawyer's best audience. His delight with his attorney's performance was quite evident to the viewing audience and he was frequently seen to throw back his head and laugh with sheer delight at Zelden's verbal joust with the reporters.

On a number of occasions when Andrews and his lawyer marched the length of the building they were accompanied by a squad of assistant D.A.'s who seemed to be running interference through the mass of newsmen and television cameramen. To many of the questions, Andrews would snap: "Read the Warren Report for your answers."

"What do you think of D.A. Jim Garrison's investigation?" asked one newsman.

"That's his problem, not mine," was the reply.

Another newsman gave voice to the rumors that abounded in the building: "Do you anticipate getting arrested?" he asked.

"I couldn't care less," said Andrews.

On March 9th he was questioned by the Grand Jury. Apparently the results were no more satisfactory. On the first day of the Shaw preliminary hearing Garrison stated in the presence of several of his aides that he was going to call Zelden and tell him that it was "now or never" and that he was "sick of fooling around with Andrews." Garrison made it clear that he wanted Andrews to testify at the Clay Shaw hearing that Shaw was Bertrand. But Andrews did not appear as a witness for Garrison.

On March 16th, the third day of the Shaw preliminary hearing, things happened fast for the cherubic, wisecracking Andrews. That morning he was suspended from his position as an assistant district attorney for Jefferson Parish. The Jefferson Parish D.A., Frank Langridge, a political ally of Garrison's, explained that this did not signify his belief that Andrews was guilty of any wrongdoing, merely that he had brought "notoriety" to the office. Later that morning, he appeared for the second time before the Orleans Parish Grand Jury.

He tried manfully to live up to what he had repeatedly stated to be his agreement with Garrison: "I won't say he is and I won't say he ain't."

Andrews was asked by one of the grand jurors: "Would you state positively that Clay Shaw and Clay Bertrand, having seen Clay Shaw recently, were not the same people?"

Said Andrews: "I could not do it—my personal opinion, if you are interested in it, I'll give to you."

"All right, we are interested in your personal opinion."

> "I can't connect the two—I can't say he is and I can't say he ain't—there is no way in my mind that I can connect the two, but if you ask me under oath, I can't give you my personal opinion—I just have to say there is no way in the world I can connect the two. The only difference—I would have to go along with Dick and Mumu [two assistant D.A.'s]—'cause I found out there is a difference, you know on the phone, there is a ten-second delay at a frequency or something in the transmission of the voices."

At this point an assistant D.A. took over the questioning and there followed a somewhat perplexing exchange.

"If you were to have a physical description in your mind of Clay Bertrand with regard to height and general build," asked the assistant D.A., "and if you were to put a physical description of Clay Shaw, whom I believe you have seen on TV, is that correct?"

"Yes."

"Is there anything grossly disproportionate about the general description in regard to height of the two men?"

"He is taller," said Andrews.

"Who is taller?"

"Clay Shaw."

"How much?"

"I don't know."

"Well, can't you give an approximation?" persisted the assistant.

"An approximation. How tall is Clay Shaw? I don't know how tall Clay Shaw is."

"You must have some idea about how much taller he would be than Clay Shaw."

Andrews tried desperately to shake his pursuers:

"I see him on TV—he is a tall cat—I don't believe the person I know as Clay Bertrand is as tall as him. I don't know. I can't say yes, and I can't say no. As God is my judge. I have to go back to the same thing I'm telling you—I go to a fag wedding reception, and he is standing up and he is well dressed, I don't measure the guy then, I don't measure him now. I don't even think about the guy. Just like you go to any wedding reception, you mingle, you drink, you talk. I had no occasion to—to have this guy impress me."

The avalanche of words did not work.

"Mr. Andrews, you stated that Clay Shaw is taller."

"While I am assuming that, I don't know. I see him tower over people when they put the TV camera on him so I figure he is a tall cat."

"About how much taller would you say he is?"

"The general build is the same—you are asking me for height, I can't tell you."

"Well, you can tell me whether it's closer to one inch or closer to eight inches, can't you?"

"How can I tell you that?" responded Andrews.

"Well, is he closer to four inches? Is he as much as a foot taller?"

"No."

"Is he as much as half a foot taller?"

Said the exasperated Andrews:

"You see, man, you are like all them people, you push and push for something—that's how I got two descriptions in here before. I don't know. I really, honestly, don't know. All I know is Clay Bertrand, the one I know, has a voice I know as an individual—now this was '64, seven years later when I go look for the guy that jumped up and ran out of the place—he's sitting down and I told them '58—I get in all kinds of inconsistencies, I can't give you what you want in relationship to height, except the man is in my opinion that I know as Clay Bertrand is six-foot one or six-foot two, in that area."

Andrews was in a difficult position, indeed. He came face to face with his nemesis:

"I get the impression you all want me to identify Clay Shaw as Clay Bertrand—I'll be honest with you that is the impression I get . . ."

"Well?" said the impatient assistant.

"And I can't. I can't say he is and I can't say he ain't."

"You can't say he is and you can't say he ain't?" Apparently, the assistant was beginning to feel somewhat frustrated.

"Right."

"And that is what you told us in our office?"

One final effort:

"Right. And that is what I am telling you now. I cannot say positively under oath that he is Clay Bertrand or that he is not. Even with me listening to the guy's voice on the phone, the voice I recall is somewhat similar to this cat's voice. But his voice has overtones just like Mumu said. The voice I recall on the phone as Clay Bertrand's is a deep, cultured, well-educated voice—he don't talk like me, he used the King's English. Everybody thinks I am holding something back. They think I have the key to who killed Kennedy—I wish I did. I'd sell it and make a million dollars. . . ."

Andrews was then questioned about his most recent supposed meeting with the mysterious Bertrand. Asked if he would know Bertrand at the moment he were to meet him, Andrews replied: "Instinct only. I'd really be as baffled as I am now. He is like the Holy Grail to me, you know you can see it and you know you can get it."

Andrews was asked about David Ferrie. Andrews said that as an assistant district attorney, he had once "nolle prosequied" a charge against Ferrie involving an expired brake tag on his automobile. Asked if he ever had occasion to parole anyone for Ferrie, Andrews replied that he did not.

"Do you know what parole power is?"

"You got to be joking," responded the indignant Andrews. "You ask me an intelligent question and I give you an intelligent answer. Sure, I know what it is."

After some questioning concerning discussions of fee arrangements with Bertrand for representation of Oswald, an assistant D.A. asked: "Now, what was the nature of your being contacted by Clay Bertrand at this time?"

Replied Andrews: "You are the only guy in all of them that ever asked me that. I'll elucidate—like in Enrico Caruso."

"You mean that you have never been asked why Clay Bertrand contacted you?"

"That's right. You are the first one who ever asked me."

"How about the Warren Commission?"

"No, they contacted in a different way—they got an answer out of me. They never got the whole thing."

"All right—will you tell us . . ."

"A voice that I identified as Clay Bertrand called me at the hospital and asked me if I would represent Lee Oswald in Dallas—nobody ever asked me about a fee or anything else—he said I would get real famous and he would get in touch with Lee Oswald so that I could represent him. That's that part nobody ever asked me. As soon as I said I heard the voice of Clay Bertrand blump—they all cut off. You're the first one who ever asked me for the whole bit."

Andrews then related the subsequent conversation with Zelden and was then asked about an investigator who had worked for Andrews. Had Andrews mentioned Clay Bertrand to the investigator?

"All I told him was we were going to Dallas to defend Oswald."

"You didn't tell him it was Clay Bertrand?"

"Man, I'm the boss—I don't tell my flunkies all my business. I pay them and they do what I tell them to do or they hit the road. I have [sic] no confidant with all my people. I run my office, the tail don't wag the dog."

At 6:00 P.M. on that day Andrews was indicted for perjury. The indictment read merely that Andrews "did testify falsely under oath." None of the testimony was set forth nor could there truly have been time for any significant portion of it to have been transcribed. The testimony was alleged to be material to the "issue and question under investigation, to wit: a conspiracy to murder John F. Kennedy." Shortly thereafter he posted $1,000 bond and was released.

Was he surprised by the indictment? "I laid eight to five on it and I will pick the money up," Andrews told newsmen.

Had he made any false statements? "Absolutely not. I testified as I could to the best of my knowledge. Apparently there is a conflict of opinion as to what I testified about."

"Why were you brought into the investigation?" asked the interviewer.

"That's a good question. Apparently, they seem to feel I have a key that can unlock certain locks. I don't even know where the locks are."

The day after Andrews was arrested, Garrison was interviewed by Hugh Aynesworth of *Newsweek* magazine.

"What part does Dean Andrews play in this? What does he know?" asked Aynesworth.

Replied Garrison: "Andrews doesn't know anything, but he's been bull shooting me for weeks now and I am going to get him."

Andrews's case was allotted to Judge Frank Shea. Five days later Andrews appeared with Zelden for arraignment and pled not guilty. Shortly thereafter, the defense filed a motion to dismiss the charge on the grounds that the indictment did not set forth specifically the testimony alleged to be false. The matter was taken up on April 7th, at which time Andrews asked that his name be placed as attorney of record representing himself along with Zelden. The State asked for a delay of seven days in order to permit study of the seventy-three pages of testimony given by Andrews before the Grand Jury. When the delay was granted, Zelden filed additional pleadings.

The motion to quash was never heard, nor were the other pleadings filed by Zelden. On April 12th, the indictment was dismissed and Andrews was indicted anew, this time on five counts of perjury all based on his testimony of March 16th. The bill of indictment was approximately eleven feet in length and contained, among other things, practically all of the baffling exchange between Andrews and his interrogators about the Shaw-Bertrand identification. Andrews was again required to post a $1,000 bond and upon his appearance at the building to do so he was again besieged by newsmen. He predicted new developments in the near future. "There's some guy not involved down here who's been keeping a clock on the whole thing and when it comes out, they're going to put the hat on the giant."

Pressed by newsmen about this comment, Andrews elucidated:

"I don't have nothing to do with it. I just met these two guys in a bar last week and I asked them what they're doing down here because I know what kind of business they're in. They asked me what do I know about Big Jim and I say, 'Ho, ho, ho, what can I do for you?'"

On April 18th Andrews was arraigned for the second time. Zelden remarked to newsmen that the new indictment was "just as bad as the other one" and he was given by Judge Frank Shea until May 1st to file pleadings.

Later the same day Andrews filed in his own behalf a $100,000 lawsuit against Garrison in Federal Court. Andrews complained in his Federal Court petition that Garrison placed him before the Grand Jury and compelled him "to answer questions designed to trap him, full knowing that plaintiff had no knowledge of any conspiracy or any facts

material to a conspiracy to murder John F. Kennedy." Further, said
Andrews, the D.A. caused him to be indicted "two separate times for
perjury knowing the plaintiff has and did not commit perjury at any
time."

On May 1st Zelden filed motions seeking to permit him to inspect
transcripts of the complete Grand Jury testimony. The motion was
ultimately denied and the defense was never permitted to see any part
of the transcript, save that which formed the basis for the indictment. A
motion to quash the indictment was likewise denied. The only motion
granted was one filed by Andrews himself on June 5th without the
knowledge of his attorney. It was a motion for a speedy trial and the
case was set for trial on August 9th.

In the meantime, however, Andrews still had much to say. He took
part in the National Broadcasting Company one-hour documentary
televised nationally on June 19th. He was quoted as saying, among other
things: "I wouldn't know Clay Shaw if I fell over him on the street
dead." More importantly, NBC commentator Frank McGee, serving as
narrator for the program, claimed that NBC knew who the real Clay
Bertrand was and that he was not Clay Shaw. The network identified
Bertrand as a homosexual who resided in the New Orleans French
Quarter and said that it was withholding his real identity to save him
embarrassment.

The sequel to these nationally televised remarks was inevitable. At the
June 28th meeting of the New Orleans Parish Grand Jury, Ed Planer,
news director for WDSU-TV, the local NBC affiliate, was subpoenaed
to appear before the Grand Jury. There could be little doubt about the
purpose of the subpoena. Planer had assisted in the preparation of the
NBC documentary and there was every indication he would be asked
about the identity of the party whom NBC claimed was the real Clay
Bertrand. He would undoubtedly also be asked from whom NBC
learned the identity of the "real Clay Bertrand."

Likewise, there could be little doubt but that Planer could not in
good conscience reveal either the information or the source. The confidence of informants and sources of news has been traditionally protected by newsmen and the Grand Jury appearance of Planer appeared
to be the inception of a legal battle to force this information from the
NBC representative.

Dean Andrews, notorious clown and buffoon, already twice indicted
for perjury, had no desire to see Planer so embroiled. He asked to be
allowed to testify. The Grand Jury and the assistant D.A.'s present
readily agreed. As he waited to be called, he was served with an "instanter" subpoena issued by the assistant D.A.'s who feared he would

change his mind. He hadn't. Late that afternoon he entered the Grand Jury room.

Asked one of the assistants: "Dean, do you know the real Clay? . . ."

"The man, I believe, is Gene Davis, and if you ask him he'll call me a crocker sack of lies. . . ."

"Now, what leads you to believe that this is Clay Bertrand?"

"Because I believe it. I am the only one that has to account for myself."

"What basis do you have?"

"Helen Gert back in the '50's at the fag wedding reception I was telling you all about, introduced me to Davis as Clay Bertrand."

"And this was the man that was introduced to you as Clay Bertrand?"

"Right."

"Have you talked to this man on the phone recently?"

"I talked to him almost every day. I have known him a long time."

Andrews stuck by his story. This was indeed the man he had referred to as Clay Bertrand. Asked one of the assistants:

"I asked you if you ever heard from Clay Bertrand after the time you were called about representing Lee Oswald in the assassination and the answer was 'I ain't seen nor heard of him since.' "

Replied the resourceful Andrews: "Not from Clay Bertrand. Because I call him Gene Davis . . ."

Did Gene Davis still look the same as he did years ago?

"No, he has changed," said Andrews. "He is fat like me. He has aged. Time has gone by."

There was no uncertainty on this occasion in Andrews's Grand Jury testimony: "If this case is based on the fact that Clay L. Shaw is Clay Bertrand, it's a joke."

Who was Helen Gert? She was also known as "Big Joe" or "Butch," said Andrews. Turning to the assistant D.A.'s he said:

"Y'all sent her to Gola (Angola State Penitentiary). You put her on the Ponderosa. . . ."

Andrews told the Jury that he had several times informed the "jolly green giant" that Bertrand was not Shaw.

Said Andrews: "I may have said a thousand times one thing, but the one time I say Clay Shaw ain't Clay Bertrand clears me of all the rest.

"It doesn't make any difference to me if I am convicted.

"Clay Shaw is not Clay Bertrand. Indict me if you want to."

Andrews repeated to the Grand Jury his version of what he persistently claimed to be his deal with Garrison: "I kept my deal with the giant. I said I can't say he is and I can't say he ain't and I got indicted for it."

Even before Andrews finished testifying, Eugene Davis was picked up by two D.A. investigators from his French Quarter bar and brought to the Criminal Court Building. Waiting outside the door of Garrison's office was attorney G. Wray Gill who thereupon announced his representation of Davis. Gill handed out copies of an affidavit executed by Davis, notarized by one of Garrison's assistants, and witnessed by two others.

Gill, in behalf of his client, consented to a television and press interview outside of Garrison's office and did most of the talking for his client. He stated that his client "is apparently the man" that the National Broadcasting Company identified as Bertrand but, continued Gill, Davis "is not Clay Bertrand and has not passed as Clay Bertrand."

Davis's affidavit branded Andrews's identification of him as Bertrand as "utterly and completely false and malicious and damnable . . . Dean Andrews has known me for a long time and knows that I have never been known by the name of Clay Bertrand or any other person. I want to state unequivocally for the record that I have never used the name of Clay Bertrand, nor have I called Dean Andrews in reference to representation of Lee Harvey Oswald."

Said Gill, quite irrelevantly, of Davis: "I ask you to look at him and say if any human being with one eye could say he looks like Mr. Shaw."

Andrews was right. He was indeed being called a crocker sack of lies. The complexity and confusion surrounding the Bertrand myth had truly grown from nothing to heroic proportions. But Ed Planer's crisis was over. He was no longer important to the Jury.

Andrews appeared to experience a rejuvenation as though borne of the lifting from his back of a heavy burden. On July 17th he addressed the Press Club of New Orleans to a packed house. He acknowledged that the much discussed Clay Bertrand never existed. "Clay Shaw ain't Clay Bertrand . . . and I'm the only one that knows it," he told his audience. "The emphasis on Bertrand's identity is a waste of time because he never existed in the context most people seem to imagine."

There is only one important point about Bertrand, said Andrews and that is "Clay Shaw ain't Clay Bertrand. Amen." Andrews talked about the plight of the man charged with the crime. "You have to get used to attention like the "old lady in the elevator who sticks you in the backside and says, 'Why don't you tell Big Jim the truth?' "

Continued Andrews in the same vein: "In some instances you hustle a fix. . . . Me, though, I'm a harpooned whale dragged up on the beach. I got nowhere to go."

Trying to duck the press is a waste of time, lamented Andrews. You can "no comment, no comment, no comment, or you can open your mouth and put your foot in it," Andrews complained. Almost consistently, he chose the latter course.

On July 18th Andrews was indicted once more for perjury. The basis of this indictment was his June 28th testimony concerning Gene Davis.

This was not the sum total of his problems by any means. His law practice had dwindled to practically nothing. His wife had recently delivered the couple's fourth child and he no longer had even his part-time job as assistant D.A. in Jefferson Parish as a source of income. He capitalized to some extent on his increasing fame as a clown and found a job as a master of ceremonies at a Bourbon Street nightclub called Mahogany Hall where he made twelve dollars a night. During the short period of his employment he brought laughter from the capacity audiences with jokes and ditties about Garrison's investigation. He sang a song about a dope addict who saw two men at the lakefront—"one named Clay and one named Lee." Probably Andrews did not note a lone unsmiling face in the audience. It belonged to an assistant D.A. who was sent by Garrison to scout the performance. Shortly thereafter, Mahogany Hall was sold and Andrews lost his job.

*   *   *

On August 9th, 1967, Dean Andrews went to trial on the five counts of perjury growing out of his March 16th testimony. Andrews was, of course, a favorite of the press. Here was genuine New Orleans flavor and who knew what hilarious and memorable phrases might flow from the little round man during the course of his trial?

When court convened, "Monk" Zelden filed a motion to withdraw as counsel for Dean Andrews. The motion was granted. Andrews later told newsmen that the reason for Zelden's departure was a matter of two lawyers "disagreeing on the best procedure to follow." Andrews took over his own defense. More hilarity.

The press duly noted that a sign on the lawn outside at Tulane and Broad, advertising a police benefit show, read "Biggest Show in Town."

Andrews's first step was to file a motion seeking to "recuse" Jim Garrison and his assistants prosecuting the case, alleging a personal interest in the prosecution inconsistent with the duties of the D.A. toward the impartial administration of justice. The Andrews's motion read:

> The personal interest in me individually by the office of the D.A., knowing that I possess no information material to the assassination of President Kennedy, and knowing that I know nothing of a conspiracy to assassinate the President,

and knowing that I had absolutely no contact with Clay Shaw, deliberately embarked, using the powers and weight of the office, to destroy me individually and make me a person unworthy of belief, in order that they may pursue a conspiracy that was planted in Raymond Perry [sic] Russo's head through hypnotic techniques and anchored there until enlarged by Russo to include his knowledge of the assassins, and additional possible conspiracies against Eisenhower and the Presidents of the United States and Mexico.

Andrews asked Judge Shea for a delay of several days due to the fact that he would need to subpoena additional witnesses, who were not present in court, to testify in support of his motion. The Judge denied the delay and Andrews sought a brief delay to apply to the State Supreme Court for extraordinary writs. He was granted fifteen minutes in which to call an attorney to file a writ for him. Andrews retorted that that would not be enough time "if my life depended on it." The Judge resolved the matter by appointing Zelden temporarily as attorney merely to file the writ. When Court resumed, Andrews asked Shea for a second recess so he might collect his thoughts. "I just can't pop up and say da-da-da-da . . ." explained Andrews.

Placing his hands over his eyes as though frustrated beyond human endurance, Shea snapped, "We will give you a half-hour recess, Mr. Andrews, and that is the last recess we are going to have. Then we're going to start the trial."

A half hour later the hearing started on the motion to recuse Garrison. Later, word came that Andrews's application for writs from the Judge's refusal to delay was denied by the Supreme Court.

Andrews had charged that the case against him was the result of a "carefully prepared plan to force me to identify Clay Shaw as Bertrand or keep quiet." He called to the stand a number of newsmen, as well as Bill Gurvich, the D.A.'s former special investigator, all to testify about various statements made by Garrison concerning Dean Andrews. Objections were made repeatedly by the two assistant D.A.'s prosecuting the case and frequently sustained, the issue being closely confined to statements made by Garrison about Andrews and only about Andrews.

At one point, in response to the Judge's impatience as he fumbled through papers strewn across his desk, Andrews asked the Court's indulgence for a few moments while he got his "ta ta ta" together.

In the midst of his troubles, Andrews could not break the habits of a lifetime. He spoke freely to the press. He was quoted on one occasion as saying "I don't know from nothing. What I got is a vivid imagination. The moral to all this, brother-in-law, is keep your big mouth shut." But he could not follow his own advice. He promised the press action. "I hope to bust something loose some place," he said.

Crowds gathered about as TV cameras bore in on the roly-poly comedian in dark glasses. "The fat man's got to go to the whip today," he said. "Most paupers got more than I got. I've had good times, it's been fun, but not lately."

Those lucky enough to be on the inside of the crowd that surrounded the star saw tears forming behind the dark spectacles. Andrews was crying.

The motion to recuse the D.A. was denied.

A motion to quash the indictment on grounds that the Grand Jury had been improperly selected and did not represent a true cross section of the citizenry was likewise denied.

The trial began. A five-man jury was selected. Under Louisiana law, certain types of felonies, perjury included, are triable by the five-man "bob-tail" jury.

Andrews lamented during a recess that he would go down in history as the only man convicted in connection with the Kennedy assassination. He would rather go down as an assassin, said Andrews, than as a perjurer. But he had little choice. The charge was perjury.

Help arrived in the form of a young attorney named Harry Burglass, who volunteered to assist.

Andrews's statements returned to haunt him throughout the trial. Out of the presence of the Jury, he tried to prevent introduction of his Grand Jury testimony of June 28th by claiming that he was emotionally upset. He had, he explained, volunteered to appear before the Jury, but upon walking up the courthouse steps to testify was served with a subpoena. He had heard rumors he was to be arrested, said Andrews, and the subpoena upset him to the point that he was unsure of what went on during the Grand Jury proceedings. Burglass argued the point without success and the testimony was admitted. So were a plethora of other statements. The Warren Commission testimony of Andrews went before the Jury, on the basis of State law providing for the admissibility of official government reports of commissions created pursuant to Executive Orders. This was the same basis for admission previously urged by Irving Dymond during the Clay Shaw preliminary hearing. In the Shaw hearing, the State objected, and the report was held inadmissible. In the Andrews trial, the Warren Commission testimony of Andrews offered by the State was admitted over defense objections.

Two New Orleans police officers testified that in the course of a chance encounter with Andrews on April 12th, he had stated that he would rather "take five" than be known as a "fink," meaning that he would rather spend five years in prison (the possible penalty for perjury) rather than be known as a "stool pigeon."

The interrogation of Andrews in the District Attorney's office on March 2nd had been taped. The tape was now introduced into evidence.

The Jury was literally deluged with statements of the talkative Andrews. And the trial moved at breakneck speed. Despite the late entry of Andrews's attorney, the Court held sessions nightly and on the weekend. A Sunday session was held for the first time in memory of any of the Court attaches.

When it was all over, the lawyers argued to the Jury. Burglass tried gamely. He argued that the only evidence introduced against Andrews was statements of the defendant himself and that no man can be convicted only on his own statements. The D.A. had charged that the Grand Jury testimony itself was knowingly false and hence that contradictory statements were not enough. The falsity of the Grand Jury statements themselves must be proved.

Arguments were not confined to issues of law, however. Said Burglass: "He likes attention, most of us do. He got swirled up into the biggest investigation of a murder this country has ever seen: The State v. Shaw. They wanted him to change his story. They wanted Andrews to equate Shaw and Bertrand, but he ain't that kind of a guy.

"Up comes that massive foot. It was coming down on Dean. You are the only thing between that massive foot and Dean."

Burglass claimed that there was a consistency in Andrews's inconsistencies: "He told them the truth, but he's got a jivey way of doing it. He told them Clay Shaw wasn't Clay Bertrand. They said he lied.

"Most of us live humdrum lives. But something exciting happened to Dean—Bertrand. Up until that time he didn't have an enemy in the world. He was on TV. He was here. He was there. He got swirled up into something a lot bigger than anything he had dreamed."

Andrews was convicted on two of the five counts of perjury—both of them having to do with his inability to identify Clay Bertrand as Clay Shaw.

The next the television viewing public saw of Dean Andrews, he was being escorted by deputy sheriffs to the Parish Prison. He was treated as a V.I.P. by the Criminal Sheriff and was quartered in the prison hospital until his release on bond two days later, pending his appeal. He was sentenced to serve eighteen months in prison on each count, the sentences to run concurrently. Execution of the sentence under state law is stayed until review by the State Supreme Court.

Andrews could not have been surprised by the conviction. He had lamented to newsmen that he would probably be the only one convicted in the entire Garrison probe. He had undoubtedly seen the shadow of the jailer during his March 16th testimony when he grinned at the Grand Jurors who pursued their investigation with holy zeal and said: "Y'all are looking down my throat with a loaded shotgun. . . . You guys are looking for the slightest flaw, and unfortunately I ain't St. Peter."

But perhaps it was best summed up when he told the jurors: "I get the impression you want me to identify Shaw as Clay Bertrand." That did seem to be what it was all about. And that was the pity of it. Andrews's ordeal was so unnecessary; probably it all could have been avoided. If only he had told them that Clay Shaw was Clay Bertrand! Then he could have ridden to glory with Jim Garrison.

13

FOLLOWING GARRISON'S ARRIVAL at the "truth" resulting from the various interrogations of Russo, the D.A. set about to obtain the necessary corroboration from those who must necessarily be in a position to furnish it. Time was of the essence, as the preliminary hearing was scheduled to begin March 14th.

On Sunday, March 5th, I received a telephone call from Layton Martens who was in town for the weekend and was scheduled to return the following day to his classes at the University of Southwestern Louisiana. I had not previously known Martens; he had been referred by friends.

He asked to see me that day and we met at my office late Sunday afternoon. He explained that he had already been interrogated twice by Garrison's men, most recently in December, 1966, and that he had submitted to a polygraph test which, he had been informed, indicated complete truthfulness on his part. He expected to be called as a witness in the Shaw preliminary hearing in view of the fact that he had known practically all of the principals involved. This included Clay Shaw, whom he had met on Mardi Gras day, 1965.

Martens's main concern was publicity. He asked that I contact the District Attorney's Office on his behalf and appear with him at any hearing. He also asked that I request that he be allowed to appear voluntarily and inauspiciously. He loathed the thought of extensive publicity and feared possible jeopardy of his standing both as a student at U.S.L. and as a part-time high school teacher of music in the public schools in Lafayette. The circus atmosphere that surrounded the Garrison probe caused similar fears in many others who had known some of the participants, as Garrison's subpoenas were being strewn throughout the city like buckshot. The name of every recipient was splashed across the front pages of the daily papers, together with complete biographical information and considerable speculation as to the possible connection of the witness with the case.

Early that week, before I had any opportunity to inquire as to the D.A.'s plans for Martens, he was contacted by a D.A. investigator and was asked to appear at the office to give a statement. Martens referred him to me.

The investigator was cooperative. At my request, he agreed to permit us to appear at the building on Sunday, March 12th, a day when the hordes of newsmen and cameramen were not likely to be present.

We appeared without fanfare. The press was absent, having little reason to expect any developments on a Sunday. The interrogation in the D.A.'s office was by two assistants and was tape-recorded and later transcribed. Before any questioning occurred, I asked the assistants if Martens was being interrogated merely as a witness, or if he was, in fact, himself a suspect. I received their complete assurance that Martens's own conduct was not at all the subject of suspicion; that he was being interviewed only as a possible witness in connection with the charges against Clay Shaw and possibly others. I advised Martens to answer all questions fully. I saw no reason to claim the Fifth Amendment for him and the unreserved assurances of the assistants afforded no basis for such advice.

Martens was questioned exhaustively about his acquaintanceship with David Ferrie and his own activities between 1958 and 1963. He was asked about the Civil Air Patrol and about "Latin type" people he had met. He was asked about his acquaintanceship with Clay Shaw whom he met on Mardi Gras day in 1965. Mardi Gras that year was in early March, and Shaw was dressed at the time as a monk wearing a long black cloak and hood. In his hand he carried a whip. Martens was shown photographs, most of which he could not identify. He was asked about Guy Bannister and the Newman Building and any possible acquaintanceship between the various targets of the D.A.'s interest. As far as he knew, said Martens, he never knew Oswald. Further, to his knowledge, neither Ferrie nor Shaw knew each other, nor had he ever heard one mention the other. The name Clay Bertrand he had heard only when Garrison had asked him about it the previous December.

At the conclusion of the interrogation, we were again asked about the possibility of Martens submitting to a lie detector test, though the two assistants were not certain that they would request it. I suggested that they contact me at such time as they might determine the desirability of a polygraph. No such request was ever made.

Before leaving, I asked if Martens would be called as a witness at Shaw's preliminary hearing. They did not know. I advised them as to Martens's desire to avoid unnecessary publicity and assured them that Martens would be made available any time upon a simple request through my office. We also advised them that Martens would be available should further interrogation be desired and that he would appear voluntarily at the office of the Sheriff to accept any subpoena if that were deemed necessary. Both assistants assured us that this procedure would be followed and that the office would cooperate as much as possible in respecting my client's privacy.

I had known both assistants for several years. One of them was a member of the staff from the time of Garrison's assumption of office in May, 1962. We had worked together during my seventeen months in the D.A.'s office and had always maintained an amiable relationship. I had no doubts whatever of the sincerity of the assurances by either man, nor do I have any reason to suspect that subsequent events were controlled by them.

*   *   *

Martens was not called as a witness during the preliminary hearing. The next I heard from him was by telephone from Lafayette to advise that while driving home from teaching a class on March 22nd, he heard on his car radio that he had been subpoenaed to appear as a witness before the Orleans Parish Grand Jury on March 29th. The subpoena was served a day later.

A few days thereafter during one of many trips made by D.A. investigators to the home of Alvin Beauboeuf, Beauboeuf was warned by one of the investigators: "You know, Al, Layton Martens didn't cooperate with us and that's why he got subpoenaed."

I had come to something of the same conclusion myself. I had pondered the possible reason for this Grand Jury subpoena, particularly in the face of the assurance given by Garrison's assistants, and could come to but one conclusion. I thought of Dean Andrews and I reflected on the thorough interrogation to which Martens had submitted on March 12th, his third on the same subject matter. There was little doubt but that Martens was being set up for a perjury charge.

What to do about it was a tougher question. The only possible basis for refusal to answer was fear of self-incrimination as to some suspected offense previously committed. If Martens was now suspected of some complicity in the "conspiracy," there would be some valid basis for refusal to answer.

The day before Martens's scheduled appearance, I again spoke to one of the assistant D.A.'s, one of the two who had interrogated him on March 12th. I wanted to inquire if Martens was, in fact, now a suspect. Responded the assistant, "Jim would like to see you tomorrow about that before Layton goes before the Jury. Come out a half hour early—he will clear the matter up."

I had been following Garrison's numerous public statements about his investigation and I doubted very much that "Jim" was going to clear up anything. Nonetheless, I agreed to appear with Martens at 1:30, a half hour in advance of his scheduled 2:00 P.M. Grand Jury appearance. I knew that we were going to be set upon by the flock of newsmen who roamed the building in packs and decided that a short statement by Martens could serve two purposes: First, it might sate to some degree their rapacious appetite for news and render a little less determined their insistence upon answers to all manner of questions that would be hurled at him; and secondly, we could make public the previous as-surance of the D.A. that he was not suspected of any wrongdoing whatever and was appearing merely as a witness.

We arrived at the building at 1:15 P.M. and were quickly besieged by reporters. The barrage of questions quieted when Martens read the innocuous statement we had previously prepared. He refused to answer further questions and we retreated to the relative quiet of the District Attorney's office.

We were more fortunate than Andrews or Quiroga. We waited but a half hour. Garrison, however, never spoke to us. I was called aside by one of his investigators who spoke for him.

I was assured that the D.A. was not at all interested in trapping Martens. I found the assurance curious, for no one had suggested that he was. However, it was felt, said the investigator, that Martens had not been as helpful as he might be and it was suspected that he was holding back information. Particularly I was advised that there were three areas in which the D.A. was interested and that Martens should be told that it was primarily in these areas that his help was sought.

First, I was told that certain notes recovered from Clay Shaw's home during the March 1st search indicated that Martens had been an acquaintance of Shaw's since well before Mardi Gras of 1965. No such notes were ever revealed and I doubt that they ever existed.

Secondly, the D.A. felt that Martens could say a lot more than he had about the trip to Houma in 1961.

Thirdly, the D.A. felt that Martens had not revealed all of the Cubans that he had known. Martens could, I was told, tell about a lot more Cubans, if only he would. Martens was clearly being told how to avoid a perjury charge.

I could not have known at the time, but apparently Garrison was obsessed with the idea that Martens knew a lot of Cubans. The more denials by Martens, the more obsessed Garrison was to become. I conveyed the message to my client. Martens shrugged. He had told the D.A.'s Office everything he knew several times and he did not feel inclined to lie, even to avoid being charged with perjury.

He subsequently went before the Grand Jury and was questioned for about ninety minutes. He was badgered consistently about the trip to Houma in 1961 and at one point was told by an irate juror: "Do you know you're implicated in a burglary!" I, of course, was not present in the Grand Jury room. The remark would have been a signal to any attorney to advise silence to any further questions. Martens did not perceive this clear right to refuse to respond to further questions and, under the circumstances, could hardly be expected to have the presence of mind to react properly in any event. Although we had discussed the question of possible self-incrimination, he had no way of knowing that lurking in Garrison's mind was the thought of using the Houma episode as a means of charging some of the participants with burglary for the purpose of exerting pressure and maintaining a hold on them—the same purpose that underlay his charge of sale of narcotics against the fictional Manuel Garcia Gonzales.

Martens, of course, had not been advised of his constitutional rights by Garrison or any of his assistants. They had little interest in such niceties.

It was clear from Martens's reaction that he had been roughly treated and that he had not been believed by the Grand Jury. They had obviously received the "truth" from Garrison well before the witness's appearance. Now his testimony would be transcribed and studied. I had little doubt that a perjury indictment was in the offing, probably at the following week's Grand Jury meeting.

Since Martens could not give any further information about the laundry truck that had been used in the trip to Houma, or about the Cubans who had captivated Garrison's imagination, it was necessary to get Novel and Sergio Arcacha Smith back to the jurisdiction where they would be available for questioning and perhaps other forms of pressure. The day after Martens's Grand Jury appearance, Arcacha Smith and Novel were charged with conspiracy to commit burglary of the Houma munitions bunker. The burglary in question was the removal of explosives prior to the Bay of Pigs invasion of April, 1961. It will be recalled that there had never been a complaint of a theft, and Garrison knew nothing about the operation except what he had been told by Gordon Novel himself. Information from Rancier Ehlinger, one of the young men who had accompanied the group, revealed little of value to Garrison. Garrison's affidavit charged that Novel and Smith each "between the 1st day of August 1961 and the 31st day of August 1961 conspired with Ferrie and others to commit simple burglary of a munitions bunker located in Houma, Louisiana. . . ." They could not be charged with the burglary itself because that had obviously occurred in another Parish. It was equally true, however, that the plans to journey to Houma were made in Ferrie's apartment located at the time in Jefferson Parish and that the group did not even pass through Orleans Parish on its way to the Schlumberger Well bunker.

Why the deed was said to have been committed in August is not completely clear. It may be coincidence that were it alleged to have occurred in March, 1961, prosecution would be barred by operation of the six-year statute of limitations.

The following Thursday I received a call from a newsman who advised that the Grand Jury had returned an indictment against Martens for perjury, setting forth, out of the entire ninety minutes of testimony, three questions and answers, supposedly false:

Q.—How often—how well do you know Gordon Novel?
A.—I don't recall ever hearing of or meeting Gordon Novel.
Q.—Are you telling me that even when the boxes were being removed from the bunker, you did not know the purpose of the trip?
A.—No. As best I can remember, I was there. Yes, I do remember being there, the purpose of the trip was not revealed to me.
Q.—You do not remember Sergio Arcacha Smith being on the trip?
A.—No, I don't.

Contacted at his home in Lafayette by newsmen, Martens, in his dismay at the indictment, responded that he was not at all surprised by the indictment, that this appeared to be Garrison's manner of dealing with witnesses whose testimony contradicted his theories.

*   *   *

Efforts to obtain the names of the all-important Cubans from Martens continued concurrently with efforts to force the return of Novel and Smith to the D.A.'s lair.

About a week after the perjury indictment Martens was approached in Lafayette by three friends of Garrison's, including Jack Martin. They explained to him that they were sure that there had been a misunderstanding between Martens and Garrison, but if the two would meet that the misunderstanding could be cleared up and the charges against him dismissed.

Martens had been frightened by the indictment and worried about its possible effect on his job, his status as a student, and on his future. Throwing caution to the wind, he felt he could not resist the opportunity to meet with the D.A., clear up whatever "misunderstanding" there was, and to be relieved of his anxieties. He was later told that Garrison would be happy to see him and a few days thereafter was received by Garrison privately in his home.

I knew nothing of the contact by Garrison's friends or of Martens's visit to Garrison, though my representation of Martens had been well publicized. Personal contact by any attorney with an opposing litigant without the consent of the litigant's attorney is contrary to every code of ethics ever devised by the legal profession. But Garrison was busy solving the assassination of Kennedy and he had no time for trivia.

Garrison explained to the young music student that he did not really feel that he, Martens, had lied, but simply that he had not been completely candid. Martens noted with discomfort that Garrison talked in hushed tones. His house was bugged by the F.B.I. he explained.

"What is it that you think I know?" asked Martens.

"We don't think you have given us the names of all of the Cubans," said Garrison.

"You know all the Cubans I know," said Martens.

The conversation was brief, Martens possessed neither the imagination nor the audacity to pull Latin names out of the air like Dean Andrews. It is well that he did not.

I filed numerous pleadings in behalf of Martens. Like Andrews's attorney, I felt entitled to the transcript of the entire session. How else could we determine the proper context of the supposedly false answers or even determine the specific incident to which the questions referred?

In August, this request was denied.

Following the court appearance at which the ruling was rendered, I received a telephone call from Jack Martin. He had read the account of the ruling in the press and was very surprised, he said, to learn that the charges against Martens were still pending. He spoke of the April meeting between Garrison and Martens which he had arranged, assuming I knew of the meeting. In a remarkable example of understatement, he explained to me that "Garrison sometimes thinks people know more than they do." Martin would talk to his friend, the D.A., and try to have the charges dropped. They were not dropped.

When I next spoke to Martens I asked if such a meeting had in fact occurred. I had doubted it and had assumed it existed only in Martin's beclouded brain. Martens confirmed, however, that the account was correct. I was at first more furious with Martens's naïve act than with Garrison, whose ethics I had long ago accepted as nonexistent and I read him the riot act for his foolish personal encounter with the D.A.

The efforts to learn the names of the elusive Cuban assassins continued. Martens's aged and mentally infirm mother was confined in a mental hospital north of New Orleans. She was visited on several occasions by D.A. assistants and investigators. She was treated politely, but pressed for certain information. The information? Names or descriptions of her son's Cuban friends in 1963. Mrs. Martens could furnish no such information. She knew of no Cuban friends.

Later in the fall, Martens more sensibly reported to me another contact from the D.A.'s office. Jack Martin had called and advised that Garrison had met with Mark Lane, who was now living in New Orleans as an "unpaid investigator," and Harold Weisberg. The three had put their heads together and decided that it was all important that they get from Martens certain information. Accordingly, if Martens would submit to a sodium pentothal test by a doctor of his choosing, Garrison would be happy to forget any past misunderstandings. The information about which he was to be questioned: the names of some more Cubans.

I advised Martens to report back to Martin that any offer should be made through me, as his attorney. I thought no more about the matter until about ten days later I asked Martens during the course of a conversation if he had received any response from Martin. I was advised that the D.A. would not deal with me as I was in the pay of the C.I.A. and of the National Broadcasting Company whose newsman, Walter Sheridan, I now represented in connection with charges of alleged bribery of Garrison's star witness, Perry Russo.

If Garrison could not extract from Martens the names of the mysterious Cubans there was some solace in the fact that neither could Martens's recollection of past events be too helpful to Clay Shaw. For what jury could believe a man who was charged with perjury?

14

ANDREWS AND MARTENS WERE
charged with perjury. Alvin Beauboeuf was not charged with any offense, nor was he ever served with a subpoena. His ordeal was more subtle, but undoubtedly no less painful. He was repeatedly summoned to the D.A.'s office and visited at his home by D.A. investigators. Interviewing Beauboeuf was the special project of two investigators, Lynn Loisel and Louis Ivon, who had been with Garrison since his induction into office. The episode beginning on March 9th, 1967, has been among the most controversial and complex of the entire investigation.

In early 1967 Beauboeuf resided with his wife in Arabi, Louisiana, in St. Bernard Parish, just south of New Orleans proper. He was employed as a filling station attendant. Visits to Beauboeuf's home by the two investigators and his visits to the D.A.'s office increased considerably following Ferrie's death. Finally, the two told Beauboeuf that he "had to know something about the assassination." Beauboeuf replied that he knew nothing.

About 10:00 P.M. on Thursday, March 9th, 1967, five days before the start of the Shaw preliminary hearing, Loisel and Ivon again appeared at Beauboeuf's home. After a few routine questions, including a request that he identify a photograph he had already identified numerous times, they asked Beauboeuf to step outside. Loisel took over the conversation.

"You know, Al, my boss has got unlimited money and we know you know something so we're in a position to do something for you, perhaps pay you $5,000-$10,000-$15,000 and a guaranteed job with an airline," was Loisel's opening pitch. According to Beauboeuf, when Loisel said "airline" he did not hear much more. Beauboeuf has always been fascinated by anything connected with planes or flying. He does recall that Loisel specified that he wanted the truth. Beauboeuf said that he would do anything he could to help.

Replied Loisel: "Al, we want you to fill in the missing links in the story." According to Beauboeuf, he assumed that Loisel was talking about Ferrie's personal life and the people he had met, and Beauboeuf replied that he would. Beauboeuf told the investigators that he would like to talk to his wife about it and to his attorney. Loisel assured him that "a positive contract or any other form of writing you want to put it in will be all right." Continued Loisel: "We'll guarantee that you will be the hero, not the villain, and if your attorney wants to draw up any type of papers, he is perfectly welcome to do so." The attorney was to contact Loisel the following day and set up an appointment for himself and his client, Beauboeuf, to meet the investigators in the D.A.'s office.

The next morning Beauboeuf called his attorney, Hugh Exnicious, whose office is in Jefferson Parish, and described to him the meeting that had occurred the previous night. On his attorney's advice, Beauboeuf went to his office and they discussed the conversation further. Exnicious suspected an attempt to buy false information. He called Loisel at the D.A.'s office and asked that the two investigators meet in his, Exnicious's, office because of the "Roman circus" that was taking place at Tulane and Broad. Loisel first refused, but after discussing the matter with Garrison called back and advised that he would be right out. In the early afternoon of March 10th, as Exnicious and Beauboeuf waited for Loisel to arrive, Exnicious placed a tape recorder behind the curtain in his office which could be activated by a switch under his desk.

Loisel arrived about 2:30 P.M. Exnicious got up from behind his desk and introduced himself to Loisel. "I thought you were coming with your partner," he said as he walked to his seat behind the desk. He then clicked on the recording machine as he continued speaking: "What's his name?"

"Ivon?" said Loisel.

"Ivon. He didn't come out with you?" asked the attorney.

"No. We've got too much to do. Now, let me bring you up to what Al and I were talking about last night. I told him we had liberal expense money and I said the boss is in a position to put him in a job, you know, possibly of his choosing, of Al's choosing. Also, that there would be . . . we would make a hero out of him instead of a villain, you understand. Everything would be to your satisfaction. There's no . . . I mean, we can . . . we can change the story around, you know, enough to positively beyond a shadow of a doubt, you know . . . eliminate him, you know, into any type of conspiracy or what have you."

Exnicious nodded in approval and murmured agreement from time to time as the uninhibited investigator continued: "The only thing we want is the truth, you know, no . . . no deviations on his part, you know. We want to present the truth. We want the facts and the facts of the assassination. That's what we want." Exnicious again nodded his agreement.

"And for this," continued Loisel, "the release, you know, the thing will be typed up in such a way that Al, you know, will be free and clear."

"Now, in other words," said Exnicious, "what you want him to do, he will come up and give you such evidence that you will be able to couch him in terms of being a hero?"

"That's correct," Loisel affirmed.

"And you'll also . . . you have an unlimited expense account, you said, and you're willing to help him along?"

"I would venture to say . . . well, I'm, you know, fairly certain we could put $3,000 on him just like that, you know," replied Loisel as he snapped his fingers. Again Exnicious indicated understanding and agreement.

Continued Loisel: "I'm sure we would help him financially and I'm sure we . . . real quick we could get him a job."

Exnicious was assured by Loisel that the D.A.'s Office was not at all interested in Ferrie's personal life or "the homosexual thing."

". . . Now, about the job, what do you mean by that?"

"Al said he'd like a job with an airline and I feel like the job can be had, you know."

"Well, now, these are tough things to come by. What makes you feel that you would be in a position . . ." Exnicious wanted to furnish all of the rope that he could.

"Well, let's say that . . . well, his connections. For instance, he was talking about a small operation such as Space Air Freight. I know with one phone call he could go out to the Space Air Freight and write his own ticket, you know. That's just Space Air Freight. That's not Eastern or something else. But I feel like we have people who are stepping stones to the larger airlines and so forth." Added Loisel: "They're politically motivated, too, you know, like anything else."

Exnicious meant to make a complete case. He was leaving nothing to chance. "Well, now, Lynn, let me ask you this: You're speaking about the District Attorney, Jim Garrison, and his ability to place Al in a responsible pilot's position with an airline?"

"That's correct, according to Al's own ability." Loisel explained that Beauboeuf would have to advance through the ranks. The first year or two he might "stay in a room in the back with the charts, or something, I don't know." Then, according to Loisel, he "advances a little further, then he's a copilot, then he's a pilot."

"Now, let me ask you this, Lynn: Is this something that you have thought up yourself or that Garrison . . . He knows about the situation?"

"That's right," said Loisel. He apparently did not share Garrison's suspicious nature about electronic bugs.

"And he's agreed that if we could in some way assist you, that you will be able to give him these three things?"

"That's correct."

"Well, now, supposing you tell me . . . I don't want to lead you down any pathway . . ."

"No, no. Look . . ." Loisel did not feel at all that he was being led down any pathway.

". . . What you think that Al has that he could help you with?"

"We had a man sitting . . . well, first off, I feel . . . Well, we feel that Al is as close to Dave as anybody could have been," explained Garrison's investigator. "All right. Now, we know this is a rough . . . I'm drawing you a rough sketch. We have a man who has come forth recently, told us he was sitting in a room with Ferrie, Clay Shaw, two Cubans, and Oswald."

It was getting interesting. "Oswald was in it?" asked Beauboeuf's attorney.

"Oswald was in it," assured the investigator.

"Where was this meeting, in his home, Ferrie's home?"

"If I'm not . . . if I'm . . . correct me if I'm wrong. I believe it was."

"Uh huh, I don't know," said Exnicious, apparently wondering how he could correct Loisel.

"All right. I'm not going to . . . I'm not going to go into . . . you know . . ." stuttered Loisel.

"Yes, I understand. I don't want you to," said the sympathetic attorney.

"But anyhow, the assass . . . Ferrie said, 'The best way in which the assassination can be done is to get the man . . . to get the President in cross fire,'" continued Loisel as Exnicious nodded to indicate his continuing interest. "And went on to discuss that. And then Clay Shaw and Ferrie . . . I believe it was Clay Shaw and Ferrie, or maybe it was Clay Shaw and Oswald, having a little heated argument. Clay Shaw wanted some of his methods used or his thoughts, you know, used, but anyhow, that's what we have in mind, along that line."

If Al did not know anything about the conspiracy prior to this day, he should know something now.

Exnicious wanted some elucidation as to what it was that Beauboeuf was supposed to know: "Was Al supposed to have been at that meeting?"

"No, Al wasn't at the meeting," explained Loisel patiently.

"Well, how is Al supposed to be able to help you with that meeting?"

A fair question.

"Well, Al is in . . . Al, being as close to Ferrie . . ."

"Yes," nodded Exnicious, apparently feeling that he was getting a firm bite indeed.

". . . has to know the whole thing from beginning to end. He has to know it," Loisel was emphatic. Garrison's brand of logic was contagious.

"I see. And you're convinced from all the evidence that Al could not be as close as he was to Dave without knowing something in some way?"

"That's right," agreed Loisel.

"Now, let me ask you this, Lynn," said the attorney. "You don't mind my calling you that, do you, Mr. Loisel?"

"No, positively not," Loisel assured him.

"Let me ask you this: Do you think that . . . that . . . of course, if . . . if my client, Beauboeuf, if he knew about this and didn't tell you, he's committing a crime, he's an accessory after the fact, isn't he?"

"No, he's not. I tell you how we go about that. Well, Dave Ferrie, bless his poor soul, is gone. Al was scared of Dave. Al has a family, you know. When Al first met Dave, he was a single man. Al has a family now. Al was threatened by Dave, you know, to . . . never to divulge this. Al or his family would be taken care of."

Exnicious nodded understandingly. "I see."

"You understand, now that poor Dave is gone Al has voluntarily come forward and told of his knowledge. I mean, there's 99,000 ways we could skin that cat, you know. I mean, it's something, you know . . . that's his patriotic duty. He's . . . now he's placing his family, you know, the safety of his family at the hands . . . at the mercy of the District Attorney's Office because he must clear his conscience and . . . as an upstanding young American."

Exnicious was now ready to go to the heart of the matter.

"All right," said the attorney. "Now, let me ask you this, Lynn: Supposing Al in his own consciousness does not know anything and you run him through . . . you said something about hypnosis, you would be willing to take him through any truth serum and polygraph and so forth and so on. I read his statement. There's nothing in his statement that indicates that Al consciously knows or willingly told anything about the conspiracy of Dave Ferrie's or certainly didn't even know Clay Shaw. Now, how can that be changed?"

"When was the statement made?" interrupted Loisel.

It was agreed that the statement was made in late 1966. "Ferrie was living, wasn't he?" continued the investigator.

"Yeah . . . oh, I see," said Exnicious, as though ashamed of his naïveté.

"He had no choice. He was scared, you know, I mean he . . . married man, father-in-law, you know, wife and kids, and this and that and everything else. He's scared."

"Well, have you any real . . . let me ask you this: Besides your personal opinion, have you anything really on Al Beauboeuf that he knows anything we might clear up?" asked Exnicious.

"Umm, no. Really, the only thing we're doing or have been trying to do is to have Al tell us."

"Well, he's already been up there the one time. Now, what more do you want now?"

"We don't believe him," said Loisel, "let's put it that way."

As to whether or not Beauboeuf would have been guilty of being an accessory, Loisel acknowledged that technically that might be true, but that "we have no choice, you know. I mean, we are seeking the information."

The two men then talked at some length about the merits of Garrison's case against Shaw. Exnicious was not impressed and there was little Loisel had to offer that seemed impressive. Finally, Exnicious again turned to Loisel with the crucial question.

"Yeah. Lynn, let me ask you this: Supposing we agree to this and it's all drawn down and after you run Al Beauboeuf through the three deals, it comes out he knows nothing about the whole thing, what . . . what then? Will you still give him the money and still give him the position?"

Loisel was quite specific: "No. That's not the deal."

"What is the deal?" asked Exnicious.

"The deal is that Al fills in the missing links."

"Well, supposing he doesn't know what . . . who are the other assassins?"

"Well, he can't fill in the missing links if . . . if he doesn't know. And that is what the deal is predicated on."

"That he knows?" asked Exnicious.

Both men laughed. "Oh, yeah," said Loisel.

"Oh, boy," said Exnicious, still laughing, "you better let me get to talk to him some more in order to find out if we can . . . He told me, and I'll be frank with you, that he knows nothing at all about the assassination, same thing he told you and told the D.A.'s Office early in November, and now this is going to have to change his story. If he does, in fact, feel that he knows something about it, perhaps he will then say all right."

Loisel again assured that there would be no embarrassment to Beauboeuf and that they were not at all interested in Ferrie's personal life. What they wanted, explained Loisel was "the places, the times, you know, and what have you." If after talking to Beauboeuf it appeared to Exnicious that Beauboeuf did have the information, then he, Loisel, was going to ask a few questions just to satisfy his own curiosity, questions that "only a man in his [Beauboeuf's] position could know." Loisel would have to know the answers, of course, before "the deal is clinched." If Loisel satisfied himself that Beauboeuf knew what he was talking about, then they would go right into the boss's office and "the man himself" would sit down.

"You're talking about Garrison?" asked Exnicious.

Loisel assured that he was and, further, that any type of contract would be agreeable. Loisel chortled a bit as he thought of the reaction of the "Federal Government" when "this thing is broken."

Loisel was asked to step outside for a few minutes while Exnicious spoke privately to his client, Beauboeuf. Beauboeuf reiterated to his lawyer that he knew nothing at all about any assassination plot.

"You realize that if we turn him down, they're going to subpoena you?" advised Exnicious.

"I didn't think they thought so screwed-up," said Beauboeuf.

The two men pondered the dilemma. It would do no good to take the tests, for Beauboeuf knew that in the end he would have nothing of value anyway. He would then not get his money or the job. They finally agreed to tell Loisel that Beauboeuf would submit to the test. The plan was to bargain. If Beauboeuf submitted and if the information he possessed did not suffice, then would the D.A. just go along with the job with the airline?

Loisel was called back into the room and the proposition was put to him. Just a job at an airline in the event Beauboeuf, despite full cooperation, turned out not to know a thing. "That doesn't seem to be too much," said Beauboeuf.

"No, but it's not what we're looking for," said the investigator.

"But suppose the facts are that Al doesn't know anything," persisted Exnicious. "Suppose that there was a conspiracy, but that Al knew nothing about it? You can't accept that?" asked Exnicious.

"Right. Our investigation has led to Al himself, you know, and we just feel like he has to know." After more conversation back and forth between the investigator and Beauboeuf's lawyer, it was finally agreed that Loisel would speak to Garrison.

Nonetheless, Loisel decided to throw out a few hints. He didn't want any answers at the time from Beauboeuf, but there were "a few things that don't add up."

Continued Loisel: "Number 1, after the assassination, they went to a skating rink. Now, we interviewed this man at the skating rink. Dave didn't skate and the man said, 'You know, this man didn't come up here, you know for . . . he came up here for only one reason. And that was when everything . . . you know, at the proper time, Dave Ferrie said, "I'm Dave Ferrie from New Orleans! I want you all to know I'm here," in a loud voice.' "

Loisel then described Ferrie's flight to Hammond the night he was being sought by the D.A.'s investigators. "There's just too many things," said Loisel.

Also, Loisel mentioned an informer who had been a friend of Ferrie's.

"You're talking about Jack Martin?" asked Exnicious.

"No. No. No. Phew!" exclaimed Loisel.

"I wondered, you know."

"Oh, no, that sack of roaches," Loisel hastened to explain.

Exnicious laughed. "Well, I'm relieved to find you're not swinging this whole thing on this man's reputation and Garrison . . ."

"What do you mean?" said Loisel. "He will never enter into this investigation. I mean he . . . he entered and exited so quick."

The two exchanged exclamations of mutual relief that the prime witness was not Jack Martin. "Man, we will be torn to pieces, but not like that," said Loisel.

"Well, I just can't see how you can prevent it, unless you come up with a key figure in the whole thing, a guy that knows a lot about it."

"Well, we know we'll win the preliminary, and it gives us a little more time to gather additional evidence."

It was suggested that Beauboeuf would be made available on Monday, the 13th of March, the day before the Shaw preliminary hearing and that he would be available for all of Garrison's tests. But Loisel wanted him available for the weekend, and it was agreed.

*　　*　　*

Loisel left. Exnicious was now in possession of a tape which he strongly felt to be an offer of money and a job for false information. The two men, Beauboeuf and Exnicious, discussed now what should be done. During the days that followed they explored the possibility of selling the tape to some of the national news media for money. Beauboeuf was out of work and desperate for funds. But he never did submit to any of Garrison's proposed tests.

Evidence of the tape, as well as attempts by Exnicious to have Loisel charged with public bribery by Garrison's political friend, Jefferson Parish D.A. Frank Langridge, were soon known among lawyers and others close to the probe. It was in Langridge's bailiwick that the alledged bribe attempt had occurred.

It was not long before word got back to Garrison's office. Undoubtedly, Garrison and Loisel were as piqued over the transmittal of a transcript of the tape to the United States Attorney General as by any other aspect of the entire episode.

On April 11th Beauboeuf received a visit at his home from Loisel and Ivon at about 11:00 P.M. The two investigators asked Beauboeuf if they might come into Beauboeuf's home to show him a picture. After entering the house, Loisel said, "You know, Al, you play dirty politics, you get hurt."

"What do you mean, Lynn?" asked Beauboeuf.

"You know what I mean," replied Loisel.

Ivon asked if Beauboeuf was aware of what was going on. Beauboeuf acknowledged that he knew what had taken place. "I didn't think you would be behind this, Al," said Ivon. The two then started to leave after telling Beauboeuf that they wanted to see him the next day. Before leaving, Ivon said, "You know, Al, Layton Martens didn't cooperate with us and that's why he got subpoenaed." Beauboeuf acknowledged that he did not want his name publicized all over the country. "It's a little late for that now," responded Ivon. The two investigators again started to leave, whereupon Ivon asked Beauboeuf to come outside with him. The three men went to the front of the house and Loisel repeated: "You know, Al, you play dirty politics and you get hurt."

"Well, Lynn, you all didn't want to do anything for me, why should I do anything for you?" said Beauboeuf.

"Al, I hate to see one of my men get in trouble over that tape recording," said Ivon. As to how he had found out about it, Ivon replied that they had "certain connections."

Continued Ivon, "Before I'd see any of my men get in trouble over a minor thing like this, I might go through some extent of hurting you by subpoena for some of the files that you seen."

It will be recalled that at the time of Beauboeuf's arrest in Ferrie's apartment on November 25th, 1963, the D.A.'s men had confiscated from him certain obscene photographs, including several of Beauboeuf himself.

According to Beauboeuf, Loisel said, "Al, I don't want to get into any shit and before I do, I'll put a hot load of lead up your ass."

Beauboeuf responded: "Well, what do you want me to do? I said you all didn't do anything for me and you want me to come through with everything that is not true."

According to Beauboeuf, Ivon continued: "Al, you want to let it go like that?" To which Beauboeuf responded that he did not want any trouble.

Again, according to Beauboeuf, Loisel interjected: "Al, while you are trying to sell your story, we are going to be passing out these pictures and all this information like it was going out of style."

"Well, what do you want me to do?" asked Beauboeuf.

Said Ivon: "I think you better come up to the office tomorrow." Beauboeuf agreed and did, in fact, appear at the D.A.'s office the next morning.

When he appeared in the D.A.'s office on the morning of April 12th Beauboeuf was assured that the offer to exchange information for money was not considered a bribe and was not in violation of any law. Beauboeuf states he was told he would be required to sign an affidavit to the effect that he did not understand the conversation to be a bribe. He was left alone in Ivon's office for approximately an hour and a half while the statement was prepared. He then read the statement that was presented to him, but he decided that it appeared too damaging to him. Certain changes were made and the statement was signed.

Approximately a month later, Beauboeuf was to tell the police he did not consider the statement to be true, but was forced to sign because of blackmail and threats. Beauboeuf stated that he "signed willingly under the full understanding that I was backing out and was guaranteed to be left alone." According to Beauboeuf, Loisel sat next to him in a chair and spoke "loudly" to Beauboeuf, saying, "Al, I know you're lying, you've been lying to us all along and I know you've got to know something." According to Beauboeuf he asked to be given a lie detector test, to which Loisel responded that they did not have "six hours out of every day to fool with you."

In a second statement to the police on June 2nd, Beauboeuf stated he signed the affidavit because he was threatened by Loisel that "they would be handing out pictures and my entire file out to the press." The threat referred to by Beauboeuf was that made at his home the night of April 11th. Beauboeuf also denied that the verbiage and thoughts of the affidavit were his. They were thoughts and words used by someone else, claimed Beauboeuf. The affidavit was approximately two and one-half pages in length. It stated in part:

> I want to state again that no representative of the Orleans Parish District Attorney's office has ever asked me to do anything but to tell the truth. . . . I understand now that the rumor has been going around . . . that Lynn Loisel . . . supposedly offered me money to produce some sort of false statement. At that time, when Mr. Loisel was asking me what I knew about the case, after talking to him for awhile, I told him that I could not afford to continue to take the time to tell the District Attorney's Office what I knew about the case until I found a job and solved my financial problems. I said I was broke and that it took too much of my time and it had already taken too much of my time answering questions about the case. Mr. Loisel replied that if I told the entire truth about the case, as I knew it, and that if these facts led to the capture of the men who killed President Kennedy, he felt I would not have to worry about either a job or money. He said, however, that it had to be the truth because the District Attorney's Office would require me to take a lie detector test and other tests because they were not interested in building their case on any statements about which there was any question. . . . The next time the matter of money and a job was brought up was in the office of Mr. Hugh Exnicious. . . . He started a tape machine before Mr. Loisel came in. . . . Mr. Exnicious turned to Mr. Loisel and said "Is it true that you offered my client a job or some money to tell the truth about the assassination?" Mr. Loisel replied that this was correct; that his office was interested only in

getting the truth and that anything less than the truth would be useless. . . . Then Mr. Exnicious said, "What do you want to know?" Mr. Loisel said, "We want to know what part Dave Ferrie played in the assassination of the President. We know a lot of his involvement already, but we feel that Alvin Beauboeuf knows some missing links that will help us get all of the men involved in the assassination." This is when Loisel said that they wanted nothing but the truth and no deviations from the truth. . . . The purpose of the questions being asked by Mr. Exnicious was obviously to attempt to get Mr. Loisel to offer me money and a job while the tape recorder was on. However, Mr. Loisel said that there would be no help of any kind for me unless I told the complete truth. . . . Mr. Exnicious told me that he thought he would sell this tape and make some money. . . . I have not heard the tape played lately, but I would be surprised if anybody would pay money for it if Mr. Loisel's statement about me having to tell the truth was still left on the tape. If Mr. Exnicious had left this on the tape, I don't know who would want to pay money for it, but he seemed confident that he could sell it to someone. . . .

Hugh Aynesworth of Newsweek magazine became interested in the entire incident, and talk of the alleged bribery was compounded by rumors of impending publication of the story in Newsweek magazine. Exnicious advised Beauboeuf to get other counsel to prevent further complications in his legal representation of the witness.

* * *

Beauboeuf retained Burton Klein, a former assistant district attorney under Dowling and, for a short period, under Garrison. On May 5th Klein made the first of many efforts to obtain redress for what he deemed a flagrant attempt at bribery. He referred the matter to the New Orleans Police Department which thereupon commenced a lengthy and detailed investigation with a somewhat curious conclusion. Subsequently, Klein attempted to bring the matter to the attention of the Orleans Parish Grand Jury, but found the Jury most unreceptive. With the encouragement of three or four of their "legal advisers"—all Garrison's assistants—they hooted their scorn for Klein and ridiculed his claim of bribery. The Jefferson Parish Grand Jury, the Jury with direct jurisdiction over the occurrence itself, was more receptive but, under the guidance of Garrison's friend, Frank Langridge, did nothing.

The May 15th, 1967, issue of Newsweek magazine contained a story by Aynesworth entitled "The J.F.K. 'Conspiracy.'" The article summarized Garrison's investigation in generally derogatory terms and reserved special emphasis for the Beauboeuf incident. Garrison barely deigned to answer the article, referring contemptuously instead to the magazine ownership: "Who owns *Newsweek?* The *Washington Post.* What is the *Washington Post?* One of the main mouthpieces of high offices in Washington. It's an administration paper."

Pressed by reporters, Garrison's response was that the matter was unimportant. "The only thing important is the truth," said Garrison.

On May 9th Hugh Exnicious filed a formal complaint with the Committee of Ethics and Grievances of the Louisiana State Bar Association. Garrison's response was to forward a copy of the April 12th affidavit. No action was taken by the Committee.

Following the publication of the *Newsweek* story, Beauboeuf and Klein appeared on local television news programs. Klein reiterated the substance of Beauboeuf's complaint.

On May 12th Garrison made a complaint of his own to the Ethics and Grievances Committee. The complaint was against Klein and contained some of the D.A.'s more mystifying statements. His complaint?

> Mr. Klein has recently appeared on television and issued statements to the newspapers in which he has represented himself to be the attorney of Alvin Beauboeuf. He has used this as an opportunity to lead a counterattack against an increasingly successful investigation by the District Attorney's Office into the conspiracy to kill John F. Kennedy.
>
> There is, of course, nothing wrong with an attorney being an advocate of his client's cause. However, Mr. Klein does not really represent Mr. Beauboeuf but has been hired, instead, by individuals whose only objective is to prevent a successful conclusion to the investigation. It is to be noted that in his public appearances with Mr. Beauboeuf, Mr. Klein makes his attack on the District Attorney's investigation while his "client" sits silently beside him. . . .
>
> The point is that Mr. Klein has to know that what he is saying is not true. The point is that Mr. Klein has not been retained by Mr. Beauboeuf, who is simply an unfortunate pawn in this matter. Above all, the point is that Mr. Klein, for purposes of money and personal gain, is engaged in a serious and dedicated attempt to obstruct the course of justice. . . . I know of nothing more serious than the participation on the part of a lawyer in a cool scheme to sabotage justice, to halt the course of a serious inquiry into the assassination of a President. In my considered judgment, a man who would engage in such conduct, which is essentially

criminal in nature, should not be allowed to continue to pose
as "an officer of the court."

Klein answered the complaint by letter. No action was taken by the
Committee.

In the course of the police investigation, both Ivon and Loisel denied
any threats against Beauboeuf following the March 10th session and
further denied that they ever solicited false information. Both Exnicious
and Beauboeuf confirmed to the police investigators that it was their
definite opinion from the entire manner of Loisel that false information
was solicited. Beauboeuf also confirmed his opinion that false information had been sought the previous day by Loisel and Ivon. At one point
in his statement to the police, Beauboeuf stated upon reading the
transcript of the tape that "there might be particular statements that
may have been omitted." However, he made it explicit that he was
referring to that portion of the transcript when Loisel left the room and
during which the recorded conversation was between Exnicious and
Beauboeuf. Nonetheless, Garrison subsequently seized upon these comments to claim specifically that the tape had been found to have been
"demonstrably altered." Neither Beauboeuf nor Loisel ever indicated
any portion of the conversation that was not accurately reported in the
transcript of the conversation between Loisel and Exnicious. On June
10th the police sent a letter to Charles Ward requesting advice as to
whether D.A. investigators had available to them, subject to approval,
funds to pay informers for information about inquiries being conducted.
Two days later Ward replied:

> . . . the answer is yes.
> In the past we have paid informers, both confidential and
> overt, to provide information relative to criminal activity.
> Any agreement to pay informers is always conditioned upon
> verification of the information given and the absolute truth
> and veracity of the information.

Concluded the police: The Department failed to "detect that Loisel
or Ivon have violated any rules of the code of conduct of the New
Orleans Police Department."

Public bribery is defined in the Louisiana Statutes as the giving or
offering to give anything of value to any witness or person about to be
called as a witness with the intent to influence his conduct in relation to
his duty as a witness. The statute says nothing about a corrupt motive
and it does not appear to be necessary that the "something of value" be
offered for false information.

The point may be minor. Except that about six weeks later NBC reporter Walter Sheridan and WDSU reporter Richard Townley were charged by Garrison with supposed bribery of Garrison's star witness, Perry Russo. The charge was that the two newsmen offered Russo employment and residence in California for the purpose of "affecting his duty as a witness."

It was claimed that the employment and residence were to be furnished in the event Russo had to flee Garrison's jurisdiction should he recant his testimony. Sheridan and Townley both vigorously denied having offered Russo anything at all. However, no one, including Garrison, ever accused the two newsmen of having offered these "things of value" for anything but the truth.

15

TO DETERMINE PRECISELY THE
number of persons subpoenaed or questioned by Garrison's staff or the
Grand Jury would be extremely difficult. The estimate must be placed,
at a minimum, at close to two hundred.

For some, their contact with the mushrooming probe was a lark or
high adventure. For others it was neither, but was, at least, mercifully
brief and relatively painless. But for many others it was traumatic, and
in some instances lives were tragically altered.

A glance at a selected few reveals something of the odd conglomeration of personalities that characterized the Garrison spectacle.

*   *   *

One of the most widely publicized adventures was the strange odyssey
of Gordon Novel. His troubles began with the Shaw preliminary hearing
and the attendance at the hearing of NBC reporter Walter Sheridan.

Sheridan has never been content with the role of passive observer, nor with surface appearances. He sought out information from every available source, and among the sources was Garrison's electronic expert, Gordon Novel. Novel spoke freely with Sheridan, as he did with most others. He related to the newsman Garrison's interest in the truck that had been used in the trip to Houma in 1961 and gave him the photograph of one of the laundry trucks taken by the D.A.'s men.

Garrison somehow became convinced that Novel had been paid $1,000 by the National Broadcasting Company for the photograph. He hadn't. He had, in fact, been paid nothing at all. But the D.A. had good cause for chagrin nonetheless. Novel, like Andrews, had quickly spotted the D.A.'s solution to the assassination as a fantasy and, like Andrews, he had gone along for laughs.

Novel received a subpoena to appear before the Grand Jury on March 16th. Upon appearing at the building on that date, he speculated to newsmen about the reasons for his appearance: "I think Mr. Garrison wants to know something about activities during 1961 which are related to Mr. Sergio Arcacha Smith."

After testifying before the Jury, he quickly concluded that the game was over. It will be recalled that this was the day of Andrews's second Grand Jury appearance and likewise the day of his first indictment. Novel reasoned that there was little future for him in New Orleans. Probably figuring Garrison's bubble to burst sometime in the near future, he decided to pull up stakes and lay low until the D.A. should fall on his face.

Like Andrews, Novel was the target of two Grand Jury subpoenas. Following his appearance on the 16th, a new subpoena was issued for March 22nd.

But Novel was never served with this second subpoena. By the time of its issuance he had sold his Jamaican Village Bar and departed the state. His lawyer, Steven Plotkin, said that his absence was not at all to avoid the subpoena or not to cooperate with the District Attorney, but purely for "personal reasons." He was in Washington, said the attorney, and would return in "due course."

However, a Columbus, Ohio, newsman reported Novel's presence in that community for at least three days prior to his scheduled Grand Jury appearance. The day following his failure to appear he was ordered arrested by Garrison as a material witness. Bail was fixed at $50,000.

On the night of March 22nd Novel told reporters in Columbus that "Political ambition lurks behind Garrison's probe," and thereupon left Columbus for Chicago. This was the first fusillade in a long-range duel between Novel and Garrison. The elusive witness flitted about with great agility as Garrison swatted with all the powerful clubs in his armory. From the safety of several thousand miles separating Novel from the borders of Louisiana he jeered and mocked the D.A. like a small boy from the safety of his home making faces through the window at the neighborhood bully. Meanwhile, the D.A.'s long arms reached out for him.

On March 24th a material witness charge was filed, but Novel was found only by the Hearst Headline Service and the National Broadcasting Company in an undisclosed "hideaway." He was transported at NBC's expense to McLean, Virginia, for interviews and a lie detector test. The test indicated that all questions were answered truthfully.

Garrison and his men were incensed. "I think it odd that he can be found by newspaper and television media and not by the people who are trying to arrest him," said one of them. From his still undisclosed hideaway following the test, Novel referred to Garrison's investigation as "the most enormous fraud ever perpetrated in the annals of the legal history of the State of Louisiana."

Furthermore, he was in "international jurisdiction," said Novel. "If Garrison wants me, he will have to go through the World Court." He also announced his plans to sue the members of "Truth and Consequences," Garrison's affluent backers, as well as Garrison himself. "I'll have half the fortunes of the city in my back pocket," he boasted.

He was going back to New Orleans, said Novel, but not to be browbeaten by Garrison. "His mad ambitions have run away with him," said the pesky witness.

Confronted by newsmen with this barrage of unflattering statements, Garrison contemptuously dismissed them as "unworthy of comment." "What difference does it make what he said?" sneered Garrison.

On March 31st, two days after Layton Martens appeared before the Grand Jury, Novel and Arcacha Smith were charged with conspiring to burglarize the Houma bunker on August 19th, 1961, in a bill of information filed by Garrison. Arrest warrants were issued for both men. Novel was now wanted, not merely as a witness, but, supposedly, to stand trial for a felony.

The following day, Saturday, April 1st, he was apprehended in Gahanna, Ohio, a suburb of Columbus. The arrest accelerated, rather than slowed, Novel's loquacity. "Unless I am kidnapped or killed . . . their days of perpetrating this monstrous fraud are numbered," said Novel. He issued a written statement: "I would like to congratulate Chief Robert F. Brandon of the Gahanna Police Department . . . in his apprehension of myself. His office and men are to be praised in doing what the supposed master crime solver—Mr. Jim Garrison— couldn't do. My attorneys will fight extradition, if necessary, to the United States Supreme Court. . . ."

Novel spent the night in jail, unable to post bond in the amount fixed by the Columbus Municipal Court, the sum of $10,000. He showed up the next morning in Municipal Court and began arguing his own case for a bond reduction. In the middle of his argument, he was joined by attorney Jerry Weiner, who thereupon took charge of the long battle to resist return of Novel to New Orleans.

On April 4th, Novel posted his $10,000 bond and was released. Referring to the Houma episode, Novel told newsmen: "You will see that it was the most patriotic burglary in history." But his favorite subject was Garrison. He "wants to make a name for himself," Novel insisted. "Jim Garrison is the greatest character assassin of all times, and I've got the stuff in here to prove it," he claimed as he indicated an attaché case he carried.

On April 6th, Novel announced that he was willing to go back to testify before a Grand Jury that wasn't "loaded." He did not like the idea, however, that the Jury was composed of some of Garrison's best friends. Weiner telegrammed the Jury foreman offering Novel's return provided the burglary charge was dropped and provided any questioning by the Grand Jury was conducted without Garrison's presence. Novel also asked immunity from any "further charges, intimidation and harassment." Finally, he wanted assurance that he could return to Ohio after testifying and that his Grand Jury testimony would be made public. Crowed an assistant D.A.:

> He's not going to dictate conditions to us. He's not in a dictating position. Mr. Novel is a fugitive from justice and we're going to get him back on our own conditions.

Replied the Grand Jury by telegram: "Conditions impossible."

Extradition proceedings were started. Papers were filed in the office of Governor McKeithen for further forwarding to Governor Rhoades. Included in the extradition papers was an affidavit by Novel's ex-wife, Marlene Mancuso.

Garrison, seldom content with one charge, filed two new ones. These were theft charges, the "thefts" involving unpaid services and goods purchased over a period of several months between June and September, 1962.

In the meantime, the extradition papers had been received in the office of Ohio Governor James A. Rhoades. There Garrison's plans to return his elusive witness hit a snag. They were returned to Louisiana with the request that certain "technical defects" be corrected. A legal aide to the Ohio Governor remarked to newsmen that "certain reports indicate that the extradition was for a purpose other than the simple burglary charge and we want clarification." The Governor wrote Mc-Keithen asking assurance that the request for extradition was not a subterfuge to obtain Novel for questioning on the assassination probe. He apparently did not like being a pawn in Garrison's game. Garrison termed the request "the most incredible thing I have ever heard."

Governor McKeithen tried to reach Rhoades by telephone, but soon determined that the Ohio Governor must be "the busiest man in the country." He was never successful in reaching him. An assistant to Rhoades advised that "when the papers are in order, Ohio will certainly return Novel to Louisiana." Garrison, sensing a run around, never returned additional papers. After a delay of several months, the entire matter was dismissed in the Ohio courts.

Novel had his attorneys file in Louisiana a $50,000,000 lawsuit against Garrison and the members of "Truth and Consequences." Attorneys for Garrison and his financial backers moved to take Novel's deposition in New Orleans. When the motion was granted by the Court, Novel withdrew his suit.

Garrison still had one more arrow left in the quiver. A Uniform Compulsory Attendance of Witness Act provides that, as between the states subscribing to the Act (all but six of the states in the Union), if immunity for all past transgressions be afforded, a witness residing in one state will be compelled to return to any of the other subscribing states under tender of travel expenses and a per diem allowance. Garrison had never felt inclined to offer Novel immunity.

On February 20th, 1968, Garrison decided to make this last effort and had a subpoena issued under the Uniform Witness Act.

Novel's immediate response was a lengthy blast with a hint of desperation:

> . . . I never committed any burglaries and am most certainly not a material witness except to Mr. Garrison's attempts to fraudulently and maliciously involve myself, who was his former personal chief of security in his alleged investigation of the alleged conspiracy to allegedly assassinate John F. Kennedy.
> . . . In reference to his new subpoena, I, personally, haven't read it. So I will just have to see it before deciding whether to play my game or his.

For a brief moment Novel appeared winded. Shortly after his initial blast he told reporters: "I'm tired of fighting. I think it's time to bring this to a head. I want to have a home and raise a family."

He regained his breath quickly. He resisted the subpoena before the

Franklin County Court in Columbus, Ohio. His lawyer argued that "if he testifies he knows anything about Kennedy's assassination, he will be charged with conspiracy to assassinate the President. If he says he knows nothing, he will be charged with perjury." The trial judge overruled all objections and ordered Novel to comply with the subpoena.

On appeal, however, Novel fared better. The Appellate Tribunal ruled that Novel, already under charges, should not be required to return to Louisiana. The reason? ". . . It appears he will not be afforded protection against arbitrary arrest," said the Appellate Court and suggested that depositions could be taken in Ohio. The opinion further stated quite pointedly, that it was the thinking of the presiding Judge that there was no showing that Novel was a "material and necessary witness to an investigation of a conspiracy to assassinate John F. Kennedy."

Garrison had shot the last arrow. Novel could not be forced to return to Louisiana. He had won his battle with Garrison. But he could not come home to celebrate the victory.

*   *   *

When Sergio Arcacha Smith left New Orleans in 1962, he moved to Houston where he was living at the time of the assassination, and later to Dallas. It was in Dallas that he resided with his wife and five children when the Garrison assassination probe went into high gear in early 1967. He was employed at the time by a Dallas air-conditioning manufacturing firm.

In early February an assistant D.A., at Garrison's direction, called Smith on a number of occasions and asked him to come to New Orleans to answer questions. Smith was not, assured the assistant D.A., a suspect. Some of the Cubans whom Garrison had already interviewed, however, felt otherwise and had told Smith in no uncertain terms that the Orleans Parish D.A. was trying to "frame" him. Smith declined to come.

On February 25th the assistant D.A. flew to Dallas with Bill Gurvich and called Smith for the purpose of asking for an interview. Mrs. Smith answered the first two telephone calls and stated that her husband was not at home. On the third call, the phone was answered by a Dallas Police Department detective. Smith was present, advised the detective, but he preferred to be interviewed at Police Headquarters, and Garrison's men were asked to meet Smith and the detective there. About 10:00 P.M. on the 25th, Gurvich and the assistant met Smith with detectives at headquarters.

They wanted certain information, explained the assistant. "O.K., shoot," said Smith. Garrison's aide balked. The questioning could not take place in the presence of anyone else except Smith's attorney, he explained. It could only take place in the presence of the detectives, responded Smith. A heated argument ensued, but Smith and the detectives remained firm and Gurvich and the assistant D.A. flew back to New Orleans.

Garrison made one more attempt. He sent word via a Newsweek reporter that he did not suspect Smith of anything, that he knew Smith was a family man like Garrison himself, and that Garrison would stop in Dallas on his way to Las Vegas to have lunch with Smith. Smith agreed and a date was set. Garrison never appeared.

His attorney wrote the D.A. a registered letter offering to meet with him or any member of the D.A. staff in any place but New Orleans. The letter was never answered.

On March 31st came the charge of conspiracy to commit burglary filed jointly against Novel and Smith. On April 2nd, he was arrested at his home by the Dallas police, taken to headquarters, photographed, and fingerprinted, then transferred to County Jail. Bond had been set by the New Orleans court at $5,000. The Dallas Justice of the Peace set the bond at $1,500, however, and Smith was released. He was quoted as telling the Texas officers "Garrison hasn't got anything. . . . There is nothing pertinent I could tell the New Orleans people."

Smith then lapsed into silence. He said nothing, refusing all comment whatsoever, as a legal battle was fought over his extradiction. Smith's extradition was ultimately refused by Governor Connally. Garrison was finding to his chagrin that public officials beyond his jurisdiction were far less cooperative than those in New Orleans and Baton Rouge.

The publicity to Smith was considerably less than it might have been but for his persistent silence. He did not escape unscathed, however. He lost his job as the result of the arrest and publicity and was unfavorably portrayed in Spanish-language newspapers in this country and abroad. But his name dropped out of the news shortly following the death of Garrison's extradition attempt in the summer of 1967 and, compared to other Garrison suspects, he has fared well.

*   *   *

In early 1967 Sandra Moffett was living in Omaha, Nebraska. She was now Mrs. Harold McMaines. Her husband was a truck driver and a part-time minister at an Omaha church. She had renounced her past, she claimed, and turned to religion. She married McMaines "because he was the first guy that took me out and took me to a movie instead of a beer tavern."

On March 8th two D.A. investigators arrived in Omaha and went to the McMaines residence. They arrived about 10:00 P.M. and identified themselves. They were, they said, investigating the assassination of President Kennedy and they needed Mrs. McMaines to accompany them back to New Orleans to identify photographs and give any information that she could furnish. Mrs. McMaines looked at her husband. McMaines objected and asked if the officers had a warrant. They did not. Mrs. McMaines, Lillie Mae was the name she now used, was not in any trouble, explained the officers, but was merely wanted as a witness. All expenses would be taken care of by the D.A.'s Office. The investigators asked that McMaines call in the morning to advise as to their decision.

Mr. and Mrs. McMaines went to the office of the County Attorney, Donald Knowles, who called the D.A. investigators. The pair from New Orleans then met with the McMaines couple and Knowles in his office. Knowles advised them that he had apprised Mr. and Mrs. McMaines of their rights and that the choice was up to them. McMaines was undecided. He and Lillie Mae and the two officers left the County Attorney's office to discuss the matter over breakfast. The investigators tried to calm the fears of both husband and wife. They would furnish both Mr. and Mrs. McMaines new clothes in addition to paying all expenses to New Orleans and they would be located in a very nice hotel.

McMaines had some fear of not returning as the officers requested and he advised the investigators he wanted to telephone his attorney in a nearby town. Upon doing so, McMaines was advised that if the officers had no legal papers to force his wife's return they should not voluntarily leave Omaha. McMaines returned to the restaurant and gave the officers his decision: They were not returning. He and his wife then left. The investigators followed them down the street and continued their attempts at persuasion. McMaines turned abruptly: "Don't bug me, leave us alone."

The investigators never saw Mr. or Mrs. McMaines again. About 11:00 P.M. when they returned to their quarry's apartment, they were advised by the landlord that the couple had left the residence, taking all of their belongings. The following day the investigators were informed by Knowles that he had received a telephone call from an attorney, Richard Duskin, who was now representing the McMaines couple, and that any contact with the couple should be through him.

The investigators returned to Knowles's office where they were joined by Duskin, who quickly became irritated at their refusal to furnish any details of the investigation. Duskin made it clear that he felt that the entire thing was a "cloak-and-dagger" operation and that "Mr. X," referring to Garrison, seemed to be "pulling all the strings." Duskin didn't understand how the investigators could be flown to Omaha without being allowed to disclose details of the investigation. Further, he could not understand why Lillie Mae could not be questioned in Omaha. He would not, he advised, permit his clients to return to New Orleans with the investigators. Should they return to New Orleans, said Duskin, he doubted that his clients would be permitted to leave. The investigators gave up and returned to New Orleans.

During the cross-examination of Perry Russo at the Shaw preliminary hearing, Sandra Moffett was mentioned by Russo as having accompanied him to the party at Ferrie's home. The resultant publicity intensified the ordeal that commenced with the arrival of the investigators on March 8th. McMaines lost his employment as a truck driver. Lillie Mae lost two consecutive jobs for the same reason, ultimately finding work in a cleaning firm in Omaha.

On March 27th a warrant was issued for the arrest of Sandra Moffett McMaines, now known as Lillie Mae McMaines, on a charge of being a material witness. Bond was set at $5,000.

She was interviewed by newsmen in Omaha. She could not have attended a party at Ferrie's apartment prior to Kennedy's assassination, said Lillie Mae, because she had not been introduced to Ferrie until 1965.

Two days later Knowles filed a fugitive charge against Lillie Mae and she was arrested about 4:00 P.M. on that date. An extradition hearing was set for April 25th and she was released on $1,000 bond.

On April 10th Judge Bernard Bagert in New Orleans signed a "certificate of attendance" asking the Nebraska courts to compel Lillie Mae's return to New Orleans to appear before the Grand Jury April 18th, 19th, and 20th. This was the procedure ultimately used against Gordon Novel involving the Uniform Attendance of Witness Act. The certificate, in effect, granted immunity to Lillie Mae and she was tendered a check for traveling expenses.

A few days later Knowles's office announced that he could not find Mrs. McMaines and that no active search was being made for her. Apparently, she had left Nebraska and his office was, he said, abandoning attempts to enforce the New Orleans court order. "A subpoena is no good across state lines and I assume now she is no longer in Nebraska," his office stated. The McMaines couple had, in fact, moved to Iowa, where they resided with friends. Iowa is one of the half dozen states in the Union which had not enacted the Uniform Witness Act.

On April 25th the material witness charge, the original effort to force the witness's return, was heard in court. Mrs. McMaines remained in Iowa and was not present. County Attorney Donald Knowles moved for forfeiture of the $1,000 bond. "I believe that motion is premature," said Municipal Court Judge John Clark. The Judge referred to a motion previously filed by Lillie Mae's attorneys to dismiss the proceedings, claiming that her life would be in danger should she return to New Orleans to testify.

The motion to dismiss was granted. "That's what I call instant justice," said her attorney. With regard to the certificate of attendance under the Uniform Witness Act, Knowles said, "If she ever sets foot in Nebraska, it will be served." She never did.

Said one of Garrison's assistants: "We're frustrated on her. There's nothing we can do. Our material witness charge against her will not hold up apparently." He had, said the assistant, sent a letter to the police in Des Moines. Nothing had come of it.

Like Novel, Lillie Mae was safe as long as she remained in exile.

*   *   *

Carlos Quiroga was contacted intermittently for various reasons by D.A. investigators following his questioning in the early part of 1967. His next contact of consequence with the D.A.'s office began in mid-April and lasted approximately six weeks.

Quiroga is an intense, fiery, short-tempered individual. His eyes still bristle when he speaks of his escapade with Garrison's office. As he tells his story, the words flow quickly and the anger is obviously deep.

On April 14th he was contacted by a D.A. investigator. The subject discussed was one of Garrison's favorites, another request for a lie detector test. Quiroga agreed. He already had experience with the D.A.'s Office, however, and spoke first to an attorney. The attorney was loath to advise consenting to the test, but pointed out certain dangers that might be faced from the indictment-happy D.A. upon refusal. He urged caution. Quiroga finally agreed to the test, but requested by letter that he be given copies of the questions to be asked. He was informed that this would be done.

Quiroga was directed to the office of the same operator who had first given the polygraph test to Perry Russo in February. He was accompanied to the office by his wife. The operator informed Quiroga that he could not be allowed to see the questions prior to taking the test, but Quiroga refused to submit to the polygraph unless he were shown the questions, as agreed. The irritated operator called Garrison and was told to inform Quiroga to take the test at once or that he would be arrested immediately. Faced with this threat, Quiroga agreed and was then given a routine statement to sign to the effect that the test was taken voluntarily. This he refused to do. A heated argument ensued and the operator informed Quiroga that he would not be given the test and would face arrest unless this statement was signed. Quiroga's wife began crying and the harassed Cuban finally signed the statement and submitted to the test. The following day he made a complaint to the Federal Bureau of Investigation, neither the first nor the last complaint to be made to that Bureau by witnesses in the Garrison probe.

On May 10th Quiroga was subpoenaed to appear before the Grand Jury. Upon arrival at the building, however, he was not take before the Jury. Instead, he was confronted by an assistant district attorney who bluntly informed him, "You failed the lie detector test." He was also told that he must get a lawyer, for unless he changed his testimony, Garrison said, he would be indicted. Quiroga again consulted with an attorney.

Shortly thereafter, he was again subpoenaed before the Grand Jury, this time for May 24th. Prior to going into the Grand Jury room, he was warned again that unless he testified "truthfully," contrary to previous statements he had given, he would be indicted as an accessory after the fact to the murder of Kennedy, and for perjury. Inside the Grand Jury room Quiroga attempted to take the Fifth Amendment and refused to answer questions. He was heatedly told by Garrison, and by one of his assistants, that he could not, under the circumstances, claim the Fifth Amendment and that he must testify or that he would be held in contempt.

After repeated threats, he began to answer questions. Garrison and his assistant wanted brief yes or no answers. But Quiroga does not answer briefly. As they do from many Garrison witnesses, the words flow freely from Quiroga. The argument erupted anew. Garrison finally shouted at him uncontrollably to get out of the Grand Jury room. Quiroga left.

He was subsequently told through his attorney that if he "keeps his mouth shut," he will be let alone. Quiroga has, in fact, been let alone following his Grand Jury appearance. He has also kept his mouth shut.

* * *

To those who admire excellence, John Cancler, commonly known in New Orleans as St. John the Baptist, is an interesting, if not an admirable, character. When asked his occupation, he will respond that he was "formerly" a burglar. But he is too modest. He is generally reputed to be one of the most skilled craftsmen in the business. He has been in many of the finest houses in New Orleans and is not seriously challenged as the most expert burglar in the community.

St. John the Baptist is a tall, well-built Negro of about forty years. He is smart, glib, and cunning. He has never been known to engage in force or violence, however; his field is stealth, chicanery, and connivance.

In early February, 1967, John Cancler was confined in the Parish Prison awaiting trial on a burglary charge. In mid-February he was tried and following a three-day trial, was found guilty by a jury. He had quarreled with his attorney during the course of the trial and he contacted me a few days following his conviction. He wanted me to handle his appeal, which I agreed to do. Some weeks later he repeated to me, as he had to many others, both before and after our conversation, stories which he was later to repeat to a nationwide audience on June 19th on the National Broadcasting Company white paper on the Garrison probe.

According to Cancler, while he was confined in the Parish Prison the first part of February, 1967, he was contacted by a certain investigator from the District Attorney's Office who asked him to "do a job for us." The job? Cancler was to get into a house without anyone knowing that it had been broken into. Cancler replied that he could do this, and the investigator drove him to a home in the 1300 block of Dauphine Street in New Orleans. Cancler told the investigator that he could break into the house if the windows were "standard," but he was advised that he could not at that time get out of the car to look.

"What am I supposed to take out of the house?" asked Cancler. He was not to take anything out, advised the investigator. He was supposed to put something in the house. What was it all about? "It has something to do with the assassination of President Kennedy," he was told. Cancler claimed he was frightened by anything "as big as that" and refused to go through with the plan.

Cancler had still another tale to tell. In mid-March, 1967, about a month following his conviction, he stopped a fight between two inmates in the Parish Prison. One of these was Vernon Bundy. The next day Bundy told Cancler that he thought he knew a way to get out of the Parish Prison where he was being held for parole violation. He spoke of the Clay Shaw hearing then in process. According to Cancler, Bundy asked him if he thought it would sound more plausible to say that he, Bundy, had seen Clay Shaw on Esplanade Street or on the lakefront. Further, according to Cancler, Bundy made it clear that he was planning to testify that he had seen Shaw meeting someone and that he was going to tell the District Attorney about it. He also made it quite clear that the statement he planned on giving the District Attorney was not true.

In June I was asked by certain NBC representatives as to whether I, as Cancler's attorney, objected to him repeating these statements on tape for the television broadcast that was then in the making. I advised the NBC representative, Cancler himself, and the Office of Sheriff Louis Heyd, that this had no connection to the burglary charge I was appealing and was not my concern.

The NBC telecast was on June 19th and the famed New Orleans burglar had his moment of glory on national television.

In early July I saw a press report that Cancler had been served with a Grand Jury subpoena which commanded his appearance on July 12th. I had not the slightest confidence that either the D.A.'s Office or the Grand Jury was the least bit interested in any information that Cancler could give. I doubted very much that there was any impending indictment of either the D.A. investigator or of Vernon Bundy, one of Garrison's star witnesses at the Shaw preliminary hearing. Undoubtedly, another perjury charge was in the offing. For Cancler this was doubly serious, for in the event of conviction, he would be a four-time loser and face life imprisonment.

I normally refrain from gratuitous unsolicited advice. Further, I knew that Cancler was undoubtedly as familiar with his privileges against self-incrimination as was I. Nonetheless, I felt that a simple warning to keep quiet was in order.

On July 12th I was in Baton Rouge attending to other business and was not present when Cancler appeared before the Jury. An assistant D.A., asked by a reporter if he, the assistant, felt that Cancler could contribute anything to the investigation, replied: "Absolutely not." The incongruity of subpoenaing before the Grand Jury a witness who could contribute nothing to the investigation apparently mattered little to Garrison or his assistants.

Upon returning to the city that night, I was completely dismayed to hear the account of the day's proceedings. Cancler had been asked in the Grand Jury room whether the statement he made on the NBC telecast was true. He responded that on advice from his attorney he declined to answer.

He was then taken before the Judge exercising supervisory authority over the Jury, in this case Judge Bagert, who was asked by the D.A. to order the question answered. Judge Bagert so ordered. Cancler again refused, claiming his Fifth Amendment privilege on advice of counsel. Cancler was held to be in contempt and sentenced to serve six months in the Parish Prison and to pay a fine of $500 or to serve an additional one year. He was then given another opportunity to answer the question, but persisted in his refusal.

I subsequently applied to the State Supreme Court for extraordinary writs seeking to set aside Cancler's contempt conviction and sentence. In late August Judge Bagert, on his own motion, reconsidered his ruling and dismissed the contempt conviction and sentence.

Whether the alleged incident involving Vernon Bundy happened or not is of very little importance. Whether Cancler was solicited to commit a burglary by one of Garrison's investigators is of considerable importance. His unsupported word is certainly not sufficient proof that he was. Neither, however, are Cancler's character and background conclusive proof that he was not. No serious investigation of the matter has ever been made. Nor has there been a serious denial.

*   *   *

Another participant in the NBC telecast was a Latin inmate of the State Penitentiary at Angola, Miguel Torres. In February, 1967, Torres was temporarily in the Orleans Parish Prison, having been transferred there at Garrison's request from Angola where he was serving a nine-year sentence for burglary.

Torres claimed that he was approached by two D.A. investigators and told that he had his choice of serving his full nine years, or of getting out of prison. He was also told, according to Torres, that he would be given heroin and a sojourn in Miami, if he would cooperate. It will be recalled that in February, Garrison's office had questioned one Emilio Santanna, another Cuban from Florida, who was suspected of complicity in the assassination plot. The basis for suspicion of Santanna was his acquaintanceship with Torres, who had lived near Oswald, and Torres, it had developed, had once frequented an area, including the 1300 block of Dauphine Street, near Clay Shaw. This was a clear indication to Garrison of complicity.

Torres claims that the "cooperation" demanded involved testimony that he had been approached by Clay Shaw for homosexual purposes and that he knew Clay Shaw as Clay Bertrand. Torres refused.

In late August, some two and one-half months after the NBC telecast, Torres was subpoenaed before the Grand Jury. Asked about his statement on the NBC program, he refused to answer. Cancler's previous contempt conviction and sentence was still pending before the State Supreme Court, and Judge Bagert, though infuriated at Torres's obstinacy, ordered the attorney for Torres, Burton Klein, and the District Attorney to submit legal memoranda the following week. However, the Grand Jury term expired a few days thereafter and Torres was never called before the incoming Grand Jury. The matter was dropped.

*   *   *

Fred Leemans operated a Turkish bath in New Orleans which Clay Shaw, on occasion, frequented. Garrison's office was to leave no stone unturned in attempting to identify Shaw as Bertrand, and one of the stones they turned was Fred Leemans.

Leemans was contacted by an assistant D.A. and requested to come to Tulane and Broad for an interview. During the interview, in response to questions, Leemans indicated that he was trying to obtain a location for a private club in New Orleans, but that he needed $2,500 to do so. "Garrison helps those who help him," Leemans was told and arrangements could certainly be made for Leemans to get the money he needed. According to Leemans, he allowed himself to be led by the assistant who seemed more than willing to put extremely leading questions to him. According to Leemans, "When he wanted a yes, I gave him a yes."

What he was led to say, according to Leemans, was that Clay "Bertrand" whom he identified as Shaw, frequented the Turkish bath in the company of a young man named Lee and a Cuban. The assistant, feeling that he had hit upon something important, took Leemans to see his boss personally.

According to the witness, Garrison then took over the prompting. In response to Garrison's gentle leading Leemans said that Lee had a beard and was dressed in a dirty T-shirt and khakis. A statement was drawn and Leemans then signed the statement despite the fact that all of the contents were false. He later asked the assistant about the $2,500 and was told that money matters would have to be discussed directly with Garrison with no one else present.

Subsequently, an investigator contacted Leemans and asked him to return to the office to put his statement in the form of a sworn affidavit. Leemans now had second thoughts about the matter, contributed to in no small part, no doubt, by his failure to receive the $2,500, and he did not return. Leemans, too, repeated his story on the NBC telecast on June 19th. He claims that he was later contacted by a D.A. investigator and was offered $5,000 to appear on the one-half hour of network time given Garrison by NBC to reply to the June 19th telecast. According to Leemans, the $5,000 was for the purpose of appearing and testifying that his story on the NBC program was false. Leemans declined.

*   *   *

In the 1963 Louisiana gubernatorial campaign, there were a number of major candidates. In addition, there were the usual odd assortment of entries who run for publicity, amusement, or other reasons best known to themselves. One of these was a part-time preacher named Clyde Johnson. He received a certain amount of news coverage, unwarranted by the seriousness of his candidacy, as he was undoubtedly entertaining copy. He was widely telecast on TV stations throughout the state, strumming a banjo to backwoods audiences, shouting incoherently, or jumping up and down uncontrollably as though possessed of saint vitus's dance. Some were unkind enough to suggest that the preacher might be insane.

Two weeks following the Shaw preliminary hearing, on March 30th, 1967, Johnson called the District Attorney's Office from his home in Kentwood, Louisiana, Clay Shaw's birthplace. He had certain information to give the D.A.'s Office and asked that he be conveyed to New Orleans from Kentwood.

Johnson told the D.A. that in the summer of 1963, while stumping the state as a candidate for governor, he was staying in the Roosevelt Hotel in New Orleans. He received a telephone call and the voice on the phone introduced himself to Johnson as Mr. Elton Bernard. Johnson was asked to meet Mr. Bernard at the entrance to the hotel, which he did. According to Johnson, Bernard gave him a brown envelope with $2,000 in one hundred dollar bills as a campaign contribution and encouragement in Johnson's anti-Kennedy harangues. There were additional contacts. As Johnson told the D.A.'s Office, he figured that Bernard was "a Republican with more money than sense."

Sometime in the early part of September, 1963, Johnson received a call from Bernard who instructed him to meet Bernard at the Capitol House Hotel in Baton Rouge. Bernard brought three other persons with him to the meeting. One was named Leon, the second was described only as being a "big Mexican-looking fellow with a mustache," and the third party was "Jack." Shortly after the meeting got underway, Johnson left the room to use the bathroom, adjacent to the room in which the other three men were conversing. Johnson claims he overheard one of the three say something to the effect that "he would get him." He also heard Bernard say that "others were working on this" and "Well, he's got to come down from Washington. The pressure is on. He's got to come back."

As Johnson came back into the room, Jack said, "What about him?" pointing to Johnson, and Bernard replied, "That's all right. He's one of the boys." Finally Bernard opened a briefcase and gave Jack and Leon thick brown envelopes, and, as they were ready to depart, Bernard gave a brown envelope to Johnson containing fifty hundred-dollar bills.

Johnson claims he received several calls thereafter from Bernard while in Alexandria.

Now, on March 30th, 1967, in Garrison's office Johnson was shown a number of photographs and from the photographs had little difficulty in identifying Elton Bernard, Leon, and Jack.

Jack, of course, was Jack Ruby. Leon was Lee Harvey Oswald. Elton Bernard, to no one's surprise, was Clay Shaw.

Why had not Johnson come forward with his story prior to this time? He knew, he said, that Oswald was arrested shortly after the assassination and murdered two days later. He also knew that Ruby was subsequently tried and convicted for the murder and later died in prison. Only after Johnson had seen Shaw's picture in the newspaper and on TV did he associate Ruby, Oswald, and Shaw as being the persons in his room in Baton Rouge. Also, said Johnson, he had been scared and he felt that the law had been taking its natural course when Oswald and then Ruby were apprehended. But only when he associated Clay Shaw as being the other person in the room did the full impact of the events that occurred in his room strike home to Clyde Johnson.

Did Garrison believe the story of the Kentwood preacher? In early June, 1967, in response to pleadings filed in the Shaw case by Shaw's attorneys seeking the names of coconspirators of Shaw and the alleged acts done in furtherance of the conspiracy, Garrison replied in his answers filed in open court that Shaw delivered money to Ruby and to Lee Harvey Oswald in a Baton Rouge hotel in September, 1963.

Like other Garrison witnesses, Johnson apparently later suffered a change of heart. When he appeared to balk, a subpoena was issued to him demanding his appearance in Garrison's office in mid-June. He never appeared. He fled instead to a three-room cabin in southern Mississippi about seven miles south of Lacombe. He was finally located holed up in his darkened cabin by members of the press. Why was he not coming in response to the subpoena? For reasons of his own, said Johnson. He spoke to reporters from the bed of his small cabin and refused to turn on the bedroom light because he said he was afraid. A reporter stood in the bathroom as Johnson answered questions from the bedroom.

"Shaw and me are the only ones that know about it now," said Johnson, as he repeated to the reporter the story he had related to the D.A. "The meeting was a mistake," he said.

Johnson also had certain new information for the reporters: During the same month in which the meetings with Bernard took place he was shot at by occupants of a car which trailed him along a highway in Mississippi. At the time, he heard sounds like cap pistols coming from the other car and he dove to the floor of his own vehicle. According to Johnson, his car went out of control and smashed into a bridge abutment. Fortunately he survived the attempt on his life.

*   *   *

There was the man from Vancouver, Donald P. Norton. Norton was a musician, a native of Columbus, Georgia, who claimed to have met Clay Shaw in Alabama in August, 1962. Shaw was with a man who gave Norton an attaché case containing about $50,000 to be delivered to a "Harvey Lee" in Monterrey, Mexico, in exchange for another case containing documents. This, said Norton, was a C.I.A. assignment. The documents were delivered to a C.I.A. operative in Calgary, Canada.

This was not Norton's first C.I.A. assignment. He claimed that in 1958 his contact man on behalf of the C.I.A. was David Ferrie. On one occasion he was given $150,000 to carry into Havana to another C.I.A. operative.

Norton claims that he lost his job with the C.I.A. in November, 1966, as a result of the Garrison investigation. Said Norton: "I was told . . . that I should take a long quiet vacation." He had been operating, he claimed, his own record promotion and production company in Albany, Georgia, until that time, but thereupon spent seven months crisscrossing the United States and Canada, finally arriving in Vancouver in July. He first told his story in Vancouver a few days thereafter to a representative of the CHCT television station, where he had been employed. The story was discounted. It was then related to the Vancouver Sun. A representative of the paper contacted Garrison who promptly agreed to send First Assistant Charles Ward to interview Norton in Vancouver. A few days later, in mid-July, Norton returned to New Orleans for further questioning.

Why had not Norton come forward with his bizarre story following the assassination? No explanation was offered despite his immediate recognition of Oswald in 1963: "During the publicity of the assassination when the man known as Lee Oswald was revealed to the public, I almost immediately recognized him as being the same Harvey Lee I had met in September, 1962, in Monterrey, to whom I delivered the money."

Norton was given a lie detector test by a Vancouver news media which had been negotiating for his story. Like Perry Russo, however, he was highly nervous and the test was inconclusive. The Vancouver news media refused to deal with him for that reason. The story was ultimately

published by the *Vancouver Sun* in early August and a few days thereafter in the *Albertan* in Calgary.

*   *   *

There was Raymond Cummings, a Dallas cab driver who contacted
the D.A.'s Office in early March, claiming to have important information. He had seen a picture of David Ferrie in a Dallas newspaper, he
told the D.A., together with the story of Ferrie's claim he had never
been in Dallas.

Cummings, however, claimed to know otherwise. He had been a part-
time Dallas cab driver from January 11th, 1963 to March 15th of that
year. Sometime during this period Cummings was driving his cab when
he took a man from the Dallas bus station to suburban Irving. The
passenger, said Cummings, was Lee Harvey Oswald. Cummings claimed
to have remembered this man because both he and his passenger were
ex-Marines, and they talked about the service. Cummings claimed that
Oswald stated before the trip that he did not have enough money for
the fare, but that Cummings took him anyway.

A few weeks later, Cummings claimed to have picked up three men
on a Dallas street and was told to take them to the Carrousel Club of
Jack Ruby. Cummings recognized one of the men as Oswald from the
previous trip and they again spoke about the Marine Corps. The second
of the three he could not identify at all, but the unusual face of the
third man caused Cummings to keep glancing at him in the rear view
mirror. He noticed a wig and false eyelashes. Cummings had little
trouble in identifying No. 3 as David Ferrie.

*   *   *

There was Clyde Limbaugh, who claimed to have worked for Jack
Ruby as a singer in one of Ruby's nightclubs in 1961, 1962, and 1963.
He showed up in Garrison's office on March 7th. He claimed to have
evidence that Ruby had been part of a conspiracy, but was chased away
by Gurvich, who claimed he was totally unreliable.

*   *   *

Howard Rice Knight from California claimed to be a reincarnation of
Julius Caesar. He wore a red toga to prove it. He also claimed to have
been offered $10,000 by Jack Ruby to assist in the final plans for the
assassination with Oswald, Ferrie, and Shaw. He was brought to New
Orleans for questioning. His tab for travel and a four-day stay in the
Crescent City was picked up by the District Attorney's Office.

*   *   *

There was Arthur Strout, a 26-year-old Boston dishwasher, who wrote to Garrison claiming to have a photograph showing himself with Oswald, Jack Ruby, Perry Russo, and two other men, made in Ruby's Dallas nightclub a month before Kennedy was killed. Garrison's office purchased a one-way airline ticket for Strout providing transportation for him from Boston to New Orleans in late March. Strout received the ticket, but never showed up in Garrison's office. His whereabouts were a mystery for a few days until he reappeared in his home town, Auburn, Maine, and acknowledged: "There's no photograph . . . and I never was in Dallas."

Why had he said that he had? "I had been drinking when I called Mr. Garrison's office. I don't want to call Mr. Garrison myself, but I'd like him to know that I've changed my mind about the whole thing and have nothing to testify about."

This did not come as news. Garrison's office had already decided to drop him as a witness after Strout's father had claimed: "There was no photograph. There never was one. Arthur would say that he was with John Wilkes Booth at Lincoln's assassination if he thought he could get publicity out of it."

*   *   *

They came in a never-ending stream. Some were volunteers; some were quite reluctant. Many were subpoenaed from outside of the state. Some resisted appearance; others meekly complied.

And the subpoenas showered like confetti. One went to Allen Dulles, former head of the C.I.A. One went to Life magazine ordering production of the Zapruder film, a home movie of the assassination fortuitously taken by Abraham Zapruder. One went to Mrs. Ruth Paine, former landlady of the Oswalds' in Irving, Texas. One went to Marina Oswald herself, now Mrs. Marina Porter.

Following Marina's appearance before the Grand Jury, a Garrison assistant termed her testimony "very helpful." Asked by a reporter if she felt she had furnished any information of value, Marina replied in one word: "No."

Subpoenas went to many whose possible knowledge about any of the events surrounding the assassination was most difficult to discern—often to the witnesses themselves.

One of those complying with Garrison's subpoena issued under the Uniform Attendance Act was Kerry W. Thornley of South Tampa, Florida, a former Marine Corps buddy of Oswald's. Garrison insisted,

Thornley's denial to the contrary, that Thornley had known Oswald in New Orleans in 1963. Thornley appeared and submitted to questioning and was charged with perjury for his pains.

A man named Edgar Eugene Bradley found himself charged one day with conspiracy to assassinate Kennedy. This was puzzling as he had been living and working in North Hollywood, California, since 1962 and had never lived in New Orleans. Actual basis for the charge was a letter from a resident of Van Nuys, California, repeating reports of suspicious activity.

Many wondered, however, if he had not been mistaken for a Leslie Norman Bradley, who had worked as a flight instructor in 1962 at the New Orleans Lakefront Airport. Further, Leslie Bradley, now residing in Miami, had once been imprisoned in Cuba for anti-Castro activity.

There does not appear to be any reason, however, to believe that he knows any more about the assassination than the Edgar Eugene Bradley charged by Garrison. In the fall of 1968, Governor Reagan of California refused extradition.

Two men in New Orleans were subpoenaed for reasons totally unknown except that the name of both men was Oswald.

The *Washington Post* described this as a "rather peculiar way to run an investigation." Just think what might have happened, said the *Post*, "if the District Attorney of New York had called Bud Costello to ask about Frank's activities? Or if the marshals of the old west had called Henry and William James to ask about Jesse?"

"The field for Mr. Garrison is unlimited," continued the *Post*. "After he finishes with all the Oswalds in New Orleans, he can move his show elsewhere. And, of course, he can call all those people named Ruby. There must be enough Oswalds and Rubys in the country to keep Mr. Garrison's investigation going for some time, maybe enough to last through the next election.

"We hope Mr. Garrison is enjoying the show he is supervising. Nobody else is."

Least of all Clay Shaw. Neither he nor his attorneys ever knew quite when or from where the next witness was coming who might link Shaw with Oswald, Ruby, or Ferrie, or with any two or all three of them. Each one had to be investigated and the story disproved—if possible. When the Reverend Clyde Johnson placed Jack Ruby in a hotel room in Baton Rouge in early September, 1963, Shaw's attorneys journeyed to Dallas seeking evidence to disprove Ruby's absence from Texas during that period. The task was rendered considerably more difficult by the Reverend's inability to recall the exact date of the alleged meeting. When Mr. Norton from Vancouver placed Oswald at a hotel in Mexico

City during a certain period, evidence as to Oswald's whereabouts during that period had to be ferreted out.

And it all cost money. It may not have been entirely true, as the *Post* concluded, that no one besides Garrison was enjoying the show. But certainly Shaw was not. Unless he enjoyed being slowly, but inexorably, financially gutted.

16

WITH THE ADVENT OF THE UNEX-
pectedly thorough coverage by the national and international press and
TV in the early stages of the investigation, the realization came to
Garrison that he was now facing an audience far larger than that of his
earlier career. He was speaking now not merely to the citizens of New
Orleans or even Louisiana. His audience was international. He was no
longer exposing sinister influences among the New Orleans Police Department, the State Legislature, or the Judges of the Criminal Court.
He was now faced with the challenge of exposing darker and more
dangerous conspiracies in the agencies and high offices of the United
States Government. Garrison intended to do his duty by the people of
the United States just as faithfully as he had by the citizenry of New
Orleans and Louisiana.

Any doubts as to his intentions or resolve must certainly have been
dispelled shortly after the preliminary hearing in mid-March. After
Shaw's indictment was allotted to Judge Edward Haggerty, Jr., the
Judge promptly ordered both the prosecution and defense in the case to
refrain from making public statements about the case.

> The canons of professional ethics must be used to prevent
> the flow of prejudicial pre-trial publicity from members of
> the Bar. This includes the prosecution, as well as defense.
> . . .

Garrison seemed wryly amused. "The Judge was just making a suggestion when he handed out the guidelines. The District Attorney can
make any statement he wishes," was Garrison's response to the Judge's
orders.

Nonetheless, all was quiet for approximately six weeks following the
hearing, though Garrison's theory that the "conspiracy" included Central Intelligence Agency involvement was widely rumored and was the
subject of news articles by reporters friendly to Garrison. The supposed
involvement of the C.I.A. could also be gleaned from many aspects of
the court proceedings of the several defendants.

The first public blast against the supersecret intelligence agency,
which, by official policy, makes no public statements, comments, affirm-
ances, or denials, came in early May. Following news stories speculating
that Garrison claimed to have proof that Oswald had been acting as an
undercover agent for that organization, the D.A. ventured forth with a
relatively mild attack. He challenged the C.I.A. to produce what he said
was an important photograph of Oswald which had been suppressed for
more than three years. The C.I.A. had, the District Attorney claimed,
produced a "fake photograph" when the Warren Commission asked for
a picture of Oswald and a Cuban companion leaving the Cuban
Embassy in Mexico. "It is perfectly obvious that the reason the true
picture of Oswald and his companion was withheld and a fake picture
substituted was because one or both of these men were working for
agencies of the United States Government here in the summer of
1963," said Garrison.

It is difficult to argue with anything that is "perfectly obvious."

The next day came harder blows. The C.I.A. and the Federal Bureau
of Investigation cooperated in concealing the facts behind the assassination from the Warren Commission and the American public, said Garrison, and he was going to ask for a Senate investigation. He had learned
the truth behind the assassination, and the C.I.A. had known all along
that the Commission's report was untrue. They had deliberately duped
the Commission by flooding it with a "gush of irrelevant information in
order to obscure the truth."

> Oswald's Fair Play for Cuba actions in New Orleans consti-
> tuted a transparent sham. These actions were designed as a
> cover while he was in fact engaged in no Communist activity
> whatever.

> His associations here were exclusively—not merely fre-
> quently, but exclusively—with persons whose political orien-
> tation was anti-Castro, all of whom were plainly connected
> with federal agencies here.
>
> . . . These activities were carried out with the full knowl-
> edge and consent of the C.I.A. and the F.B.I.

Then, Garrison's ineluctable conclusion:

> They would positively—not just probably—know of Os-
> wald's total involvement with those individuals engaged in
> anti-Castro planning and operations.

> And yet they remained silent while evidence was presented
> to the Warren Commission, to the American people and to
> the world that this man was an individual engaged in mean-
> ingless, lonesome activities—that he was a freelance Com-
> munist who had no connections, no case agents or compan-
> ions. . . . And they would know well that when Lee Oswald
> was in Dealey Plaza in Dallas he was not alone.

Garrison next brought to light an insidious plot to thwart his investigation. Such a problem was not new to him, however. He had been
confronted with a similar problem with the Judges of the Criminal
Court who tried to block his investigation into organized vice and he
would expose this combination of federal agencies as surely as he had the
previous efforts of the Judges:

> The plain fact is that our federal intelligence agencies are
> implacably determined to do whatever is necessary to block
> any further inquiry into the facts of the assassination.

> The arrogant totalitarian efforts of these federal agencies to
> obstruct the discovery of the truth is a matter which I intend
> to bring to light when we have finished doing the job they
> should have done.

At this juncture the Warren Commission was not yet suspected of
having been members of the conspiracy. They were innocent dupes,
according to Garrison. This relatively tolerant view of the Commission
was not to last, however.

Garrison subpoenaed an F.B.I. agent, Regis Kennedy, who had investigated Oswald's New Orleans background, and a former agent,
Warren DeBrueys. United States Attorney Louis LeCour moved to

quash the subpoena on grounds of executive privilege. Garrison's reply
to the move was prompt:

> Obviously, what has happened is that the federal agents
> involved are taking the Fifth Amendment. This isn't going
> to stop our investigation. There's no way in the world they
> can stop it. All they can do is slow it down.

He also subpoenaed from C.I.A. Director Richard Helms a "true
photograph" of Lee Harvey Oswald and a "burly Cuban" that he had
previously alluded to. Nothing more was heard of the subpoena.

On May 11th Garrison made the first of many charges that the
Central Intelligence Agency was paying lawyers who represented key
figures in his investigation.

> Naturally they are paying lawyers involved. There's no ques-
> tion about that.

Again, the difficulty of quarreling with a statement about which there
was no question, was considerable. Garrison explained the basis for his
positive conclusion: "We have reason to believe that Mr. Klein (attorney for Alvin Beauboeuf) has recently been to Washington, D.C."

"We know that Plotkin (attorney for Gordon Novel) has been receiving money, if only through an intermediary, from the C.I.A.," continued the D.A.

Both Plotkin and Klein immediately denied the statements. Nonetheless, Garrison continued to repeat these accusations long after Klein and
Plotkin tired of denying them.

Garrison also pointed to other evidence establishing irrefutably his
claim of C.I.A. financing of lawyers for assassination figures:

> We know that Sandra Moffett up in Iowa, who has no
> money, is represented by the Chairman of the Thirteen State
> Regional Democratic Organization. There's no question in
> our minds what's happening. This is because we're making
> progress. If we weren't you'd hear nothing but silence.

*   *   *

On May 13th Garrison's assistants filed in open Court a response to
the request by Shaw's lawyers to have returned to Shaw much of the
property seized from him on the day of his arrest, March 1st. The
answer alleged that a certain notebook taken from Shaw was vital evi-

dence in that Garrison had deciphered a coded telephone number in the book, which number was identical to one contained in a notebook belonging to Lee Harvey Oswald.

The memorandum in Shaw's notes reads: "Lee Odom, P.O. Box 19106, Dallas, Texas." In Lee Harvey Oswald's notebook was a notation containing two characters which did not appear to be English characters at all, and which experts claimed to be Russian letters. They admittedly possessed some similarity to Old English printing of "P" and "O" followed by the numbers 19106. The number, Garrison explained was, in coded form, the unpublished 1963 telephone number of Jack Ruby, the killer of Lee Harvey Oswald. How did Garrison convert the "P.O. 19106" to the number he claimed was Ruby's unpublished number, WH (WHitehall) 1-5601? It was simple. He personally accomplished the decoding process himself.

First, he explained, it was necessary to unscramble the numbers by selecting the nearest digit, then the farthest digit, then the next nearest digit, then the next farthest digit, and so on. When the process of unscrambling is applied to 19106, the number obtained is 16901. However, Oswald always added a standard "outside" number, Garrison said. Oswald invariably added 4900 or 1300. Said the D.A.

> In this connection, it is of some interest to note that Lee Oswald lived in the 4900 block of Magazine and Clay Shaw lived in the 1300 block of Dauphine.

It was further explained that when 1300 was subtracted from the unscrambled number, 16901, the result was 15601.

The letters P.O. standing for Post Office can be converted to the letters of the telephone exchange WH for Whitehall by using the telephone dial. The numbers corresponding to P and O on the dial are 7 and 6. They add up to 13. The only other two numbers on the dial that add up to 13 are 9 and 4, said Garrison, conveniently forgetting 8 and 5. The letters corresponding to 9 and 4 are WH standing for Whitehall.

Earl Ruby, brother of Jack Ruby, claimed to reporters that he was certain that his brother never had an unlisted telephone number. "I didn't know anything about such a listing and I believe he would have told me," he claimed. Shaw's lawyers, admitting that it was all very interesting, pointed out that any number could be converted to any other number using that system. It was undoubtedly coincidental that the series of numbers in Oswald's book and Shaw's were the same, but the fact remained, insisted the defense, that P.O. Box 19106, Dallas, Texas was an address left by Lee Odom, a real person, who visited Shaw in 1966 while in New Orleans trying to promote a bullfight in the city. Odom was quickly located in Dallas and he confirmed that while in New Orleans he stayed at the Roosevelt Hotel and that he inquired of the manager of the hotel as to whom he should see about finding a place for a bullfight. The manager of the hotel suggested Shaw so, said Odom, he contacted Mr. Shaw. Further, according to Odom, Shaw came to the hotel and the two talked for about twenty minutes and Shaw gave Odom his card. Odom gave Shaw his address, which was P.O. Box 19106, Dallas, Texas. "The bullfight didn't come off and we never communicated again—that's all there was to it." Odom said.

People just didn't understand. "We are well aware there is a Mr. Lee Odom," said Garrison. "The fact that there is a real Lee Odom, however, is not the point. The point is that Clay Shaw and Lee Oswald have the same Post Office box number in their address books and this was, in coded form, the unpublished phone number of Jack Ruby in 1963."

Dallas postal authorities confirmed that the box had not come into existence until 1965 and Odom exhibited evidence of his acquisition of the box that year. But "the fact that someone acquired the post office box when it came into existence in late 1965 does not change the oddity of that circumstance at all," said Garrison.

Mr. Odom was beginning to look mighty suspicious. "We are very interested in knowing who introduced Mr. Odom to Mr. Shaw, how many bullfights Mr. Odom has actually produced, and a few other things. We are particularly interested in clarifying now why there is also coded in Lee Oswald's address book the local phone number of the Central Intelligence Agency.

> Since it is obvious that it is no longer possible to get the truth in any form from officials of the C.I.A. agency in Washington no matter how highly placed, we are looking forward to talking to this businessman from Irving, Texas, about some of these coincidences.

Odom was not at all reluctant to talk to anyone about his meeting with Shaw. He called Garrison collect and told him what he had told the reporters. Garrison did ask Odom some questions. According to Odom, Garrison wanted to know his address and next of kin "in case something happened to me, but I wouldn't tell him." Added Odom: "He also told me he didn't want me to leave Irving."

Odom, in fact, had no intention of leaving Irving. He told reporters: "This is where I'm settled with my wife and two children . . . I don't have any idea about why the same number appeared in Oswald's notebook." Further, said Odom, he never knew Oswald.

*   *   *

All was quiet for a few days and then Garrison gave the public a real glimpse of the "truth" behind the assassination:

> The President was killed by a fatal bullet that was fired from the front. That was not the only time he was hit from the front. There was a cross-fire situation set up which involved at least two pairs of men in the front—apparently two men behind a stone wall and two behind a picket fence, which is a little bit back of the stone wall.
>
> The role of the second man in each case was to pick up the actual cartridges taken on the bounce, so to speak, so that the cartridges could be disposed of as quickly as the guns, which were apparently tossed in the back of cars. There were cars parked immediately behind.
>
> In addition to those men in front, they had at least one man in the back who was shooting, although it is becoming increasingly apparent that he was not shooting from the sixth floor of the book depository.
>
> We have located one other person who was involved in the operation. He was one of the adventurers who was involved in anti-Castro activities, who was not using a gun, but who was engaged in a row in Dealey Plaza in order to aid those who had guns. You had, in effect, a group of men operating as a guerrilla team. It was a precision operation and was carried out very coolly and with a lot of coordination.

Garrison had thus explained why there were no cartridges found. Spent cartridges were picked up by the "second man." What about the fact that no spent pellets were discovered that would support such a theory? There was a reason for that, too:

> It appears they used frangible bullets. They are forbidden by the Geneva Treaty, but are the kind of bullets that are quite often used—or would be used—for an assassination project by intelligence forces or forces employed by an intelligence agency, because there is assurance, even beforehand, that there will be no bullets, no slugs remaining, with any of the land marks of the guns to help authorities identify the guns. Frangible bullets explode into little pieces.

According to firearms experts, however, the frangible bullets to which Garrison referred are soft, compressed graphite bullets used for target practice and are not capable of piercing more than a tin can at a maximum of fifty yards. Insofar as is known, no bullets combine the characteristics necessary to shatter upon impact and to leave a large gaping wound and much internal damage. Garrison's inspiration for the frangible bullet theory, however, was unshakeable. It had been based on an anonymous letter, and the statements of firearms experts did not even merit an answer.

Did Lee Harvey Oswald take part in the actual assassination:

> There is no question at all about the fact that Lee Harvey Oswald did not fire a shot there.

It had been pointed out to Garrison that a slug had been removed from one of the two stretchers bearing Kennedy and the wounded Governor Connally at Parkland Hospital in Dallas immediately following the assassination and that the slug was proven to have been fired from Oswald's rifle. Garrison's answer: It was planted by the conspirators. "It was dropped on one of the cots at the hospital," said Garrison.

This had been advanced as a theory by Lane and Popkin, among others. Garrison claimed that he knew this "without any question."

How did the assassins escape without a trace after the killing? The D.A. did not know exactly how they escaped, but

> we know they left the scene in cars . . . and headed in all different directions.

Who were they?

> It's quite obvious that the C.I.A. knew who they were because they had previously been C.I.A. employees.

The C.I.A., as usual, was silent. It has remained silent throughout.

A few days later on a local telecast he repeated his charge that the C.I.A. was deliberately concealing evidence. If Richard Helms, the C.I.A. Director, were in his jurisdiction, Garrison assured his audience, he would not hesitate to charge him criminally. Few doubted that he would.

Appearing before a nationwide television audience on "Issues and Answers" aired by the American Broadcasting Company, Garrison was asked how he would judge himself if, after all, he failed to prove his allegations. Garrison retorted that the question would not arise because "we have already proved it and we have the evidence." However, said Garrison, "hypothetically" if he were to fail, his evaluation would be:

At least I have made an attempt to find out the truth and so far as known, this is the first objective investigation by any official agency in the assassination.

* * *

On June 19th NBC ran its hour-long documentary on Garrison's investigation. A few days later William Gurvich, Garrison's top investigator, in connection with his assassination probe broke publicly with Garrison claiming that there was "no basis in fact and no material evidence in Garrison's case for an assassination plot." Said Gurvich to newsmen:

". . . There's nothing to it."

He urged that the Shaw case be dropped and that the entire situation be reevaluated. "Up to now," he said, the "standard and professional method of criminal investigation was not always used in all phases of this investigation."

It was clear that the conspiracy was widening. Said Garrison:

There will continue to be developments—all of them mysteriously coordinated—which are designed to create the idea that our investigation should be stopped immediately, if not sooner.

A tremendous amount of federal power is being brought to bear on anyone connected with our investigation. . . . It is obvious that the official Washington attitude is that our inquiry must be stopped at all costs. . . . As far as I'm concerned, there is not enough money in the United States Treasury and there is not enough printers' ink in this country to keep us from developing the facts about the murder of President Kennedy.

Garrison made clear the connection between the NBC program and the power of the United States Government:

It helps to clarify the role of the federal government in obstructing the investigation, if it is kept in mind that the NBC is owned by RCA—the Radio Corporation of America. RCA is one of the top ten corporations with regard to defense contracts with the federal government.

Further, said Garrison, Gurvich had only been given limited information about the investigation and had really only been used as a photographer and chauffeur. Garrison issued another voluminous blast now linking Gurvich to the growing apparatus aligned against him:

> I am sure that almost everyone will recognize Mr. Gurvich's statements as the latest move from the eastern headquarters of the establishment to attempt to discredit our investigation into the true facts of President Kennedy's assassination. I presume that when he [Gurvich] says that the members of my staff do not have a professional approach that he means they cannot be bought.
> If that is the case, I am glad that they are amateurs and I am confident that they will remain that way.
> It is because they are amateurs and because there is not enough money or power in this country to corrupt them that we are going to work to expose the entire truth of the assassination to the people of this country.

*   *   *

On June 22nd Garrison told newsmen for a Nashville newspaper that Kennedy had been killed by a fourteen-man team of Cuban guerrillas who trained secretly in St. Tammany Parish in the summer of 1963. He also claimed that David Ferrie had been connected "in some capacity" with the guerrillas. The men he was now looking for, Garrison said, were "definitely among the Cuban trainees."

But apparently Manuel Garcia Gonzales and the others had still eluded him.

*   *   *

Garrison's next revelation concerning the assassination involved the death of Officer J. D. Tippit of the Dallas police force. Contrary to the findings of the Warren Commission, Tippit was not killed by Oswald. The death of Patrolman Tippit, said the D.A., was planned by the assassins as a goad to infuriate other members of the police force so that they would shoot Oswald on sight rather than take him prisoner." Speaking on a CBS news broadcast, he was interviewed by Mike Wallace:

> It's well known that police officers react violently to the murder of a police officer. All they [the conspirators] did

was arrange for an officer to be sent out to Tenth Street and when Officer Tippit arrived there he was murdered, with no other reason than that. . . . After he was murdered, Oswald was pointed to sitting in the back of the Texas Theatre where he had been told to wait, obviously.

According to Garrison, the plan was that a police unit would be dispatched to the theatre and upon finding Oswald armed, Oswald, the patsy, would be shot on the spot thus eliminating the possibility of his being interrogated. Why, then, was Oswald not shot on the spot?

But the Dallas police, apparently—at least the investigating officers—had more humanity in them than the planners had in mind, and this is the first point at which the plan did not work completely. . . . So Oswald was not killed there. He was arrested. This left a problem because if Lee Oswald stayed alive long enough, obviously, he would name names and talk about this thing that he had been drawn into. It was necessary to kill him.

On July 15th Garrison was afforded the network facilities of NBC for a half-hour response to its June 19th telecast. He consumed but twenty-two minutes of the response. He said little that was new:

I'm going to talk to you about truths and about fairy tales, about justice and about injustice.

In the months to follow you are going to learn that many of the things which some of the major news agencies have been telling you are untrue.

You are going to learn that although you are citizens of the United States, information concerning the cause of the death of your President has been withheld from you. . . . Personally, I don't want to be calm about the assassination of John F. Kennedy. I don't want to be calm about a President of my country being shot down in the streets and I don't want to be calm about the fact that for reasons of public policy, or national security, or any other phony reason the true facts have been withheld from the people of this country. . . . I want to assure you that as long as I am alive no one is going to stop me from seeing that you obtain the full truth, nothing less than the full truth, and no fairy tales.

Garrison had lost none of his forensic ability. It had, if anything, improved with age. Though containing little of substance, the address was delivered in the best Garrison manner, which is good indeed.

On September 5th Chief Justice Earl Warren was interviewed in Tokyo where he was vacationing. In response to questions by reporters he stated that he had "seen absolutely nothing that conflicts with the Warren Commission Report." Asked specifically about Garrison's investigation, Warren said: "I've heard that he claims to have such information, but I haven't seen any."

Garrison's lengthy press release followed promptly. The announcement, Garrison said, "should be recognized for what it is, heavy artillery whistling in from Tokyo means that everything is in place, all the infantry is lined up and the lull is over." Continued Garrison: "It is a good sign that the big push is on. Judging from the careful coordination which the establishment showed in its last offensive against the case, it is safe to expect that the other elements of the federal government and the national press will now follow up with a new effort to discredit the case and the prosecution."

Continued Garrison:

> Finding out what happened in Dealey Plaza and why it happened was not that hard. The hard part is keeping elements of the federal government and great news agencies from being successful in this systematic effort to prejudice potential jurors in advance of the trial. It is a little disconcerting to find the Chief Justice of the United States on his hands and knees, trying to tie some sticks of dynamite to the case. However, the Chief Justice is a practical man and I expect he knows what he is doing.

*   *   *

September was a good month for Garrison. The October issue of *Playboy* magazine appearing early that month contained a lengthy interview in which Garrison expounded in his usual convincing style. He appeared on no less than four radio and television interviews in New York during the week of September 22nd. His freewheeling blasts at the federal apparatus and the broad sweep of his conspiracy theory undoubtedly reached their zenith.

Appearing on Station WGLI, Babylon, Long Island, on September 22nd, Garrison claimed that upon finally reading the Warren Commission Report in November of 1966 he found out that the conclusion of the lone assassin was "totally untrue, and it was not an objective, honest inquiry. It was, in effect, a carefully organized concealment of the facts." The radio interview continued:

In other words, the lone assassin theory, which the Warren Commission developed, is a complete fraud. This is why you now have elements of the United States Government, and a large part of the news establishments of the United States doing everything it can, literally desperately, to try and conceal whatever news comes from New Orleans about this, because the United States Government has in this case perpetrated a major fraud.

Garrison had gone easy on the Warren Commission long enough. "Well, was this done purposely?" asked the interviewer.
Said Garrison:

Yes, of course. The main objective was to fool the people of the United States and, I presume, the rest of the world, into thinking that this was a lone assassin. . . .

Then, the first hint of a new wrinkle:

. . . The objective was to keep the people of this country thinking that they were still living in the best of all possible worlds; that they were not living in a world in which the big business, Texas style, financed the assassination, as it did; in which the right wing—paramilitary right-wing elements which were financed and encouraged in their training and given weapons by the Central Intelligence Agency was involved.

Were members of the Dallas Police Department involved?

Oh, yes, it couldn't have been done effectively without it. They were involved—some of them were involved at Dealey Plaza, others in the Oak Cliff operation, in connection with covering up the killing of officer Tippit. . . .

Just as in the New Orleans Police Department, a majority of the Dallas police officers were good officers, according to Garrison. Not all of the Dallas police force was involved in the assassination any more than all of the New Orleans Police Department was involved in the systematic brutalizing of prisoners.

. . . But you have within the Dallas police force, you have an element, essentially the Minute Man element, the extreme militant right-wing group, which is actively involved in assassination.

The assassination plot did not begin in New Orleans, according to Garrison, it began in Texas.

> . . . An element of big business in Dallas, Texas, big business was involved. Oil money helped finance it. There's all kinds of money coming down to finance the assassination. . . .
>
> . . . the Dallas individuals, this portion of the Dallas establishment of oil millionaires, Minute Men, and so forth, and a handful of White Russians who got control of Oswald actually started this as early as 1962. The point of moving Oswald to Dallas was really—I mean to New Orleans—was really to de-Dallasize him so that he would become an individual not from Dallas.

"De-Dallasize" now took its place in the vocabulary along with "objectify."

> . . . Employees of the Central Intelligence Agency were keeping control of Oswald and were persuading that he was still engaged in C.I.A. work, as he was in Russia.
>
> And so he was brought to New Orleans to de-Dallasize him, so that when the time came, he would not be a Dallas man.

Garrison was hamstrung in the investigation to an extent, as his jurisdiction was limited to New Orleans. New Orleans was "simply a corner of the tapestry":

> But the main part is still in Dallas. I doubt that it will ever be investigated in Dallas because of the fantastic financial power of the elements of the establishment that are involved. You can't become head of the police force, and you can't become a major figure in law enforcement in Dallas without the approval of some of these very individuals who sponsored the assassination.

Garrison's charges were certainly serious, said the interviewer. Had anyone tried to stop him from making statements such as these?

> Well, they can't directly try and stop me from making statements. They have a technical problem there because one of their objectives is to try and make this appear to be, again, the best of all possible worlds. But everything that can be

done behind the scenes is being done. . . . My phones have been monitored for a long time. There's obviously a mail check through the Post Office about inspection of mail. . . . And you have the telephone company and you have a picture of your friendly telephone man taking a little boy across the street, or something, but in reality, the telephone company in a case like this becomes an extension of the United States Government, of what is now a super state. . . . The federal government does not have to tap your phone. They don't tap our phones, they monitor them. In other words, in our case, for example, our lines, the private lines, office and home of every individual connected with this case, every key witness, is—is just thrown by attaching a connection between two terminals at the phone company into a cable that goes into a federal monitoring room. So it's all monitored. This became obvious to us early.

How could Garrison operate under such conditions?

With regard to sensitive matters, new areas, say the discovery of Oswald and Ruby in another town where it was not generally known they were together . . . and we don't want it to go straight to the defendant because there's no doubt in our minds that the federal government gives whatever information it has straight to the defendant because its position is to completely protect the assassins. . . . Then we have to speak in generalities or hold off and talk face to face.

In fact, that is the reason that it has been taking so long to get the Shaw case to trial. The defense and "these elements of the federal government are coordinating pretty effectively." The elements of the Federal Government that Garrison was referring to were "Newsweek, the Washington Post, the Los Angeles Times, the National Broadcasting Company, and the Columbia Broadcasting System."

As for Oswald, he never killed anybody in his life. He was in Russia in behalf of the United States Government looking to see if U-2's left vapor trails in their high altitude flights over that country.

Exactly how Garrison came to this conclusion cannot be known for certain. However, one of many classified documents in the National Archives is entitled "Oswald's Access to Classified Information about the U-2." According to Oswald's Marine Corps buddy, Kerry W. Thornley, Oswald was stationed near a U-2 base in the continental United States. After his defection to Russia, undoubtedly his knowledge of or access to any information concerning U-2's became the subject of government interest. Nonetheless, Garrison indicated on a number of occasions that he considered the existence of such a file very sinister.

He remained firm in his conviction as to Oswald's innocence. Oswald never killed Tippit or the President and there was no question about it. ". . . That's not even close, that's not even close," he emphasized.

Did Garrison feel that all of this could be proved? Said Garrison:

> It has been proved. We've won this fight. It's a communica-
> tion problem now. . . . The fraud which was perpetrated by
> the United States Government is exposed; there's no question
> about it.

It went on and on. Garrison has never been fond of brevity:

> . . . What are you going to do when there are individuals in
> law enforcement in Dallas who are deeply involved in the
> assassination? When they are protected by a handful of
> millionaires who helped sponsor the thing in the name of
> patriotism. . . .
> The assassination's been ratified by the United States; they
> accepted it.
> . . . The men in the jurisdiction where it happened and
> where it really originated are owned, controlled by indi-
> viduals who sponsored it and they are also protected by the
> United States Government.
> . . . When we finish doing everything we can to communi-
> cate to this country the fantastic fraud that has been accom-
> plished in the name of the United States Government, with
> the gold eagle stamped on it, then I'm interested in going
> back into private practice. And Washington? I couldn't be
> less interested, especially with what I know now about
> Washington.

Garrison dwelt at length on the supposed inordinate number of deaths of people "connected" with the assassination. In most cases the connection is somewhat tenuous. Garrison spoke of a former nightclub performer for Jack Ruby, one Nancy Mooney. According to Garrison, she was arrested on a technicality, jailed, and two hours later found

hanged with her toreador pants. Garrison stated that it was a murder.
Does this imply that she was murdered by the Dallas police?

> . . . Individuals of the Dallas police force helped kill Jack
> Kennedy. Why should they hesitate with Nancy Mooney?
> . . . It is clear that individuals on the Dallas police force
> were involved in the assassination and involved in the con-
> tinuing protection of the assassins and were involved in
> things like this.

He finally concluded:

> There's something wrong with this country and it's an awful
> lot later than we think and I hope that they can see through
> the facade, and the brainwashing and the protection of the
> establishment lie which is accomplished by the *Washington
> Post* and *Newsweek* and the *New York Times* and the *Los
> Angeles Times* and NBC and all these other propaganda
> machines and try to get to the truth before it's too late.
> There's something wrong with our country.

The concluding flourish was eloquent, though nowhere near so much
so as the concluding passage of the *Playboy* magazine interview:

> As long as the men who shot John Kennedy to death in
> Dallas are walking the streets of America, I will continue this
> investigation. I have no regrets about initiating it and I have
> no regrets about carrying it on to its conclusion. If it takes
> me 30 years to nail every one of the assassins, then I will
> continue this investigation for 30 years. I owe that not only
> to Jack Kennedy, but to my country.

*   *   *

On the same day as the WGLI interview in Babylon, Garrison had
appeared on a noon telecast in New York City on Station WOR-TV.
The theme was the same though a few matters, or new variations, were
injected:

> The fatal shot came from the grassy knoll vicinity, the stone
> wall area. . . . There's no question about that. . . . There's
> no question in the minds of any objective observer; I know
> there's no question in the mind of any serious student of the
> assassination. . . . It's not even close.

The C.I.A. and other government agencies no longer have to tap your phone, they monitor it through the courtesy of your friendly local telephone company.

Does Garrison's office pay money to witnesses in investigations?

> Never, never . . . never. We do not operate that way. . . . But we don't have money to do that. Furthermore, I am strongly opposed to such things as wire tapping, to invasion of privacy, to abusing witnesses. We just don't do it. We do not record statements of people in our office, for example, without their permission.

As for the members of the Minute Men and Dallas police force and others in Dallas involved in the assassination, Garrison had the names of some of them. Lee Harvey Oswald, once again, Garrison repeated, had nothing to do with the assassination.

> Oswald did not shoot anybody on that day and that's completely demonstrable and it isn't even close.

The subject of Robert Kennedy came up. Walter Sheridan, the newsman responsible for the June 19th NBC telecast, was a former Justice Department investigator for Kennedy and the man primarily responsible for the investigations leading to the imprisonment of Teamster boss James Hoffa. Shortly after Garrison's bribery charge against Sheridan in early July, Kennedy had made a strong public statement in defense of his friend and former employee. According to Garrison, "Kennedy has without any question made a positive effort to stop the investigation and if he denies it here, he is a liar." Garrison continued:

> If he denies it he has to be . . . there's no question about it. . . . If he says he didn't, he's not telling you the truth. . . . Who was the Attorney General of the United States when this great fraud was perpetrated and the people of the United States were told it was a lone assassin?

The moderator suggested that this may just be a "loose charge." Garrison's spine bristled:

> What do you mean loose charge? I'm telling you what I know about, there's no question about that. . . . Of course, he's made an effort to stop this investigation.

The interview ended with a colloquy between the interviewer, John Wingate, and Garrison. According to Wingate, he felt that Garrison was either "all wrong, or all right."

Said Garrison:

> . . . You're going to find we're all right, John, and it won't even be close.

Repeated Wingate a moment later, "I really believe that. You've either got something or you've got nothing."

Replied Garrison: "That's a good way to put it. It's not even close."

*   *   *

Two days later Garrison appeared on a local ABC television affiliate in New York.

In the event there were any questions about Garrison's claim that the participation of the Dallas police in the plot preceded the actual assassination, it was cleared up in this interview. To a direct question as to whether they assisted before the fact or were merely accessories thereafter, Garrison replied:

> No, no, no, no, no, no. Before—before the fact. They were a part of the pre-existing structure before the fact and these particular police officers are individuals connected with the Minute Man organization.

As far as Garrison's possibly prejudicing his case by letting the Dallas police know that he was aware of their involvement:

> There's no question about it. Anything you do in this sort of activity has a plus and minus factor. . . . But . . . I'd have to wear two hats in this sort of situation because the case is not just of interest to people in New Orleans. I have to wear one as prosecutor, so you'll find me saying nothing about Mr. Shaw, whom we have to presume is innocent. On the other hand, because we have learned things that I think the country has a right to know, I try to publicize certain things that will let everybody in America know what happened. . . . There is our case against Shaw about which I make no public statements. There is the assassination as a whole, which I think is—is—has to be publicized, the true facts, in a general way so that the people of this country will understand what a fraud has been perpetrated on them. I can't keep silent when I know this.

There followed a vigorous exchange about Kennedy's involvement in the effort to torpedo Garrison's investigation. Asked one of the moderators: "Well, what you're saying, then, is that Senator Kennedy by not cooperating is, in effect, letting the murderers of his brother walk the streets."

Said Garrison: "Well, yes, that's a fair statement. Yes."

Why did not Garrison come up with specifics rather than generalities:

> One of my problems in trying to communicate about the case is that I cannot in fairness talk about the evidence before the trial. So I have a problem—I want to say, the Warren Commission is wrong. It is not even close. But I cannot talk about the Shaw case.

The interview concluded with the question as to whether Garrison was absolutely convinced that he was going to blow wide open the Warren Commission Report and say that it was absolutely false:

> We've already—it's already as dead as Humpty-Dumpty, and there's no way for it to survive. We do have the picture of how the President was killed. We do know the names of individuals involved and we will not lose any cases.

*   *   *

Garrison's final effort of his big week was an interview on the Mike Wallace "At Large" program, broadcast on a New York radio station. It was almost impossible to expand on his earlier performance, but he tried:

> The United States Government is a party to the fraud, has participated, in effect, in the biggest fix in the human race. . . . There are elements of the Dallas establishment that are deeply involved and some of the members of the White Russian community are part of it. Now, they had total control of Marina. And Marina said, in many cases, what she was supposed to say, and instructed to say. . . . The Minute Men—Minute Men, as individuals, are involved in the assassination. I might add that the central structure, the control down to the anti-Castro Latins who operated the operation, worked at the operational level in Dealey Plaza, from the insanely patriotic oil millionaires sponsoring this, the connecting link, really, the machinery which is making it work are the Minute Men elements of the Dallas police force.

And there was something new for this program, too.

> There were a number of men at Dealey Plaza, including
> radio communications, use of transistor radios, to tell when
> the parade was coming, at which point it was turning, the—
> to signal when the guns were to pick, be picked up, to indi-
> cate that the coast was clear. . . . It will be the establish-
> ment press's problem to try and readjust after we have con-
> victions, and after we continue to move forward. . . . We
> will be proved right, and it won't even be close. And I just
> wonder what they're going to say about it then.

*   *   *

By November Garrison decided that it was pointless to continue
attacking the underlings in the plot. Perhaps there was one in higher
office who masterminded the apparatus and, if so, he should not be
allowed to go unscathed.

The occasion of a major escalation in his attack on federal powers was
a convention of radio and television newsmen of Southern California in
the Los Angeles Century Plaza Hotel on November 16th. Garrison was
guest speaker. After picking apart the Warren Commission Report at
some length, Garrison homed in on his target for the evening. He
started the assault with a series of questions. After making reference to
the Tokyo remarks of Chief Justice Warren, Garrison asked:

> For whom was he performing a function? For whom was
> Ramsey Clark performing? Who is responsible for the con-
> tinuing obstruction of the first honest investigation that this
> country has had into the assassination? . . . Who appointed
> the Warren Commission? Who was aware that there was a
> C.I.A. problem and caused the seven-man Commission . . .
> to be weighted in advance by the defenders of the C.I.A.?

> Who appointed Ramsey Clark, who has done his best to
> torpedo the investigation of the case? Who controls the
> C.I.A.? Who controls the F.B.I.? Who controls the Archives
> where this evidence is locked up for so long that it is unlikely
> that there is anybody in this room that will be alive when it
> is released?

> This is really your property, and the property of the people in
> this country. Who has the arrogance and the brass to prevent
> the people of this country from seeing that evidence? Who,
> indeed?

Even the less astute among the audience must now have realized the answer to the questions, but the manner of Garrison's introduction of "the man who" was not at all anti-climatic:

> The one man who has profited most from the assassination— your friendly President!
> Lyndon Johnson.

Garrison had come a long way—from exposure of a lowly assistant district attorney in 1962 to the President of the United States—in five short years. He had been very patient, said Garrison, and had "leaned over backwards for months" while his phones had been monitored and the government had done everything it could to torpedo the investigation.

> . . . Because they know we stumbled on it, and I claim no virtue, we're not great investigators . . . But we did stumble on it, and we do know what happened and it won't even be close, there won't be any acquittals, if we can get these people to trial—if we can get them to trial. If we can prevent the U.S. Government from blowing up our case, or finding a way to remove me from office. . . .

Then back to the case against Johnson:

> Now, I don't say that President Johnson is involved in the assassination. I have no reason to know that he is, but I do think this: I do think the fact that he has profited from the assassination most, more than any other man, makes it imperative that he see that the evidence is released, so that we can know that he is not involved, rather than assuming. . . . Of course, I assume, that the President of the United States is not involved, but wouldn't it be nice to know it? Wouldn't it be nice to know if people who backed him for years in Texas are not involved. Of course, we'll assume it, but wouldn't it be nice to know that?

Following the speech, there were questions from the audience. The answers to several of them were interesting.

One member of the audience was interested in Garrison's phraseology to the effect that his office "stumbled" onto the solution to the mystery of the assassination. Explained Garrison:

> . . . What I meant was that we stumbled on to the case
> itself. If we had not got curious about the odd trip that
> David Ferrie made right into a thunderstorm all night to go
> ice skating in Houston, and the fact that he did not go ice
> skating there, if we had not seen that, and continued to be
> curious about that, we would not have found our way into
> the whole thing, because they had cutoffs and insulations of
> every possible kind.

Garrison continued by explaining exactly what part of the plot he
stumbled onto:

> We just happened to find ourselves in the intermediate area
> right below the level of the sponsors, financiers, and right
> above the level of what you might call the operating level—
> the people who pull the triggers.

One puzzled member of the audience wanted to know why Chief
Justice Warren, who has never been identified as a right-winger, would
conceal a right-wing plot? This was a tough one. Said Garrison: "I have
no idea. You would have to ask Chief Justice Warren."

One individual wanted to know what the President did to incur the
wrath of the right wing? Garrison, of course, had long since theorized
concerning Kennedy's rapprochement with the Communist world and
his ban on hostilities against Cuba. It appeared, however, that the
motivation of the Texas oil millionaires, whom Garrison had identified
as members of the plot, was nothing so glamorous:

> And as far as Texans are concerned, he left no doubt that he
> was headed directly for the 27½ percent deduction that is
> something very dear to some people in Texas.

*   *   *

In December Garrison had discovered new facts about the assassination. One was a photograph of an individual picking an object off the
ground as two Dallas policemen stood nearby. According to Garrison,
the man was obviously picking up a portion of a bullet. Garrison had
several observations about this photograph. "Obviously, he was a man
holding official investigator's status," said Garrison of the individual
supposedly picking up the bullet, "employed either by the Federal

Bureau of Investigation or the Secret Service." How did Garrison know
of his federal connection? "He had to be a federal agent," said Garrison
"because the Dallas policemen otherwise would not have allowed him to
touch the bullet."

How Garrison determined that the individual was picking up any
object at all, let alone a bullet, he never revealed, for the object is not
shown at all in the picture—merely the subject's hand as he reached to
the ground. Garrison, however, not only identified the object picked up
as a bullet, but as a .45 caliber bullet. Therefore, concluded Garrison,
inasmuch as a .45 caliber bullet could not be fired from Oswald's 6.5
Mannlicher-Carcano, the federal government "had to know ten minutes
after the assassination that Lee Oswald could not have done it."

Where had the .45 slug been fired from? Garrison showed pictures of
manhole covers leading into a drainage system. "The man who killed
President Kennedy fired a .45 caliber pistol," said Garrison, "and then
fled through the drainage system to another part of the city." To perplexed reporters, Garrison continued: "We went into the sewers one
morning in Dallas and we found that a man can fit into it very easily."
Garrison explained that a man standing in a manhole behind the picket
fence on the north side of the Plaza could easily see the occupants of
the car on Elm Street.

The source of this "knowledge" was a letter from a resident of Van
Nuys, California. It quoted an unnamed informant as having been
solicited in 1961 to use the storm-drain system in an unspecified city as
an escape route following a planned assassination of Kennedy. The
supposed solicitor was Edgar Eugene Bradley, whom, it will be recalled,
Garrison later charged with conspiracy.

Asked if he knew the name of the man who fired the .45 pistol
Garrison said: "We now have a number of names of individuals who
operated at the top level in the alleged assassination plot. I'd say four,
but I'd rather not speculate who was standing where."

It would, indeed, be unseemly of the D.A. to speculate.

One of the Dallas officials appearing in the photograph stated publicly that the object being picked up was a fragment of skull. "Of
course," said Garrison, "it would be denied that the bullet was a bullet.
If he did not, he would not be Deputy Sheriff any longer." The D.A.
used the same press conference to announce that "many witnesses who
have cooperated in the big lie by refusing to tell what they know about
the truth have been given jobs in defense plants. Our office has located
at least one participant in the assassination of President Kennedy who
now works at a military base for the United States Government."

*   *   *

In February, 1968, Garrison discovered still another facet of the conspiracy. Witnesses familiar with the C.I.A.'s operation in a "geographical corridor" from California through Texas and Louisiana, and eastward to Florida, were determined to be particularly important because "this office has succeeded in identifying the assassination of President Kennedy as an operation conducted by elements of the C.I.A. and virtually every key witness, defendant and potential defendant in the case has turned out to be originally from that geographic strip." Garrison concluded his remarks:

> This office intends to demonstrate . . . that the C.I.A. made a mistake in using Orleans Parish as a staging area for the assassination and that the federal government has made an equally bad mistake in attempting to conceal this fact and in attempting to obstruct justice in Orleans Parish.

*   *   *

In mid-February in 1968, United States Attorney General Ramsey Clark, appearing on a scheduled television interview, was asked about the Garrison investigation. He replied that he had "seen nothing new." Garrison's four-page press release followed quickly. It was not one of his more moderate utterances:

> . . . Once again he is attempting to influence potential jurors by testifying for the defendant in advance of the trial. This time his statement contains a grain of truth, which is a striking novelty for him. . . . Of course, they have seen nothing new. They knew all along that the Central Intelligence Agency was deeply involved in the assassination. That's why most of the men selected for the Commission were C.I.A. oriented. . . . The main function of the Warren Commission was to conceal the assassination of the President by an ambush of C.I.A. employees and they weighted the commission with men who had big names, but who could be counted on to help conceal the truth. . . . To the men who got control of the American government on November 22, 1963, everything we have developed is old stuff. They knew that the F.B.I. received advance notice of the assassination and did nothing to stop it. They knew that Jack Ruby had been identified as having driven one of the riflemen to the grassy knoll for the assassination. . . .

Garrison then turned all of his fire on the Attorney General who, Garrison said, was "doing his best to torpedo the case of the State of Louisiana. Apparently, it is felt in Washington that if the truth of President Kennedy's murder can be kept concealed, President Johnson's promotion to the Presidency will appear to be more legitimate."

> . . . Mr. Clark appears to be among those who think that evolution has left sovereignty (State's) behind. It was precisely this kind of thinking which caused officials of the federal government to feel so confident that they could conduct a false investigation into President Kennedy's death, follow it up with a fraudulent tableau depicting a solemn inquiry, meanwhile concealing the relevant and vital evidence. Their tacit assumption that they had absolute control over all of the territory involved was slightly erroneous.

Garrison emphasized that they certainly had no control over his jurisdiction:

> . . . He has no supervisory authority of any kind over a Louisiana prosecution. He is not even qualified to practice law here. . . . His sole accomplishment as a public official has been to make several modest contributions to the credibility gap. . . .

His final thrust at the Attorney General evoked memories of his earlier sallies concerning the Mayor and the Governor:

> . . . He is a political appointee who, if his father had not been on the Supreme Court, would probably be cleaning the street with a broom. This may qualify him to head a federal office in Washington, but it does not give him the right to interfere with justice in Louisiana.

*   *   *

On February 22nd following the charge of perjury against the hapless former Marine Corps buddy of Oswald, Kerry W. Thornley, Garrison revealed the full extent of Thornley's participation in the conspiracy. Garrison dismissed as lies Thornley's denial that he had ever known Oswald in New Orleans. He explained that "evidence indicates" that the two did meet in New Orleans in 1963 and that both were "part of the covert federal operation operating in New Orleans." He described

Thornley as the Warren Commission's "star witness concerning Oswald's early left-wing orientation."

However, since Oswald was never a Communist, Thornley was obviously a government dupe. Said Garrison:

> It is thought-provoking that the only one of Oswald's former Marine comrades who testified that he was a Marxist . . . is also the only one who was in personal association with Oswald in New Orleans in 1963. . . . Thornley's associates and pattern of activity plainly mark him as an employee, like Lee Oswald, from the Central Intelligence Agency.

*   *   *

There was a final ironic twist. In late February, 1968, Garrison held an interview with a Dutch newsman. He had to speak out in Europe, he said "because it is impossible in America." Said the redoubtable Garrison: "The United States press is controlled to such an extent by the C.I.A. that we can no longer say the truth. They throttled us."

*   *   *

So there it was. If the conspiracy was not now fully revealed, certainly those who had followed the D.A.'s public statements had good reason to feel confident that they had been shown a major part of it. And it was a big one:

Accessories included the F.B.I., the C.I.A., the Attorney General, the *Washington Post, Newsweek,* the *New York Times,* the *Los Angeles Times,* the National Broadcasting Company, the Columbia Broadcasting System, the President of the United States, the Warren Commission, and Robert Kennedy.

Principals to the former President's murder included David Ferrie, Jack Ruby, anti-Castro Cuban adventurers, a number of C.I.A. employees, part of the Dallas police force, some White Russians, psychotic Texas oil millionaires, *possibly* President Johnson—and Clay Shaw.

"Certainly," said many in New Orleans, "Garrison must have something." A man in his position would be stupid, indeed, to make such statements without some solid evidence—and Garrison was certainly not stupid. Overlooked by many who so reasoned was the clear possibility that the man was stark, raving mad.

17

CLAY SHAW WAS THE FORGOTTEN
man of the Garrison investigation. Two weeks after the preliminary
hearing, he held a press conference at the home of Ed Wegmann, one
of his attorneys. He spoke of his past, his philosophy, his politics, and
the effect of the pending charge on his daily life. There was no discussion of the charge itself. Then, for the next twenty-two months while
the battle raged about him, Shaw remained a silent, pervasive figure
lurking somewhere in the background of what became loosely referred
to, for lack of a better name, as "the Garrison thing." Precisely where in
the background, however, was sometimes difficult to determine—particularly for Shaw and his attorneys. For them the twenty-two months that
elapsed between the end of the preliminary hearing and the commencement of the trial was an ordeal of frustration, heightened by the D.A.'s
deft ambivalence on the connection between his September conspiracy
in New Orleans and the November assassination in Dallas.

As a public official, explained Garrison, he had a duty to inform the
American people of what he had uncovered of the nefarious activities of

the Federal Government. The public was entitled to be made aware of each of the ugly tentacles of the giant plot. What had this to do with Clay Shaw? He couldn't say, persisted the D.A. Clay Shaw was charged with a crime and it would be improper to say anything that might prejudice that case or the rights of Mr. Shaw.

Thus protected by an impregnable shield against all such queries concerning the link between Shaw and Garrison's mushrooming conspiracy, his barrage against all other facets of the gargantuan plot all but unnerved the defense lawyers. They had neither the wherewithal nor the motivation to defend the Warren Report, the mass media, or virtually the entire federal structure.

Nor could the D.A. be silenced by the strict guidelines laid down by the Trial Judge, Edward A. Haggerty, Jr., prohibiting all principals from commenting on the case—particularly, so long as Garrison did not reveal publicly his "case" against Shaw. The plea of the defense that the continuous crescendo went far to condition the public to the first element of a case against Shaw—the existence of a conspiracy—went unheeded by the Court. There could be "fifty conspiracies throughout the United States," intoned the Judge, "that had nothing to do with what happened in Dallas." Whether the conspiracy charged in his court culminated with the actual assassination need not be proved, explained Haggerty, therefore, what did it matter what was said about Dealey Plaza? Meanwhile, the deep and melodious voice of the District Attorney could be heard from New York and Califorina, promising still more shocking revelations concerning the events of Dealey Plaza at the impending trial of Clay Shaw. Subpoenas for witnesses and documents connected with the Dallas tragedy, including one to *Life* magazine for the home movie film of Abraham Zapruder, proclaimed the necessity of these documents and witnesses as part of the State's case for the trial of Clay Shaw. Only in open court was the possibility that Dealey Plaza and the New Orleans conspiracy were not connected ever publicly voiced by the District Attorney's Office. Courtroom evidence of the extra-judicial statements by Garrison fell on deaf ears.

And by every available yardstick, Garrison's rapport with the silent public continued unabated. The increasing popularity of the cliché that "Garrison *must* have *something*" was unaffected by the local critics and heightened by the ridicule of the national press. The National Broadcasting Company's hour-long documentary on the Garrison case on June 19th had completely backfired in New Orleans. Though the telecast was praised editorially throughout the country and, no doubt, let considerable air out of Garrison's balloon at the national level, local reaction was one of sympathy for him and outrage at the temerity of NBC for its vigorous attack on a local hero. "My heart goes out to you in your fight for justice . . .," said one letter to Garrison. "I ask that you not be discouraged by this horrible unfortunate abomination . . . May God bless you," said another. Still another, with unintended accuracy, informed Garrison that "the poor ignorant public (me) is searching for a champion, so don't let us down . . ." Several months later, despite successive exposures of incidents suggestive of bribery or intimidation by Garrison's office, a secret statewide poll by a reputable concern with a history for accuracy indicated Garrison to be the most popular public official in the state; and his highest rating of popularity was in his own bailiwick of New Orleans. The public was not polled specifically on the question of the Shaw case. It did not matter. Garrison's credibility was irrevocably tied completely to his one consuming interest.

None of this was lost on Shaw's attorneys. And none of it indicated any sound reason for departing from the dogma by which most defense attorneys live: time is on the side of the defendant. If it is true that a defendant cannot lose a preliminary hearing, it is equally true that, unless confined, there is comparatively little for him to win at a trial. The removal of the cloud from his name and reputation, and of the scant restriction on his freedom is little justification to run the risk of immediate confinement that accompanies conviction. Maximum sentence faced by Shaw was twenty years. Under Lousiana law, a defendant sentenced to more than five years is not permitted his freedom on bond pending an appeal. He remains confined while the appeal works its tortuous way through the Appellate Court. Nor is the time thus served credited against his sentence if the conviction be finally sustained. Even those who felt the odds to favor Shaw's acquittal saw little reason, upon sober reflection, to indulge in Russian roulette.

There were many, however, who did not engage in sober reflection. "No conviction would ever stand up," said some who followed the pretrial rulings and the barrage of public statements by Garrison. But this was scant comfort to the defense, for the course of an appeal of a complex trial is measured not in months, but in years.

There were other factors that could not have been seriously considered by the defense's critics who yearned for a fast acquittal to put an end to the ceaseless verbal barrage from Tulane and Broad. The scope of review of criminal cases is limited to errors of law; the Appellate Court will not review the sufficiency of the evidence.

But only those errors complained of in the trial court will even rate consideration on appeal. It would be too late to claim for the first time on appeal, for instance, that Shaw's jury had been prejudiced by the extravagant statements of the persuasive D.A. The complaint must first be made prior to trial.

Appellate courts make quick work of arguments raised initially on appeal. Does the defense feel that it has been harmed by public statements of the prosecutor? Then why did the attorneys not seek a delay until public passions had cooled or a change in the location of the trial to a place less influenced by the New Orleans news media? Was the defense hampered in its trial preparation by the total absence of any allegations of facts or circumstances in the indictment? Was it hampered by the absence of information concerning times, dates, and places of the supposed conspiracies or overt acts? Then why was such information not sought prior to trial? Did the defense feel that it was unfair that Mr. Shaw be tried on an indictment returned by a specially selected Grand Jury, one not representing a true cross section of the community? Why, then, was the issue not raised and these facts proven prior to the trial?

The record must be made in the lower court and most of it prior to the trial. Where there is not much to complain of in the action of the District Attorney, as in the usual routine, uncomplicated cases, the lapse of time between charge and trial may be relatively short. Shaw's lawyers felt they had much to complain of. Absence of specific information and the barrage of public statements must necessarily loom large in the thinking of any defense attorney. Any temptation to quickly establish the client's innocence in a trial on the merits of the charge will be resisted by any but the most impetuous and imprudent.

If the impression gained by much of the public was that complicated, incomprehensible pretrial activity indicated guilt on the part of Shaw, it was indeed a painful, even dangerous side effect. In criminal cases, however, nothing can be thrown away. The record must be made, for there will be no second chance. One might hope for the best, but the worst must be expected.

The inevitable inference of guilt from such "legalistics" was no doubt heightened by skillful innuendo that pervaded many of Garrison's statements. Even many to whom Shaw's innocence was quite obvious were apprehensive with the long drawn-out pretrial procedure. "Shaw is being convicted by his lawyers," said some of the more impatient. They had apparently observed only the ludicrous nature of Garrison's words, but misjudged completely the effect of his convincing manner on the New Orleans public.

*   *   *

On April 5th, the day after his press conference at the home of Ed Wegmann, Shaw was arraigned before Judge Haggerty. His chief defense counsel, Irvin Dymond, asked for and was granted thirty days in which to file legal pleadings on behalf of his client.

A month later, pleadings were filed. Shaw's lawyers filed a bill of particulars, a request for more specific information. They noted that Shaw was charged with having conspired with Ferrie, Oswald, and "others" to assassinate President Kennedy, the conspiracy occurring allegedly sometime between September 1 and October 10, 1963." Dymond wanted to know who were the "others." Specifically, asked Dymond, was one of the conspirators Niles Peterson? Was Dean Andrews a conspirator? Miguel Torres? Julio Buznedo? Carlos Quiroga? Manuel Garcia Gonzales? Gordon Novel? Sergio Arcacha Smith? Perry Russo? If any of these were the other conspirators, what specific acts did they commit in furtherance of the conspiracy? On what specific day was the conspiracy? At what location did they conspire? Was there more than one meeting between the conspirators? What overt acts were committed?

Dymond also filed a prayer for oyer, a plea that he be allowed to inspect or receive copies of any document that the State intended to use, including letters, correspondence or notes taken from Shaw, photographs that the State intended to use and other objects, including weapons.

He also filed a motion to suppress the use of all evidence on grounds that the search of Shaw's house had been illegal and further sought the return of all items confiscated.

A motion to quash alleged that the indictment was not sufficient because it gave no details. The accused cannot tell, said Dymond, or "intelligently guess" the crime with which he is charged. As further grounds for quashing the indictment, it was stated that the Grand Jury was improperly selected and was not a true cross section of the community. This was the same Grand Jury that Bill Gurvich was later to describe as consisting of "Legionnaires from the New Orleans Athletic Club," a reference to the inordinate number of American Legion members serving on the Jury and also to an all but unanimous membership in the N.O.A.C., one of Garrison's favorite haunts.

A further reason for quashing the indictment was alleged by Dymond to be the financing of the investigation with private funds emanating from the "Truth and Consequences" group. For the hearing on this motion, Dymond subpoenaed the records of "Truth and Consequences" for the purpose of determining the amount of money contributed and the identity of the contributors.

The State was granted thirty days in which to reply. In its reply to the prayer for oyer, the State agreed to furnish none of the items sought. In its reply to Dymond's application for a bill of particulars, the State did agree to name "some" of the acts committed by the conspirators. These included: the meeting testified to by Russo at the preliminary hearing during the month of September, 1963; discussion of the means of executing the conspiracy; Shaw's trip to the West Coast during November, 1963; Ferrie's trip to Houston on November 22, 1963; Oswald taking his rifle from the home of Mrs. Ruth Paine in Irving, Texas, to the Texas School Book Depository on November 22nd; and neither last nor least, the brainchild of the Rev. Clyde Johnson:

> Clay L. Shaw travelling from New Orleans to Baton Rouge, Louisiana, in the fall of 1963 and there meeting Lee Harvey Oswald and Jack Ruby at the Capitol House Hotel and delivering to Lee Harvey Oswald and Jack Ruby a sum of money.

During July, Judge Haggerty was on vacation. In mid-August the Court held a hearing on the various pleadings.

The prayer for oyer in its entirety was denied.

With minor exceptions the application for particulars was denied.

The motion to suppress the evidence was denied.

The Court ruled on one other motion at this hearing. On August 1st, the first day of the Judge's return from vacation, the State filed a curious document asking for a "speedy trial." The motion, like all other proceedings in the Shaw case, received wide publicity and no doubt contributed to the impression that the State was anxious to proceed with the trial and was hampered only by the delaying tactics of the defense. The legal basis for such a motion was difficult to discern, for the District Attorney sets his cases at will once they are ready for trial. Until the pretrial pleadings are disposed of, the case can be set neither by the D.A. nor the Court. The motion was, of course, denied, but undoubtedly, it had served its purpose.

At the end of August, Dymond filed new motions to quash the indictment, alleging his belief that one or more members of the Grand Jury were also members of "Truth and Consequences." Among other allegations in the new bid to quash was one that full information was being furnished *Life* magazine, but not to the defense. At the same time, Dymond asked for additional particulars with regard to the overt acts mentioned by the State. Precise dates, precise times, and precise places were asked for. Particularly, he pointed out, one of the overt acts, the meeting at the Capital House Hotel in Baton Rouge, was apparently prior to the supposed conspiracy meeting in mid-September. How could there be an overt act prior to the conspiracy? What is alleged to be an overt act and what meetings are alleged to constitute the conspiracy? asked Dymond.

In mid-September, the hearing was held on the various motions to quash. Among the witnesses subpoenaed for the purpose of testifying to the use of tainted evidence was Jim Garrison. Practically none of Dymond's questions were permitted. The attorney attempted to ascertain from Garrison, among other things, whether, in fact, Russo and Bundy had failed polygraph tests, whether *Life* magazine had been permitted to use a one-way mirror in his office to photograph Clay Shaw, and whether *Life* was given a copy of the master file in Shaw's case.

Judge Haggerty solicitously advised Garrison not to answer any question until his counsel had a chance to object. Garrison readily accepted the generous offer, except when asked if Perry Russo had failed the lie detector test. "He certainly did not," boomed Garrison, before the objection could be entered.

A few days later, the motions to quash were denied. Two weeks later, the application for a bill of particulars as to the overt acts was likewise denied.

Following the hearing on the motion to quash, Haggerty told reporters that he had heard "rumblings" around the courthouse that the defense planned to file a motion for a change of venue (location of the trial). If there were such a request, said the Judge, it would be incumbent upon the defense to prove that it could not get a fair trial in New Orleans. "It simply can't allege this," said Haggerty.

In the face of this comment, the fate of a motion for change of venue or for further delay, filed by Dymond on October 4, 1967, appeared very questionable. The motion was to the effect that Garrison's publicity barrage had so prejudiced any prospective jury that under prevailing circumstances, Shaw could not receive a fair trial.

The ˜ooler heads in the District Attorney's office were delighted. Additional time could well be used to bolster the State's slim case against Shaw. A favorable court ruling, however, appeared unlikely in the event of resistance by the State. The solution was a reply to Dymond's motion containing an exasperated preamble professing the State's desire for a speedy trial, but agreeing out of a sense of justice and an abundance of caution to a "reasonable delay." On October 3rd, Garrison's office filed its answer to Dymond's request.

If it was not possible to get a fair trial, it was because of the actions by Shaw and his attorneys, said the D.A.'s reply. Referring to Shaw's lone press conference, it accused the defendant of making public statements "calculated to influence prospective jurors." "If a prejudiced atmosphere exists, he is the author of his own misfortune and to that extent he cannot be heard to complain," continued the D.A.'s answer. Shaw's request was termed "unreasonable and capricious."

However, the answer concluded, if the continuance be granted to the defendant, it should be for a "reasonable" time. Three months was considered proper. A trial date was selected for February.

The Judge attempted to obtain Dymond's waiver to State law which permits application for change of venue to be filed anytime up until two days prior to the trial. Dymond refused. He had no way, he said, of determining what the atmosphere would be in February.

In February, a motion was filed for a change of venue. The motion set forth in great detail Garrison's prolific efforts to educate the country to the extent of the conspiracy. Testimony was taken during several days commencing March 5th. The defense attempted to subpoena copies of all press releases of Garrison's, a copy of a letter he had written used as advertisement of the film "Rush to Judgment," and copies of all correspondence with the author of an article appearing in the National Observer in January, 1968, wherein Garrison was quoted as saying: "Clay Shaw will not walk out of the courtroom."

The application for the subpoena was denied. However, at the same time the Court was denying access to the documents by the defense, the letter to the writer for the National Observer was given to the press as part of a colorful release by Garrison accusing the defense lawyers of "lying for a fee." Said the release in part: "They [the defense lawyers] have to know that only rarely have I ever given interviews concerning the assassination . . ."

Garrison was called as a witness at the hearing. Each time he was shown the transcript of a television or news interview, he would acknowledge his authorship and inform Dymond that "if you read it, you'll see I refused to comment on Clay Shaw." "Still nothing about Mr. Shaw," he would reply on other occasions, and when confronted with still other transcripts replied, "Yes, like all this other stuff, it doesn't have anything to do with Mr. Shaw."

Then, did the charges against Shaw have any connection with the actual assassination? asked Dymond. Garrison did not have to answer that question, ruled Haggerty. "The defense is going to have to separate the chaff from the wheat," said the Judge, and he commented that there could be "fifty conspiracies" that have nothing to do with the actual assassination.

Eighty prospective jurors were called and asked if they could give Shaw a fair trial. Most said that they could.

On April 4th, 1968, the motion for change of venue was denied.

The defense applied to the State Supreme Court for extraordinary writs seeking to compel the change of venue. Though this move did not prohibit either the selection of a trial date or the trial itself, the D.A. announced that a new trial date would await action by the Supreme Court on the defense move. It was urged by the defense in the application in behalf of Shaw that an appeal following a conviction in a locale inflamed by prejudicial statements was a most unsatisfactory remedy. On April 23rd, the Supreme Court refused to review Haggerty's ruling. The Court would not, it stated, "interfere with the orderly proceedings in the trial court."

The case was set for June 11th. Asked about rumors that the defense attorneys had stated an intention to ask the federal courts to stop the prosecution, one of Garrison's top trial assistants commented: "Inasmuch as the federal courts have about as much jurisdiction over this case as the courts of England or India, we see no basis for any additional delays of the trial on this account."

Shaw's lawyers disagreed. On May 27, 1968, two weeks before the scheduled commencement of the Shaw trial, they filed in the Federal District Court in New Orleans a lengthy petition asking the Court to prohibit the trial or any further prosecution of Clay Shaw.

*   *   *

Why had Shaw's lawyers asked the Federal Court to enjoin what was, after all, a State prosecution for violation of State law? The attorneys were, no doubt, discouraged and apprehensive, but the move was not one of desperation. They were not the first to appeal to the Federal Court for protection from Garrison's excesses. By May of 1968 the path from Tulane and Broad to the stately landscaped Federal District Court Building in the heart of the French Quarter was well traveled. It was for many of Garrison's victims the sole refuge from the stifling hostility of Tulane and Broad, by now so thoroughly dominated by the D.A.

The relative merits of popular election of judges vs. appointment for life, as in the federal system, have been debated among lawyers for years. The issue of independence of the judiciary vs. control over inept or incompetent judges will likely never be completely resolved, for there are arguments on both sides too powerful to be finally put to rest. Instances and examples can be cited or imagined clearly supporting one means or the other as superior. In any such future discussion it would appear that the history of the Federal Court litigation during this period of Garrison's most prolific activity must certainly rank high among the arguments of the proponents of appointment.

While many bent and some wilted before the blustering Garrison, the judges of the local Federal Court virtually alone remained impervious. They had no favor to seek from the popular D.A., nor any reason to fear him. The task of vindicating constitutional rights went by default to the federal courts. The story is one of the brighter aspects of the Garrison episode.

It started with Walter Sheridan. Following the June 19th NBC documentary on his investigation, Garrison contented himself for several weeks with lengthy diatribes against NBC and against Sheridan and Richard Townley, a reporter for the local NBC affiliate who had assisted in its preparation. In early July, however, Garrison filed a bill of information charging Sheridan with public bribery of Russo. The "bribery" consisted of a supposed offer to Russo of a home and employment in California and free legal counsel should Russo decide to change his testimony concerning the conspiracy meeting he claimed to have witnessed. A few days later, Garrison followed with three charges against Townley, alleging bribery of Russo and both bribery and intimidation of Marlene Mancuso, ex-wife of Gordon Novel.

Despite the familiarity of the pattern, I was shocked to learn of the charges against Sheridan. I had met the newsman during his presence in New Orleans while working on the documentary. I knew that he was not capable of bribery and that the charge was a knee-jerk reaction to the carefully prepared and highly effective documentary. I pondered the similarity between Garrison's latest action and a somewhat more ambitious effort to stifle expression of unpopular opinions undertaken in 1963 by the Un-American Activities Committee of the Louisiana Legislature. The 1963 incident involved the arrest of one James Dombrowski, Executive Director of a civil-rights organization, and two other men, as well as confiscation of vast quantities of material from the offices and homes of all three. Prosecutions were initiated against them, charging violation of a broadly drawn and obviously unconstitutional Subversive Activities Law. The law could not conceivably survive a serious constitutional attack, yet the three men faced long and costly litigation with all of its inherent risks before vindication could reasonably be expected. The paralyzing effect of such a procedure on other civil-rights activities could scarcely be minimized. I represented Dombrowski, together with Arthur Kinoy of New York City, a brilliant and creative civil-rights lawyer. We sought a Federal Court injunction against State prosecution on the grounds that the purpose of the prosecution was not good faith vindication of the State's criminal laws, but rather a means of discouraging the exercise of privileges guaranteed by the First Amendment of the United States Constitution dealing with free speech and free press. Ultimately, in a landmark decision entitled "Dombrowski v. Pfister," the United States Supreme Court maintained the power of the Federal District Court to enjoin a State prosecution under such circumstances. Upon proof of the "chilling effect" of such a prosecution on exercise of free speech, said the high court, the District Court had the right and the duty to enjoin it.

I discussed these thoughts a few days later with Sheridan's personal attorney, Herbert Miller of Washington, D.C., who called to inquire as to Sheridan's prospects for a fair trial in New Orleans. Miller's question was somewhat rhetorical. He had headed the Criminal Divison of the Justice Department under Robert Kennedy and had his own strong views from the outset. We discussed the necessity of the newsman's appearance in New Orleans to post bond, and Miller inquired as to whether I felt it might be the occasion for an arrest and handcuffing of Sheridan, or for some other means to embarrass or humiliate him. I somewhat naïvely advised Miller that I did not think any such occurrence possible.

He was not arrested nor handcuffed. However, upon appearing on July 17th in the Office of the Clerk to post bond, Sheridan was served with a Grand Jury subpoena ordering his appearance before the Orleans Parish Grand Jury the following morning, July 18th, at 9:00 o'clock. Never before had I heard of forcing an individual charged with crime to testify before a Grand Jury in secret session. There was no specific prohibition, nor should any have been necessary. It was one of those things that are repugnant to anyone familiar with basic concepts of constitutional immunities and it was quite likely that until this day it had never been tried. Miller commented as we left the bulding that this appeared to be "the stuff they made movies from fifty years ago." He expressed the opinion that he would not have remained in the Justice Department twenty-four hours after using such tactics.

I reflected on the case of Layton Martens. He had been taken before the Jury for no other purpose but to lay the foundation for a charge of perjury. I was determined that Sheridan would not go before the Grand Jury until we had exhausted every possible means of preventing it.

The subpoena had been served at about 3:30 P.M. Miller and I and Edward Baldwin, a local attorney, who represented Richard Townley, discussed possible moves. Miller felt strongly that Garrison and his assistants should be recused as legal adviser to the Grand Jury and wanted to file a motion to this effect before the 9:00 A.M. scheduled appearance.

He had good reason for his opinion. In addition to the barrage of unflattering statements about Sheridan and Townley, Garrison, about a month prior to the June telecast, had ordered the two newsmen arrested and beaten. When an assistant protested that there was no basis for such an arrest, Garrison advised his assistant not to be so "legalistic." The instructions were never carried out, however. The orders had been directed to Bill Gurvich, who refused them, and shortly thereafter he parted company with Garrison's office.

There appears little doubt that the incident happened. The charge was often repeated and never convincingly denied. More than anything else, however, it probably indicated the degree to which Garrison felt the strain of aggressive criticism, for he has never been known to be addicted to violence.

My own opinion was that the strongest defense against the subpoena was Sheridan's privilege guaranteed by the Fifth Amendment against giving any testimony that could be used against him. Traditionally, the possibility of incrimination is no bar against appearance before a Grand Jury. The witness must appear, but has a right to refuse to answer any particular question that he feels could be incriminating. This the witness must determine for himself, however, for the attorney is not allowed to appear with his client before the Grand Jury.

But Sheridan was charged with a crime. Practically anything that could be asked of him, including merely his previous presence in New Orleans, could conceivably be used against him at a trial. I did not want Sheridan appearing before the Jury at all.

Miller and Baldwin wanted to make the first effort before the State courts and then appeal to the State Supreme Court, using the federal action as a final resort. I preferred to ignore the state procedure, which I feared would consume precious time, and to petition the Federal Court directly for an injunction against enforcement of the subpoena. We decided to prepare the papers necessary for both courts and to make a decision the following morning. Baldwin and Miller prepared the papers for State Court. I worked separately that night and prepared the federal papers. I felt that even if we sought relief from the State Court, we were going to need them shortly thereafter, for I did not see much likelihood of permanent help from that quarter.

The next morning we decided to start with the State Court. By appointment with Judge Bagert, who had judicial supervision over Grand Jury proceedings for this jury term, we went to his home at 8:00 A.M. and filed with him our motion to quash the subpoena or, alternatively, to recuse Garrison as Grand Jury legal adviser. The motion prepared by Baldwin set out in considerable detail Garrison's past oppressive use of Grand Juries and the details of his feud with Sheridan. Appended to the motion was an order granting a temporary stay until the motion could be argued in open court. In my briefcase I had an application to the State Supreme Court for writs from a possible refusal by Judge Bagert to grant the delay, and a petition to the Federal Court in the event we were unsuccessful with the State high court.

Judge Bagert signed the order granting the temporary delay. A week later the motion was argued in open court. The Judge denied our motion to recuse Garrison or to quash the subpoena. He allowed until noon the next day in which to appeal to the State Supreme Court for extraordinary writs. Our papers were filed that night. At 11:00 A.M. the next day, the Supreme Court granted a further delay while it took our application under consideration. On August 7th the Supreme Court, too, denied our request for relief.

We held our Federal Court petition in abeyance, waiting to see if the D.A. would persist in his efforts or if, having won his victory, he would drop the entire matter of the Grand Jury appearance. It would not have been out of character.

The next meeting of the Jury was on August 9th. Sheridan was in Detroit on a job assignment with NBC, but ready to fly to New Orleans immediately upon word from us. We received no word on the 7th, the 8th, or the morning of the 9th. It was our intention to file our Federal Court petition upon the first indication that Sheridan was wanted. Hearing nothing by noon on the 9th, Miller caught an early afternoon plane to Washington.

At about 4:00 P.M. I received an "instanter" subpoena commanding Walter Sheridan to appear before the Grand Jury immediately. I called Judge Bagert who referred me to the Grand Jury foreman. I told the foreman that Sheridan was in Detroit, and could be present the following morning at the earliest, and that he would be in New Orleans at such time thereafter as the Jury wanted him. Sheridan, indeed, would have been back at such time as the Jury wanted and would have appeared before them—provided we were not successful in obtaining the relief we wanted from the Federal Court. We had assumed there would be some minimum advance notice which would have given us an opportunity to present our papers to a federal judge. Sheridan had been permitted to leave New Orleans by the Judge to whom his bribery case had been assigned on condition he return upon forty-eight hours' notice. The foreman advised me that I would be notified shortly of the Jury's decision.

At about 5:15 P.M. the same day, we received our answer. I was served with an order to show cause on the following Tuesday why Sheridan should not be held in contempt of the Grand Jury for failing to appear "immediately" as ordered.

The next morning we filed our federal petition. This was the first of our many appearances in Federal Court to block the Sheridan subpoena.

The atmosphere was somewhat different from that at Tulane and Broad. Legal issues were seriously discussed. Arguments on both sides were heard attentively. It was like a breath of fresh air to us.

In our petition we sought not only an injunction against enforcement of the offensive Grand Jury subpoena, but also against prosecution of Sheridan or Townley on the criminal charges. Ultimately, Judge Alvin Rubin of the Federal District Court refused to enjoin these prosecutions and we took an appeal to the Circuit Court seeking a reversal of that part of his opinion.

But as to the Grand Jury subpoena, Judge Rubin ruled on August 28th that Sheridan could not be forced to match wits with the District Attorney in secret session with the Grand Jury without benefit of an attorney. "Charged as a criminal, he will sit before a Grand Jury, forced to undergo interrogation outside the presence of his lawyer, required to decide at his peril and without the benefit of counsel present at the time, whether any particular question relates to public bribery or does not relate to public bribery . . ." said Judge Rubin. The action of the D.A. would, he continued, leave Sheridan "naked to those whom he conceives to be his enemies."

It was the first clear setback to Garrison in a blitzkrieg by subpoena that was rapidly approaching its climax.

In late September, turning temporarily from his preoccupation with the Kennedy probe, Garrison sought to destroy the Metropolitan Crime Commission for its persistence in speaking of the existence of organized crime in New Orleans. Particular target of his wrath within the Commission was Aaron Kohn, its Managing Director.

David Chandler, a *Life* magazine reporter, had contributed to a series in *Life* on organized crime, including embarrassing details of organized crime in New Orleans. Garrison, suspecting that much of the information had come from the Crime Commission, perceived this to be a plot to destroy him, for there could obviously be no organized crime in New Orleans while he was District Attorney. Garrison determined to smash Kohn and the Crime Commission once and for all. His method was admittedly ingenious. Twelve years previously Kohn had served a ten-day jail term for refusing to reveal a confidential source of information in court. His zealousness in guarding his sources of information was well known, and the Crime Commission could hardly have functioned without it. Garrison's first thrust was two-pronged. He subpoenaed all records of the Crime Commission containing names of any confidential informants on any subject at all during the thirteen-year history of the Commission. He also subpoenaed all records of contributors. The Commission was supported exclusively by voluntary contributions and, understandably, many contributors did not wish their connection with his avowed enemy, the Crime Commission, known to the D.A. This aspect of the subpoena was, hence, a threat almost as serious as the first.

My law partner, Herbert Garon, and I represented the Commission. We moved before Judge Malcolm V. O'Hara, who was the judicial supervisor of the new Grand Jury, to quash the subpoena on constitutional grounds that went to the heart of Garrison's efforts. Garrison obviously wanted the information to use against Kohn and other officers themselves in violation of the guarantees of the Fifth Amendment. We argued that this was clear from the State's own motion for the subpoena which had brazenly claimed, among other things, that false testimony had been given under oath by them on prior occasions and that the members were seeking to control various rackets themselves, hence, the reason for their attacks on persons accused by the Commission of illegal activity.

Further, we claimed that the attempt to subpoena membership lists would destroy the effectiveness of the Commission in violation of the rights of its members to peacefully assemble and to express themselves as guaranteed by the First Amendment of the United States Constitution.

The State abandoned its effort to get the membership list. As to the records of informers, the bid to quash the subpoena was denied by Judge O'Hara, nor would he brook any delay for an appeal to the Supreme Court. We had anticipated the possibility of this reception and while I argued in court, my partner called a third attorney associated with us who was standing by in the State Supreme Court waiting to file immediate application for relief should the need arise. A stay order was granted by the Supreme Court moments before Kohn was to be ordered into the Grand Jury room to produce records that he had not brought with him and would not produce under any circumstances. As in the case of Sheridan, a federal petition was already prepared in the event the State high court had not acted.

In mid-December, after hearing arguments, the Supreme Court threw out the subpoena on grounds that it had been too broadly drawn, but ignored completely the constitutional issues. Under State law, the decision was not final for fourteen days thereafter, during which either side might ask for a rehearing. We had planned to do this, for we wanted to reurge our constitutional arguments. But even before the delay for rehearing expired, a new subpoena, more narrowly drawn, was served and Kohn was again ordered into court the following day to produce records and to give oral testimony.

I had assumed that the rehearing provision had been overlooked when the new subpoena was issued. Nothing that had happened thus far had prepared me for the utter disregard of our clear right to reurge this constitutional issue once more before the Supreme Court. The matter was argued in court the following day. The assistant D.A. finally agreed to delay the production of the documents until the Supreme Court decision became final. However, the State would not agree to postpone the oral testimony of Kohn. Judge Matthew Braniff, acting for Judge O'Hara, who had taken leave of absence, refused to grant any delay to Kohn, or to agree that the issue of Kohn's obligation to reveal confidential informants was a matter still pending before the Supreme Court.

At about 7:00 P.M., after approximately two and one-half hours of abuse from the Grand Jury members, Kohn was asked the name of the confidential informant who had told him of the presence in New Orleans of a notorious gambler. The presence of the gambler had been reported in the press and was widely known by anyone who was interested. Kohn refused and persisted in his refusal in open court. Judge Braniff ruled, over our objections, that he saw no reason to wait for the Supreme Court ruling on the first subpoena to become final. Nor would he permit even a few hours' delay in which to apply to the Supreme Court for a review on his present ruling. It was argued by the assistant D.A. that such a delay would interfere with the "orderly processes of justice."

Kohn was held in contempt and sentenced to remain in jail until he should indicate a willingness to respond to the Grand Jury's questions. At this hour it was impossible to obtain any action from the Supreme Court. Kohn spent the night in jail. That night we prepared our application for writs, which were filed the next morning. Kohn was released at noon by the high court pending its study of the entire matter.

A few weeks thereafter, our application to that Court for review of its previous ruling that no constitutional issues were involved in Garrison's efforts to subpoena the Commission records, was denied.

Faced with the prospect of an immediate order to produce the records, we again turned to Federal Court and sought an injunction against further subpoenas. For the second time it became clear that the D.A. had somewhat less influence on events in Federal Court than at Tulane and Broad. Issues which had been ignored in State courts were the subject of serious scrutiny by Judge Herbert Christenberry, to the acute discomfort of the assistant D.A.'s. Faced with the threat of a restraining order, they agreed to withhold any action on production of the records until the State Supreme Court acted on Kohn's sentence for contempt.

In the late spring of 1968 the high court set aside the sentence on the ground that the very issue of Kohn's constitutional right to refuse to reveal confidential informants was still pending before that Court at the time that he refused to make such a revelation before the Grand Jury.

But the Court never did pass on the merits of the constitutional question and the D.A. was free, had he chosen, to continue his efforts to subpoena the documents. However, a necessary prelude to any such order to produce documents would have been a hearing in Federal Court on our petition for the injunction and the District Attorney had already sensed the lay of the land. He called it quits. He has made no further attempt to get the Commission's files.

He did, however, make an attempt to salvage some lost prestige. The President of the Crime Commission was Dr. J. D. Grey, minister of one of the largest Baptist congregations in New Orleans. Dr. Grey is widely respected and counts among his congregation one member of the Supreme Court.

Shortly after the Supreme Court decision reversing Braniff's contempt citation of Kohn, the headlines announced that Dr. Grey was being subpoenaed before the D.A. to explain why he had visited with a Supreme Court Justice while the case had been pending. Deeming the subpoena to be one more effort at intimidation, we asked the Federal Court for a restraining order against the required appearance. Garrison, of course, had not made the slightest effort to learn from the Supreme Court Judges whether the Reverend Grey had tried to influence their decision, the only conduct that could possibly constitute a crime on the part of the reverend. Garrison's attempt to compel Dr. Grey to give testimony which could presumably be used as a basis for another bogus charge, or, at the very least, to humiliate and embarrass him was thwarted by the Federal Court. A temporary restraining order was issued and a full hearing was to be scheduled. Characteristically, however, Garrison announced that he was withdrawing this subpoena, for he had, he said, already established publicly the fact that Grey had spoken to a Supreme Court Justice during the two-month period while the case was under advisement. Dr. Grey had explained in a public statement that he had spoken to the Justice on matters involving church affairs and that the subject of the case had not come up at all during the meeting. Of course, countered Garrison through his First Assistant, Charles Ward, they did not believe that Dr. Grey would be so crude as to directly ask a Judge to decide a case favorably. The attempt at influence was much more subtle, said the D.A.'s statement. But by their procedure, it continued, they had thus forced Reverend Grey to admit that he had done something very improper, and the subpoena would now be withdrawn.

Perhaps to some unknown number of the public, Garrison may indeed have made the meeting appear as something vulgar.

David Chandler was a *Life* reporter who gathered a portion of the material used in the *Life* magazine articles published in September, 1967, on organized crime in the United States, with considerable emphasis on the City of New Orleans. As a result, he, too, was the target of a sustained and concerted effort to compel his appearance before the Grand Jury.

Shortly following the appearance of the *Life* magazine articles in September and loud disclaimers by Garrison of any organized crime in New Orleans, a subpoena was issued for Chandler's appearance before the Grand Jury. Chandler was not in New Orleans at the time, but news of the issuance of the subpoena quickly reached him. Chandler was represented by Cicero Sessions, the local attorney for Time, Incorporated, the owner of *Life*.

Sessions is a skilled and formidable courtroom lawyer, but he had had little contact with Garrison's office, not having engaged in the practice of criminal law for many years. He talked to Garrison's assistant and agreed to produce Chandler voluntarily for questioning. He could not produce Chandler on October 5th, the date the D.A. wanted, for Sessions was scheduled to be engaged in a trial in Federal District Court and another date was agreed upon with the assistant D.A.

In casual conversation, Sessions informed me that he intended to permit Chandler to testify, but would claim the newsman's privilege granted by statute to news reporters with regard to any questions concerning confidential informants.

A few days later, however, Sessions asked me for certain documents from my file in the Sheridan case. He was, he explained, going to move to quash the subpoena against Chandler. Why the sudden change in plans? Sessions had learned, he said, that the District Attorney's Office could not be trusted. While Sessions had been engaged in the Federal Court trial on October 5th, Deputy Sheriffs were trying to break down the door to Chandler's French Quarter apartment to serve him with an "instanter" subpoena. Chandler, aware of the agreement between his counsel and the D.A.'s Office, had refused to answer the Sheriff's knock, for he correctly feared an effort to take him immediately to Tulane and Broad without his attorney.

Chandler avoided service on that day, but was subsequently subpoenaed to appear on October 11th. Sessions filed motions to quash the subpoena, alleging that it was the D.A.'s intention to entrap his client and to charge him with perjury. Further, argued Sessions, Garrison's office had refused to disclaim that Chandler was himself a suspect and that, therefore, he could not be compelled to answer questions before the Grand Jury. Judge Braniff quickly overruled the motions and refused to permit any delay for application to the Supreme Court for extraordinary writs. During the lunch hour, however, after the motions had been argued and denied, Sessions filed his applications, which had already been prepared, with the Supreme Court. That Court promptly issued a stay order until it might have an opportunity to consider the application at length. Approximately a week later, Sessions's application was denied.

Prior to the next regular meeting of the Grand Jury, Sessions filed his petition in the Federal District Court seeking to restrain enforcement of the Grand Jury subpoena on much the same basis as was advanced in the Sheridan case. Faced with the threats of temporary restraining orders by the Federal Court pending a full hearing on Sessions's petition, the D.A. voluntarily agreed to withhold enforcement of the subpoena pending a ruling.

Chandler, unlike Sheridan, was not charged with a crime and the only real issue before the Federal Court was Garrison's good faith in attempting to compel his critic's appearance before the Jury. Garrison had publicly termed Chandler a liar and his protestation to the Federal Court, where he appeared as a witness, that he wanted information from Chandler on organized crime, whose existence he had vociferously disclaimed, made little impression on the Court.

On March 11th the Federal District Court enjoined Garrison from enforcing his subpoena. Garrison had publicly announced that the *Life* articles were untrue, said the Court, and that he had obtained all the information in *Life*'s files and that, according to Garrison "every bit of information . . . had turned out to be incorrect."

"Garrison has stated his lack of regard for the truthfulness of the very testimony being sought," the Court continued, and "Chandler's fear of prospective prosecution for perjury or false swearing . . . is well founded."

It was the first clear finding of fact, based on courtroom testimony, of Garrison's abuse of the vast subpoena power of his office. For the D.A. it was a stunning setback.

The intemperance of his remarks about this ruling shortly thereafter to a convention in New Orleans of a national association of prosecuting attorneys prompted a request from the president of the group that future remarks be toned down at the closing banquet. Garrison's reply was a cancellation of the banquet and a public explanation that the money already paid by the members was the price of his lesson to them in free speech.

*   *   *

So there was ample cause for optimism when on May 27th Edward Wegmann, in behalf of his client, Clay Shaw, presented to Judge Frederick Heebe of the Federal District Court a forty-six page complaint detailing at great length the history of Shaw's misfortunes beginning March 1st, 1967. The complaint stated that Shaw required a "sanctuary" in the Federal Court to grant him relief from "irreparable harm, clear and imminent" which Shaw had suffered since his arrest. Wegmann cited his inability to learn any of the particulars of the offense with which Shaw was charged. The denial of this information, said Wegmann, was a denial of due process of law. Wegmann cited at length Garrison's publicity barrage, the use of the "hallucinatory drug-induced and hypnotically-induced testimony" of Perry Russo to obtain the indictment and charged that Garrison was conducting an "illegal, unwarranted, fraudulent, and useless probe of the Kennedy assassination." Clay Shaw, said Wegmann's petition, was being used as a pawn and a patsy by Garrison for the purpose of mounting his attack on the Warren Report.

Because the petition alleged certain Louisiana procedural statutes, as well as the conspiracy statute itself, to be unconstitutional, it was necessary that the case be heard before a three-judge court. The following day, pending the appointment of such a court, Judge Heebe signed a temporary restraining order barring further prosecution of Shaw until action could be undertaken by the three-judge panel. Judge Heebe also signed an order authorizing the defense attorneys to take testimony immediately of key members of Garrison's staff in preparation for the scheduled hearing.

But Garrison ordered his staff to disregard the order on the grounds that the Judge's action was "plainly illegal and no member of this staff is to compromise or cooperate in any way with this totalitarian display of power by the Federal government." Garrison's men were instructed to appear at the deposition and give only "names, office rank, and social security numbers." The D.A.'s Office filed a motion to dismiss the complaint, alleging that the Federal Court was without jurisdiction.

On June 17th a hearing was held on the motion for dismissal. Legal briefs were submitted by both sides and on July 23rd in a lengthy, well-considered opinion, the Court refused to block the impending trial.

Unlike the situation in Dombrowski v. Pfister, or the Sheridan case, reasoned the Court, there was no serious complaint by Shaw that the action was undertaken to inhibit Clay Shaw in the exercise of his right of free speech. It was indeed true that Shaw had not been singled out for his ordeal because of personal animosity on the part of Garrison or any desire to intimidate Shaw personally. It was all quite cold and emotionless. Garrison had determined certain specifications for the elusive Clay Bertrand, and Clay Shaw fit those specifications. There was no animosity involved.

The case was again set for trial by Garrison's office, this time for September 11th. But on August 2nd Shaw's attorneys filed a notice of appeal with the United States Supreme Court and asked for perpetuation of the restraining order pending action by the United States high court on the appeal. The same three-judge court which had maintained Garrison's motion to dismiss did agree to hold matters in abeyance until Shaw's lawyers might exercise their right of appeal. This was followed by the inevitable blast from Garrison on further interference with the process of justice in New Orleans.

On December 9th the United States Supreme Court dismissed the appeal for lack of probable jurisdiction.

There was now no plausible reason for delay by the defense—or by Garrison. Garrison solemnly announced that the legal pleadings of Shaw's attorneys were "obstructions on the legal level" and assured the public that there had been "even more serious obstructions behind the scenes." He claimed that he had been contacted to learn if he would be interested in a federal judgeship in return for dropping the case. Peering intently into the TV camera, Garrison promised emphatically that "This case is going to trial" and that the only way that anyone could stop him would be to kill him. "The moment of truth has arrived," said Garrison. He pointed out that President-elect Nixon was due to be sworn in as President on January 20, 1969. President Johnson's role, at the very least in suppressing evidence of the assassination plot, had already been "established" by the D.A. and he was therefore setting the case for January 21st, he claimed, in the hopes that he would meet with less obstructionism from the new Administration. The trial was to be "a test of whether we really have justice in America."

But there was one further crisis. Shortly prior to trial, Garrison attempted to compel the National Archives to release to him for use at the Shaw trial the autopsy photographs and X rays of President Kennedy. A United States judge in Washington had asked for evidence as to its relevancy at the trial of Clay Shaw. Garrison was not used to answering embarrassing questions. He announced that he would seek an indefinite delay in the trial, for he could not try the case without this evidence. If the case never came to trial, it would be the fault of the Federal Government and its persistent obstructionism.

Whether Garrison misgauged the popular reaction to this move, suffered a change of heart, or never intended to delay the trial at all, can only be guessed. But on January 20th, the date on which the motion was to be argued, Garrison withdrew his request for a continuance. Said his chief trial assistant: "The State will trust the good judgment, common sense, and spirit of justice which the State feels prevails among the people of New Orleans. . . ."

As things developed, it was perhaps the most accurate statement to emanate from Garrison's office since the launching of his assassination investigation almost two years previously.

18

THE TRIAL NEVER QUITE GOT OFF
the ground. Garrison still had his followers. And they still expected
complete vindication of their hero and a full revelation of the true story
behind the assassination. But somehow the same excitement wasn't
there. Two years had passed and much had happened. High emotional
pitch can be maintained only for so long. Some were misguided enough
to think that Garrison was going to try the case himself. A brief pretrial
announcement explained that Assistant D.A. James Alcock would
handle the brunt of it. During the five weeks of trial, Garrison actually
spent no more than a few hours in court examining a total of two
witnesses. Practically the entire case was handled by assistants, though
Garrison would stop in briefly from time to time to observe the proceedings, and to sign an occasional autograph.

It took two weeks to pick the jury. The State was going to prove six
overt acts, said Alcock to each prospective juror, though only one need
be proved, and Alcock wanted to know if the jury could convict if any
one were proved to be in furtherance of the plot. The six acts? The

same six that had been given to the defense in the fall of 1967, including Shaw's trip to San Francisco, Ferrie's trip to Houston, and the meeting at the Capitol House at Baton Rouge. Why Shaw should travel from New Orleans to San Francisco to establish an alibi for a murder in Dallas was not explained.

Dymond wanted to know if the jurors had an opinion as to the validity of the Warren Report. The Judge ruled the question out. That had nothing to do with Shaw. But, protested Dymond, the D.A. had been promising to disprove the Report at the Shaw trial and even then was trying to subpoena the autopsy report and X rays. "We will cross that bridge when we get to it," replied Haggerty.

Finally they had a jury—all male—nine whites, three Negroes. The jurors would remain sequestered and would sleep at a local hotel under the watchful eye of a deputy sheriff throughout the trial.

Then came the opening statement.

Garrison personally delivered the State's opening remarks. The State would prove five overt acts, said Garrison. He listed them. Why only five? The Capitol House Hotel meeting was now omitted. Unknown to the jury, the D.A. had discovered that the Reverend Clyde Johnson had recently been arrested and jailed for failing to pay a hotel bill. Embarrassingly enough, on January 23, just two days after the start of the trial, he was charged in Garrison's own office. Scratch one overt act.

Further, said Garrison, the State was going to prove that Kennedy was shot from three directions. Dealey Plaza was now officially part of the case. Dymond objected. The charge was conspiracy in Orleans Parish, he said. Haggerty overruled him. The prosecution was entitled to "over-prove its case" if it wished, said the Judge. He could not tell the State how to present its case.

Dymond made a brief opening statement for the defense. He was going to show, said Dymond, that the so-called conspiracy was not conceived until after Ferrie's death. "That's when the roaches came out of the woodwork . . . Russo is a liar—a notoriety seeking liar whose name does not deserve to be mentioned among honest and just people."

Then began the parade of witnesses. A number of residents of Clinton, Louisiana, were called to prove Oswald's presence in that town in late August or early September, 1963. Three claimed to have seen Shaw with him. One was the Town Marshal, John Manchester. Another, Cori Collins, was a Negro civil-rights worker. The very diversity of their backgrounds lent credence to their testimony.

Not to Hugh Aynesworth, the *Newsweek* reporter, however. He had recently interviewed Manchester upon learning of his impending participation in the trial. At the conclusion of the meeting, Aynesworth expressed interest in talking to Collins, a worker for the Congress of Racial Equality. A deputy took the newsman to Collins's house and entered without knocking. He barked orders: "The newsman here wants to talk to you, Collins." Collins spoke to Aynesworth at the deputy's prodding. The similarity of the testimony of the Marshal and the CORE worker at the trial was no surprise to Aynesworth.

Nor could the defense have known of prior statements by Manchester to other State witnesses shortly after the Garrison probe became public that he could not identify the persons in question.

The third witness from Clinton to identify Shaw was William Dunn, a construction worker. He had seen Shaw, for the first time in his life, for about ten minutes during the late summer of 1963, sitting in his car. He had not seen Shaw again until the day the trial started—January 21st, 1969. The D.A.'s Office brought him to Court while Shaw was there to identify him. Why didn't Dunn report the incident after Shaw's arrest two years ago? "He was arrested already," said Dunn, "I'm gonna get him arrested again?"

Vernon Bundy came next. He repeated his original story, but with a new embellishment. He asked for permission to demonstrate how he knew it was Shaw who came to the seawall where he had gone to inject himself with narcotics. "Would you have the gentleman there go to the back of the courtroom?" asked Bundy, pointing to Shaw. Shaw complied. Bundy came down from the witness seat and sat in Shaw's chair. At Bundy's request that the "gentleman walk forward," Shaw complied. Bundy described a twisting of the foot by Shaw when he walked. It had frightened him that day at the seawall, said Bundy. He had watched Shaw walk at the preliminary hearing before his own testimony to be sure of his identification. For some reason, this was not mentioned, however, in the preliminary hearing.

Bundy was excused. Before plunging back into obscurity, however, his name was twice in the news shortly following the close of the Shaw case. The first publicity was Garrison's reference to him in the course of a TV interview as "a completely honest man." The second was occasioned by a twenty-day jail sentence following his plea of guilty in Municipal Court to a charge of theft of two pairs of pants.

Next came a surprise witness; no trial should be without one. In the Shaw case it was a New York accountant named Charles I. Spiesel. He had met Ferrie in a French Quarter bar in June, 1963. From the bar he and Ferrie and a few of Ferrie's friends went to a party in a building at "Dauphine and Esplanade." At the party, according to Spiesel, Ferrie introduced him to Clay Shaw. Later that night, a discussion about killing Kennedy took place. Shaw seemed amused by the conversation, said Spiesel, though at one point he asked Ferrie if the assassin could be flown away from the scene to safety. Ferrie replied that he could.

Through a leak in Garrison's office, the defense had learned of Spiesel and the substance of his testimony. The leak was the same that furnished the information about the Clinton witnesses which Aynesworth had investigated. Concerning Spiesel, there was much to investigate. The report of the probe into Spiesel's background had been flown in by the defense that afternoon from New York City. It was placed in Dymond's hands less than five minutes before the State's examination of the witness was concluded and he was tendered to Dymond for cross-examination.

It was an interesting cross-examination. It developed that Spiesel had filed a $16,000,000 lawsuit against a New York psychiatrist and the City of New York, claiming they "hypnotized" him and harassed him out of business. Why did they do this? Spiesel didn't know for sure, but speculated it might be a Communist conspiracy.

The following morning the cross-examination continued. Spiesel had also sued the New Orleans police during a stay here in 1965. Among the complaints against the New York defendants: they had injured his sex life. Had Spiesel frequently been hypnotized? About fifty or sixty times. Frequently people hypnotized him just by looking at him. It was true that fifteen suits involving false tax returns had been filed against him, but "they were part of the conspiracy." Why $16,000,000, asked Dymond, speaking of the New York suit? $1,000,000 for each year of the conspiracy, replied the witness.

Dymond asked that Spiesel be instructed to take the jury to the apartment where the supposed meeting with Shaw had occurred. The Judge arranged for transportation by bus to the general vicinity. The Judge, wearing a red sport coat, instructed Spiesel to lead the jury to the apartment. For over an hour Spiesel led the entourage around the neighborhood and into several buildings. Close on the heels of the jury, attorneys, and court personnel was the inevitable squad of newsmen. Traffic was temporarily blocked off while the cortege toured the neighborhood. A local TV station, noting the approach of Carnival, called it the first parade of the season. Spiesel led the group through several buildings on Esplanade Avenue, but could never quite identify the apartment.

Next came Perry Raymond Russo. If cross-examination of Russo had been a nightmare at the preliminary hearing, his cross-examination at the trial was every lawyer's dream. The major problem faced by Dymond for this second encounter with Russo must have been organization of the vast quantity of contradictory statements with which he planned to

confront the D.A.'s "star witness." The direct testimony was essentially
the same as Russo gave at the preliminary hearing, except that he now
declined to identify anyone as definitely attending the party with him in
September, 1963. He explained that Dymond had "forced" him to
name Niles Peterson and Sandra Moffett by constantly "pushing."

Concerning his memorandum to Sciambra, Russo explained that he
talked several hours and Sciambra made a few notes. Sciambra's memo
was wrong on a number of points, testified Russo, but he made no
mention of the omission of the September party at Ferrie's. Russo
explained that he had considered the meeting at Ferrie's to be an incon-
sequential bull session and thought that the key area of the D.A.'s
interest in him as a witness was his knowledge of Ferrie's philosophy.

Further, on the second day of cross-examination, Russo acknowledged
that he heard neither Oswald nor "Clem Bertrand" agree to kill the
President. Only Ferrie had said, "We will kill him." And Ferrie had
said that many times before.

Dymond at one point referred to the group at the party as "conspirators." "I don't call them conspirators," said Russo. Alcock objected
to the exchange and was sustained by the Judge.

"Did Ferrie ever ask you 'please don't repeat what you heard at the
meeting on Louisiana Avenue Parkway'?" asked Dymond. Alcock objected that Dymond was eliciting hearsay testimony. Haggerty sustained
the objection. To preserve the answer for the record in the event of
appeal, Dymond asked that Russo be allowed to answer out of the
presence of the jury. The jury filed out. The question was repeated.
"No," replied Russo. The jury filed back in.

Russo acknowledged that he had told Layton Martens that "this case
is the most blown-up thing I have ever seen." He did not say, however,
that he was not sure of his identification of Shaw. He was 100 percent
sure, but he wanted to see Shaw again because in a case of this magni-
tude, you have to be 1,000 percent sure. Was Russo 1,000 percent sure,
asked Dymond? One thousand percent is something you can't ever
reach, replied Russo.

Yes, Russo did tell Martens that he wasn't sure if the plot was against
Castro or Kennedy, but he needed to qualify that. Ferrie and his group
spoke frequently about Castro and Cuba and he had the feeling that
night in September that Ferrie had been speaking about Castro, too.

Russo was no longer sure that Oswald was still in New Orleans in
early October. It may have been late September. Was this because
Russo learned since the preliminary hearing that Oswald left New
Orleans September 25th never to return, asked Dymond. No, said
Russo.

Yes, Russo had told Phelan that "if Garrison knew what I told my priest, he would go through the ceiling." Russo explained that he told the priest that he would like to be in a position not to have to give his cooperation.

Yes, he did tell Phelan that he would like to see Shaw and resolve any doubts by asking him questions. But, explained Russo, "I am completely sure he was the man at the Louisiana Avenue Parkway apartment of Ferrie."

The D.A. knew of his meeting with Phelan and when Phelan came to his house thereafter, said Russo, his house was bugged. "The D.A. wanted to find our how far he would go," said Russo.

Yes, he had told Police Sergeant Edward O'Donnell that he didn't know if Shaw was at the party at Ferrie's, but he was under great pressure at the time.

Yes, he had told O'Donnell that if he had to give a yes or no answer as to whether or not Shaw was present, he would say no. Not in those exact words, said Russo, but in essence that is what he told O'Donnell.

Russo's two-day cross-examination ended shortly thereafter.

Then followed testimony by Anthony Sciambra, explaining the discrepancies in his now celebrated memorandum. He may be a lousy memo writer, said the assistant D.A., but he was not a prostitute. Phelan, he explained, was a journalistic prostitute.

The preliminary hearing testimony of Dr. Nicholas Chetta, now deceased, was read over defense objection that only Russo's present sanity, not his sanity in 1967 was at issue.

R. C. Rolland, the owner of the Winterland Skating Rink in Houston, the "communication center," appeared next. Ferrie appeared with two young men and "made it a point to make sure he was known to me," said Rolland. Ferrie introduced himself four or five times, he explained. The witness claimed he was first contacted by the D.A.'s Office about a year after the incident. It was pointed out that this was two years before the investigation started. "So I was off on the time," was the bland reply.

Next came a letter carrier named James Hardiman. Records of the Post Office Department had been introduced to show that Shaw's mail was delivered to 1414 Chartres Street for a period of time in 1966 when Shaw was in Europe. Hardiman now claimed to recall delivering several letters addressed to "Clem Bertrand" at that address during the same period. Had he delivered mail to anyone else at that address? Hardiman replied that he had. Did Hardiman deliver mail to a Fred Tate at that address? Yes, said Hardiman, he recalled that he did. To a Cliff Boudreaux? Yes, said Hardiman, not too long ago. Would it make any difference, asked Dymond, "if I told you I made up that name?" No, replied the unembarrassed mailman, "I delivered mail to that address."

There then followed an abortive attempt to obtain Dr. Esmond Fatter's opinion testimony about the hypnotic sessions. It was blocked by Dymond's objections.

A local travel consultant verified Shaw's travel arrangements to San Francisco in November, 1963. He had gone on to Portland and Chicago before returning to New Orleans.

For five days thereafter Garrison tried his case against the Warren Report over repeated objections of Irvin Dymond. A mock-up of Dealey Plaza, photographs and, most effective of all, the Zapruder film of the actual murder of the late President, were introduced into evidence. The grisly color film was shown to the jury no less than nine times. It was shown in full speed, slow motion, and frame-by-frame. It was rerun as State experts in ballistics or pathology used the film to illustrate their testimony. Seasoned reporters, in a show of cynicism often the hallmark of their profession, expressed the opinion that Shaw would be convicted by the blood and gore of the Zapruder film which the jury watched in rapt fascination.

"We object to all of this testimony on the grounds of irrelevancy," said Dymond. There was no legal connection between the testimony concerning the alleged New Orleans conspiracy and the actual assassination. "The evidence concerning Dealey Plaza will be connected up and highly corroborative of the discussions testified to by Russo and Spiesel concerning triangulation of fire and the use of the rifle in connection with the assassination," argued Alcock.

"There is no question the State can over-prove its case. I feel that evidence presented up to now indicates what happened in Dallas is relevant," was the ruling of the Judge. So the critics of the Warren Commission had their day in court and the jury heard expert opinion evidence that shots were fired from the front.

Former Governor John B. Connally, Jr., of Texas and his wife were subpoenaed as State witnesses. After first indicating that the subpoenas would be resisted, the Connallys agreed to come to New Orleans. They said they would appear voluntarily. However, an assistant D.A. announced that it was decided that the Governor was "a hostile witness" and that he would therefore not be called. The autopsy items subpoenaed by Garrison were finally ordered released to Garrison by the Washington Federal Court. The Government appealed and the State rested before the decision could be ruled on by the appellate court.

After completing the testimony concerning Dealey Plaza the State returned to the subject of Clay Shaw, whose name had not been mentioned for five days.

Mrs. Jessie Parker testified that she was presently employed by a clothing store, but had worked as a hostess in the V.I.P. Room of Eastern Airlines at Moisant International Airport from November 11th, 1966, until April 30th, 1967. She was asked specifically by Alcock about December 14th, 1966, and replied that sometime between 10:00 A.M. and noon on that date, Clay Shaw came to the V.I.P. Room with another man. There was no one else in the room except the two men and herself. Each man signed the guest register. After Shaw signed the book, he looked back over his shoulder at her twice. When the two men left, she looked at the signature. The signature was "Clay Bertrand."

Mrs. Parker remembered Shaw "because I admired his pretty gray hair" and because of his size. The other man did not interest her.

A New Orleans police officer, Aloysius Habighorst, was called for the purpose of identifying a fingerprint card on which Shaw signed his name. The card listed as an alias of Shaw, the name "Clay Bertrand." According to Habighorst, all of the information on the card, including presumably the alias, was given to him by Shaw immediately following his arrest two years previously. The State, as is customary, attempted to lay the foundation for introduction of this card out of the presence of the jury. The controversy centered around procedure by which the information was taken and the card signed. An accused person is entitled to be warned of his rights against self-incrimination prior to being questioned and he is entitled to be advised of his right to have an attorney present. Whether Shaw's rights were violated was very much in dispute. Testifying for the State were several D.A. investigators. The defense called Salvadore Panzeca, the defense attorney who had gone to the D.A.'s office to represent Shaw when arrest appeared imminent. Also testifying to the circumstances of the questioning was Edward Wegmann, who later joined Panzeca following Shaw's arrest. In addition, Shaw himself took the witness stand and, among other things, denied ever having given Habighorst any alias.

When the testimony was completed, the Judge ruled that Shaw's constitutional rights were violated because he was not allowed to have his attorney with him during the course of Habighorst's questioning. Hence, even if Habighorst asked the question about an alias, said the Judge, Shaw's rights were violated, and the fingerprint card would not be permitted in evidence.

The Judge continued: ". . . it is not admissible. If Officer Habighorst is telling the truth—and I seriously doubt it . . ." He never finished. He was interrupted by Alcock whose voice was trembling with anger.

"Are you passing on the credibility of a State witness in front of the press and the whole world?"

"It's outside the presence of the jury," Haggerty replied. "I do not care. The whole world can hear that I do not believe Officer Habighorst." Haggerty's voice was firm and he was adamant. He repeated: "I do not believe Officer Habighorst."

Alcock moved for a mistrial, though there is no provision in law for such a motion by the State. This is a remedy proffered only to the defense. The Judge denied the motion. Alcock announced his intention of appealing to the Louisiana Supreme Court for supervisory writs to reverse Judge Haggerty's rulings. That ended the day's proceedings. Haggerty announced that the trial would resume at 9:00 A.M. the following morning unless prohibited by Supreme Court action.

At 9:00 A.M. the following morning, Thursday, February 20th, Haggerty announced in open court that the Supreme Court had refused Alcock's application for writs. Shortly thereafter the State rested. There were a number of blank expressions in the courtroom and throughout the city. To the very end, many expected, or had hoped, for something more substantial.

Dymond moved for a directed verdict of not guilty. (In any jury case the Judge may direct a verdict of not guilty after the conclusion of all of the State's evidence if he feels that the evidence is not sufficient to sustain a conviction.) Both sides argued the motion briefly. Haggerty announced a thirty-minute recess, after which he would rule. About forty-five minutes later, Court was reconvened and the Judge announced that he intended to spend the rest of the day studying the transcript of Russo's testimony and that his decision would be announced the following morning.

The overwhelming weight of speculation was that the motion would be granted; that Garrison's case would never go to the jury. The Judge's actions indicated serious scrutiny of the record and, in the opinion of many, serious scrutiny would lead to a directed verdict.

But it did not. The next morning at 9:00 o'clock Haggerty took the bench and announced that the motion was denied. The ruling was greeted with applause from some of the spectators. They were "ghouls," said Garrison's critics. Of course, they were not ghouls. They had come to see a complete show and were disturbed at the prospect of a sudden, unexpected conclusion of the affair at midpoint. The applause merely served as an outlet for their relief.

The defense thereupon proceeded with its evidence. Despite remarks by Dymond in the opening statement that the defense had neither the money nor the inclination to defend the Warren Report, Shaw's lawyers tried gamely. Several of the Warren Commmission experts, including pathologists and criminologists, testified in behalf of the defense.

In answer to the State's evidence concerning the New Orleans conspiracy, Dymond called Oswald's widow, Mrs. Marina Oswald Porter. According to Mrs. Porter, her late husband had never worn a beard and never dressed like a beatnik. While the couple lived in New Orleans he was usually at their Magazine Street home by 5:00 or 5:30 P.M. Her husband did not wear dirty clothes, said Mrs. Porter. Mrs. Porter never knew Clay Shaw and she never heard the name "Clay Bertrand." Neither did she know David Ferrie either by name or photograph, nor did she know Niles Peterson, Sandra Moffett, Layton Martens, Alvin Beauboeuf, Melvin Coffee, Al Landry, or James Lewallen.

Nor had she heard of Perry Raymond Russo.

Lloyd J. Cobb, President of the International Trade Mart, testified that during the months of July, August, and September, 1963, Shaw was out of the city only one working day and that was September 25th when he was in Hammond, Louisiana, a considerable distance from Clinton.

Mrs. Ruth Paine, landlady and close friend of the Oswalds in Irving, Texas, told the jury that she never saw Oswald when he was sloppy, needed a shave, or wore a beard.

Then came Dean Andrews. He characterized his Warren Commission testimony as "page after page of bull." Concerning his story to the F.B.I., he said, "My mouth ran ahead of my brain." There was no Clay Bertrand, said Andrews.

On cross-examination Alcock accused Andrews of lying. "You can call it that if you want," said Andrews. "I say I made conflicting statements."

Alcock pressed hard. At first Haggerty sustained Andrews's right to refuse to answer due to possible self-incrimination. His perjury conviction was still on appeal and a new trial could conceivably be ordered. Finally, however, the Judge reversed himself. Andrews had "opened the door" by answering certain questions and could not now refuse to answer other questions on the same subject.

"I never identified anybody as Clay Bertrand," said Andrews. "I used it as a cover name for Gene Davis." About his statement to the F.B.I. agent, he said: "It was an informal rapid-fire questioning. I didn't think it was important. I felt I was an insignificant person being questioned about something big. I might have overloaded my mouth, but I didn't deliberately lie. The only explanation I can give you is that my mouth went ahead of my brain."

"You lied, then?" Alcock asked.

"You can call it a lie. I call it huffin' and puffin' . . . a bull session."

Why didn't Andrews tell the F.B.I. that Davis was Clay Bertrand? Andrews replied: "I didn't choose to implicate an innocent man— Eugene Davis. I didn't consider it important. It dawned on me that I could involve an innocent man in this. So while in the hospital I elected a course I could never get away from. It's been whiplashing ever since."

Why would Davis have been introduced to Andrews as Bertrand at the party, asked the Judge. It was probably done in jest, said Andrews. "I've been introduced as Algonquin J. Calhoun, but people know I'm Dean Andrews."

Andrews boasted that he was one of the early critics of the Warren Commission, registering his disapproval in 1964. "I didn't wait four or five years," he twitted the assistant D.A., "I jumped on the gravy train right away."

Then the defense called Edward O'Donnell, now Lieutenant Edward O'Donnell. He told of his June 19th interview with Perry Russo. He had reported Russo's statement to Garrison, said O'Donnell. At the confrontation with Russo in Garrison's office, O'Donnell had told Russo that he had a tape of their conversation where Russo admitted that Shaw was not at the party. "Russo did a double take," said O'Donnell. But the officer acknowledged that there was no tape. He had done this to try and shock the truth out of Russo.

James Phelan testified to his various interviews with Russo, and repeated to the jury Russo's various statements to him so completely at odds with his courtroom testimony.

Mrs. Jessie Garner, former landlady of the Oswalds in New Orleans, testified that Oswald stayed at her apartment from early May to mid-September, 1963. She had seen him about once a week waiting for the bus. She had never seen him with a beard, nor was he ever dirty or unkempt. She never saw Clay Shaw. She had seen Ferrie, however. Shortly after Kennedy's assassination, he came alone after dark. She first had thought that Ferrie was an F.B.I. agent seeking information about Oswald. "He stayed a few minutes and when I found out he wasn't someone important, I asked him to leave," said the witness.

The defense then called a retired handwriting expert for the Federal Bureau of Investigation, Charles A. Appel, Jr. He had gained fame for his part in solving the Lindbergh kidnapping in the 1930's. He testified that he was receiving no compensation for his work, for he had been informed that Clay Shaw could not afford his fee. He was appearing, he said, as a civic duty.

Appel testified that he had studied samples of Shaw's handwriting and had compared them with the V.I.P. guest book introduced in evidence following the testimony of Mrs. Parker. He came to a firm conclusion, said Appel, that the two were not written by the same hand. The "Clay Bertrand" in the guest book was not written by Clay Shaw.

The defense called Arthur Q. Davis, an architect. His name appeared on the Eastern Airlines V.I.P. lounge register for December 14th. The name Clay Bertrand was directly below it. Davis identified his signature, testified that he knew Clay Shaw, but that he did not see Clay Shaw in the V.I.P. lounge that day.

The next witness was Clay Shaw.

Shaw spent approximately one hour answering questions of his own counsel, Irvin Dymond, and another hour undergoing cross-examination by Alcock.

Shaw was icy calm; he testified without any visible show of emotion. Throughout the two-hour examination he peered directly into the faces of the jurymen seated to his left. His answers were usually brief, often one word, which heightened the rapidity of the examination. The eyes of the jury turned alternately to Shaw on their right, then to the attorneys on their left as questions followed answers quickly during the brisk examination. The jury sometimes appeared to be following a tennis match.

In response to Dymond's questions, Shaw related his education and business background. Shown a picture of Oswald, Shaw testified that he had never seen him in person, nor had he ever had a telephone conversation with him. He never knew David Ferrie and prior to this case, he had never known Perry Raymond Russo. He had never been to Clinton.

From July 8th to October, 1963, said Shaw, he was extremely busy. This was the period during which he was seeking to build a new Trade Mart, which today stands at the foot of Canal Street, the city's main thoroughfare. Bonds were to be sold to a New York syndicate, Shaw explained, on condition that during this period the Trade Mart was able to obtain leases amounting to $1,425,000 in annual income. "Had we not succeeded," said the defendant, "there would be no Trade Mart at the foot of Canal Street now." Shaw was out of town but once during that period and that was to visit his father in Hammond.

He had never seen Charles I. Spiesel before the trial. He had never attended a party such as described by Spiesel, nor had he attended a party or meeting as described by Russo.

He never met Oswald on the seawall, had never given Oswald any money, nor did he ever have any reason to give Oswald money.

He was not a Castro supporter and had not been active in pro-Castro activities.

He had never signed the Eastern Airlines V.I.P. lounge guest book and until the trial did not know that such a lounge existed.

He had never been known as Clay Bertrand or Clem Bertrand. He had never used an alias, except for a pen name "Allen White" in writing a play. He had never received mail addressed to Clem or Clay Bertrand.

He had gone to the West Coast in November, 1963, because he had been invited in early September to speak to the Columbia Basin World Trade Conference. "It was to be in Portland, Oregon, November 26, 1963, and I accepted," said Shaw.

Shaw claimed he had never talked even jokingly about assassination of the President. He had certainly never conspired with Ferrie, Oswald, or anyone else to murder the President, nor did he ever want President Kennedy to be killed.

After a brief recess, Alcock began his cross-examination. Alcock questioned Shaw at some length about his November trip to the West Coast and about the arrangements and about who, whether he or others, had initiated them.

Asked if he knew Layton Martens, Shaw replied that he did. He did not know, however, that he had been David Ferrie's roommate. Shaw acknowledged that he knew James Lewallen, but he did not know that Lewallen knew David Ferrie.

"Do you recall visiting the Lakefront Airport in 1963?" asked Alcock.

"To the best of my recollection, no. During the past ten years I doubt I have been there more than two or three times" was Shaw's response.

In response to Alcock's questions, Shaw stated that he owned property at 906 and 908 Esplanade. It was to 906 Esplanade that Spiesel brought Shaw and the jury to identify the room where the alleged party occurred where Shaw was present. Shaw had lived at 906 Esplanade from 1950 to 1952.

He was questioned at length about Clinton, and persisted in his denial that he had ever been there.

Shaw recalled meeting Gordon Novel when Novel wanted to negotiate with him for the concession at the top of the new Trade Mart building. Shaw did not recall ever seeing any attorney with Novel at this time and specifically he did not recall Dean Andrews.

The limp described by Vernon Bundy resulted, said Shaw, from a back condition from an Army injury in 1946. "Sometimes it makes me limp. Sometimes it does not," said Shaw.

Shaw did not know Vernon Bundy before this case, nor did he know of any dispute that might cause Bundy to testify against him. Nor did he know of any reason why Spiesel should testify against him, nor Mrs. Parker.

In August, 1963, Shaw had been told of the disturbance in front of the Trade Mart building. He had been told that "some nut" was passing out leaflets. He started to go down, but was interrupted by a long-distance telephone call. When he arrived at the sidewalk, everyone was gone and the television men were packing their cameras.

Shaw never knew Hardiman, the letter carrier, nor did he know of any reasons why Hardiman should testify against him.

With that, Alcock stated that he had no further questions.

The defense rested and the State then called rebuttal witnesses.

The State called Eugene Davis, the French Quarter bar owner, identified by Andrews as the real Clay Bertrand who wasn't Clay Bertrand. He denied that he was ever so introduced to Dean Andrews.

Then came two surprise rebuttal witnesses, Mr. and Mrs. Nicholas M. Taten, who testified they saw Clay Shaw and David Ferrie walk out of a hangar together, at the New Orleans Lakefront Airport in the summer of 1964. Their son was receiving instructions in flying from Ferrie, according to the Tatens. Mr. Taten said he asked Ferrie if he had a new student and Ferrie replied, "No, he's a friend of mine, Clay Shaw. He's in charge of the International Trade Mart." According to Taten, his wife made the remark, "Look at the beautiful hair he has on his head." Further, Taten testified, he had seen Shaw many times on Bourbon Street in the French Quarter.

When, asked Dymond, had Taten first got in touch with the District Attorney's Office? "This morning," answered the witness.

"Did you know about the preliminary hearing?" asked Dymond. "Yes, I knew," said Taten. He didn't want to get involved then, but now he felt it was his duty.

Mrs. Taten, likewise, didn't want to get involved before. "I wouldn't be here today if my husband hadn't made me come," said Mrs. Taten.

The Tatens were a complete surprise to the defense. Unlike Spiesel and the host of other State witnesses, there was no time to check out or investigate the Tatens or a rumored vow by Mr. Taten to even an old score with defense attorney Dymond.

The State also called two rebuttal witnesses to give further testimony about the events of Dealey Plaza.

The State called Mrs. Elizabeth McCarthy from Boston, like Appel, a handwriting expert. She was questioned by Garrison personally and stated that Clay Shaw "probably" did sign the name Clay Bertrand in the guest register at the Eastern Airlines V.I.P. Room. The "probably" drew raised eyebrows from many attorneys. It was curious testimony from a handwriting expert. In the overwhelming majority of cases, such witnesses will reach a positive conclusion, for handwriting, like a fingerprint, is a means of positive identification.

There was still another expert who examined the guest register, though he was not called to testify. Gilbert Fortier, one of the best-known examiners of questioned documents in this part of the country, had examined the book and known specimens of Shaw's handwriting at Garrison's request. Fortier is the expert most frequently called by the State to give testimony as to handwriting comparisons in cases involving forged or other questioned documents. In addition, he appears in other courts throughout this area undoubtedly more frequently than any other expert in the field. After examining the questioned guest book, Fortier conferred with Garrison. He was not called as a witness. Instead, Garrison called on Mrs. McCarthy from Boston, Massachusetts, to come to New Orleans. She examined the documents the night of her arrival and testified the following day.

When the testimony was over, the jury was allowed a short period in which to reexamine the exhibits.

They had been given the option of hearing arguments and the charge from the Court on the following day, but they chose to work through the night. So the arguments began on the afternoon of Friday, February 28th.

Alcock argued for the State and summarized the testimony that dealt with the alleged New Orleans conspiracy.

"That man," said Alcock, pointing to Shaw, "was proven a liar and unworthy of your belief. If he lies on one material issue," he continued, referring to the witnesses from Clinton and Shaw's disavowal of any knowledge of Oswald, "you can disregard all of his testimony."

"I do not apologize for Vernon Bundy or any other witness," said the prosecutor, "you take your witnesses as you find them. It would be nice to have all bank presidents as witnesses, but that is not possible."

Neither did Alcock apologize for Charles Spiesel. ". . . Just remember he has never been convicted in his life. He has a responsible job in New York and his employer permitted him to leave his work to plead his case before this Court."

Alvin Oser summed up the testimony concerning Dealey Plaza.

Dymond reminded the jury repeatedly that the case was against Clay L. Shaw, not the Warren Commission, though "For days on end, we would go by in the courtroom without hearing his name." He warned the jury that the State would show them the Zapruder film again. "I was shocked at it, too," he said, "but don't let it cause you to convict an innocent man.

"The whole world will be waiting to see if twelve men can convict a person in this Alice in Wonderland story."

He referred to Spiesel as "a poor little paranoid."

Speaking of the V.I.P. register Dymond said that it was difficult to imagine why Shaw would go to the airport for no other reason than to sign his name. "It is the act of a complete lunatic," said Dymond.

Garrison made the final remarks to the jury. He termed the Warren Commission Report "the greatest fraud in the history of our country." He told the jury that while Shaw was present in the courtroom, there might be a tendency to feel sorry for him, but reminded the jury that "you also are not free to forget the victim . . ." It is doubtful that the jury forgot the victim. They had seen the gory murder nine times.

He repeated the best known excerpt from the inauguration speech of John F. Kennedy: "Ask not what your country can do for you. Ask what you can do for your country." More than one of the newsmen present suggested that the use of the phrase in that context might be somewhat obscene.

Haggerty charged the jury on the law for almost an hour. It was close to midnight when he finished. The jury retired to begin its deliberations on March 1st a few minutes after midnight.

The same newsmen and spectators who feared the effect of the Zapruder film on the silent jurymen expressed similar fears concerning the effect of Garrison's emotional, final appeal. For five weeks they had scrutinized the faces of the twelve men for telltale signs. Whatever signs they saw, they apparently misread completely.

True it was that the system had been strained to its utmost. It creaked and groaned under loads that it was never intended to carry. It was subjected to stress and strain for which it undoubtedly was not constructed. Yet, to the surprise of many of the cynics, somehow the damn thing worked.

They deliberated a little less than an hour. They voted only once. Nine of the twelve were needed for a verdict. All twelve found themselves in agreement, however. At 1:04 A.M. on March 1st, the jury filed back into the courtroom. They gave the verdict to the Judge, who read it silently and handed it to the Minute Clerk. The Minute Clerk read it aloud to the hushed courtroom.

He announced what every sensible person who had given more than passing thought to the Garrison case had known for almost two years. Clay Shaw was not guilty.

*　　*　　*

19

SO IT ENDED. ON MANY PRIOR OC-
casions Garrison had been on the losing end of judicial contests, though
time has proven he has seldom gained less than a draw in his never-
ending battles for public approval. Within a few days following Shaw's
acquittal, signs appeared indicating the clear possibility he did no worse
in this one. Reporters from the eastern press dispatched to New Orleans
to describe the general disillusionment with Garrison were forced to
revise completely the nature of their proposed stories, and the tenor of
local opinion has left them puzzled and perplexed: Garrison alone had
gamely fought to establish the truth, but the odds were simply too great.
The entire federal establishment was arrayed against him. Moreover, it
is absurd to condemn a prosecutor for losing a case; he should be com-
mended for trying.

Only time can tell the extent, if any, to which his hammerlock on
public opinion has been weakened.

How can the phenomenon be explained? Perhaps it cannot. But if it
is true that a clearer perspective can be obtained through contrast, then

perhaps there is some insight to be gained by a parting glance at his intensely bitter personal conflict with Walter Sheridan. For no sharper contrast in nature or temperament could be imagined between two strong-willed individuals than that between the New Orleans D.A. and the NBC reporter.

*   *   *

Garrison's much heralded reticence in making pretrial statements about Clay Shaw never extended to Sheridan. Walter Sheridan, claimed Garrison, on many public occasions, had been sent to New Orleans by Robert Kennedy for the sole purpose of wrecking his investigation.

Garrison was wrong. Garrison claimed to have solved the assassination and the National Broadcasting Company had sent Sheridan to cover the preliminary hearing. The reporter had, indeed, been a close friend of the former Attorney General and, as a staff member of the Department of Justice, had played a major role in the massive effort to convict James Hoffa, the Teamster boss, but his sole mission in the city was that of a reporter for NBC. Immediately following the preliminary hearing of March, 1967, the network ran a one-half hour objective documentary on the proceedings, prepared largely by Sheridan.

However, following the first day's proceedings, he had gone to dinner with Garrison and several of his key men at a local hotel. Sheridan talks little. Primarily, he listens. He heard the D.A. and his lieutenants speaking of the information that they would get from various witnesses, as soon as the witnesses could be broken down and persuaded to tell the truth. They spoke of the vast amounts of proof and corroboration of the D.A.'s theory that was available from any number of individuals at such time as they could be persuaded to talk.

None of this sat well with Sheridan. He is a skilled professional investigator and he takes little for granted. He relies no more than necessary on his own ability to deduce or to draw logical inferences. This he leaves to the philosophers. He wastes little time expounding; he digs. He runs down every rumor to the source. Almost immediately upon arrival at any assignment, he will start using the telephone. He meets with as many people as possible who may know something of the subject of his inquiry and he listens.

All talk, whether advanced as rumor, conjecture, or fact is checked out. Also, if names are mentioned, he wants to meet those individuals. Then another round of talk, names, and appointments, until he reaches the source where he finds hard information—or nothing. His conclusions or hypotheses will yield to the facts. Sheridan is, in short, as an investigator, everything that Garrison is not.

One conclusion Sheridan did reach, however, rather quickly following dinner with the D.A. and his staff. Garrison had not solved the assassination of President Kennedy.

Sheridan personally ran down every witness possible that was involved in the bizarre case. It was Sheridan who interviewed and first heard the stories of Carlos Bringuier, Carlos Quiroga, Fred Leemans, the Turkish bath operator, the polygraph operator who first tested Russo and Quiroga, and the Police Department polygraph operator who later attempted to test Russo—Lieutenant Edward O'Donnell—among many others. It became obvious to Sheridan that Garrison meant to use any means possible of getting "evidence" of his predetermined "truth."

Sheridan had little interest in the strange workings of Garrison's complex psychological makeup or in any deep analysis of his psyche. To him, the answer to the entire episode was simple. The Garrison case was a fraud.

It is tempting to accept Sheridan's conclusion, but it may have been too simple. There is little doubt but that Garrison believed at least the central themes of his investigation with every fiber of his being. To that extent, the use of the word "fraud" as a conscious, deliberate attempt to deceive may not be quite accurate.

Many others who were never persuaded by Garrison's forensics will argue that he was simply mistaken; that he was misguided; that he has poor judgment, but that he is "sincere." They, on the other hand, are too charitable.

If Garrison is sincere, his sincerity is that of the witch burners. Except to those with a genuine interest in the Garrison episode as a study of almost uniquely erratic and unfathomable behavior, any inquiry into the degree of his sincerity is pointless. The time could better be spent determining the number of angels that could dance on the head of a pin.

If sincerity means belief in one's own convictions, Garrison was sincere. He has always possessed an unusual power to convince himself of anything he wished. And his massive ego has never permitted any suspicion that the product of his logic could be erroneous; or that a vigorous critic could be in good faith. Every stray thought that passes through any of the multitudinous recesses of his mind he deems to have divine conception, else why would it be found in such a hallowed place? This remarkable proclivity for self-deception has been the secret of his success. He has been singularly able to defraud himself before defrauding others.

If we are to use the words in their literal sense, we may be required to admit that if the case was fraudulent, Garrison may have been as much the victim of the fraud as the culprit. He was defrauded by mischievous witnesses such as Andrews and Novel as much as by those like Russo and Spiesel who took their publicity more seriously. But even more was he defrauded by his abiding faith in his own omnipotence.

His sincerity, or lack of sincerity, is not important. Nor is the Garrison case itself of any intrinsic importance. It is almost certain to be consigned to the dung heap of history and promptly forgotten. It will probably rate not even a footnote in any serious study of the assassination.

The reaction of those around it and the frightening implications involved cannot be dismissed so lightly. It brought out the sheep in human nature.

To all appearances, Garrison was a powerful individual. And many gathered round as though seeking shelter in the shade of a great oak. He is seldom alone. He is always trailed or surrounded by a goodly number of the palace guard.

Fifty wealthy businessmen contributed money and continued to contribute in the face of all the available evidence of gross oppression. Oppression didn't matter. Garrison was popular. He was obviously going places. The time to tie your fortunes to a rising politician is at the start. And when money is invested, it is clearly necessary to spend more to protect the investment.

The day following Shaw's acquittal, the local press printed front-page editorials. One expressed relief and gratification and mildly chastised Garrison. The other, in a refreshingly plain and beautifully written analysis, called him a disgrace and demanded his resignation.

Following the initial pleasure at observing this uninhibited truth in public print, even Garrison's critics experienced reactions ranging from resentment to fury at the timing. For two years, the local press and two of three local TV stations had played to public sentiment while reporting the developments of the case in headlines and leading stories as though it were legitimate news. Only the local TV affiliate of the National Broadcasting Company showed a spark of human reaction at the outrage, which the press generally all knew it to be. Under the circumstances, almost any excuse would have been better than the one offered for the inaction of the media—Judge Haggerty's guidelines. The guidelines had been left in shambles by Garrison.

To matters in which Garrison had a personal interest, many of the Judges of the Criminal District Court had long since abandoned all but the pretense of judicial independence.

A few, very few, of Garrison's aides may have believed virtually everything their boss had said. Most stayed for other reasons. The future of some was inextricably bound with the D.A.'s Office. They aspired to Criminal Court judgeships or other offices. Some were bound by economics. Others were personally attracted to the still charming and genial individual that Garrison could be, and often was when off stage. Some almost literally worshipped their leader and were blinded to the fate of his victims.

In a painfully superficial book about the investigation published in September, 1967, by the two reporters who first broke the story, the authors pondered the validity of Garrison's probe. Passing mention was made of the theory that the D.A. had been lured into the case by a "maze of mental convolutions that has finally alienated him from reality." The flaw in this argument, said the authors, was the assistance in his efforts by a "reasonably able and sane set of aides who have careers and ambitions of their own."

"Reasonably able and sane" they were—and decent and well-motivated. So, by all accounts, were the men who pushed the buttons and pulled the levers at Auschwitz, Dachau, and Belsen.

The importance of Garrison's case is not that he failed, but that he could have succeeded. The important thing is not that so many dismissed it as a fraud or a fantasy, but that so many believed it in the face of all the evidence, not because of anything Garrison said, but because of the convincing way in which he said it.

Whatever lessons may have been learned from the sorry tale may or may not make the way a little more difficult for the next charlatan to reach for power through skilled demagoguery. It is most doubtful that it will seriously impede Garrison's career. His hold on the imagination of the New Orleans public may be well-nigh unbreakable. Emotional attachments, once made, are difficult to dissolve; they do not yield to reason. Not only has he probably not been thwarted, but, as was soon made clear, he has been chastened by the fiasco not in the slightest degree. The end of "the Garrison case" is not by any means the end of the Garrison story.

*   *   *

Jim Garrison was not in the courtroom when the verdict was returned, and news of Shaw's acquittal was brought to his office by assistants. It is said that his bellows of rage penetrated the walls of his lair and echoed down the halls of Tulane and Broad. It proved that the "American people don't want to know the truth about the assassination," he roared.

Finally, however, his outburst cooled and he channeled his seething emotion into something more constructive.

He charged Clay Shaw with perjury for denying that he knew Oswald or Ferrie.

He charged Thomas Bethell, a former staff investigator and ex-school teacher from England, with unlawfully using a D.A. trial memorandum, namely, giving it to the defense.

He charged Dean Andrews, of course, with perjury.

And the charge against the Reverend Clyde Johnson for beating a hotel bill was quietly dropped.